2005
中国农产品价格调查年鉴

CHINA YEARBOOK OF AGRICULTURAL PRICE SURVEY

国家统计局农村社会经济调查司 编

Department of Rural Survey, National Bureau of Statistics of China

中国统计出版社
China Statistics Press

(京)新登字 041 号

图书在版编目（CIP）数据

中国农产品价格调查年鉴. 2005
/ 国家统计局农村社会经济调查司编.
- 北京：中国统计出版社，2005. 11
ISBN 7-5037-4747-1

Ⅰ. 中…
Ⅱ. 国…
Ⅲ. 农产品 - 价格 - 统计资料 - 中国 -2005- 年鉴
Ⅳ. F 323.7-54

中国版本图书馆 CIP 数据核字（2005）第 116893 号

中国农产品价格调查年鉴— 2005

作　　者 / 国家统计局农村社会经济调查司编
责任编辑 / 姚　立
E-mail /cbsebs@stats.gov.cn
封面设计 / 艺编广告 · 张冰　方红
出版发行 / 中国统计出版社
通信地址 / 北京市西城区月坛南街 75 号
邮政编码 /100826
办公地址 / 北京市丰台区西三环南路甲 6 号
电　　话 /（010）63459084　63266600-22500（发行部）
印　　刷 / 科伦克三莱印务（北京）有限公司
经　　销 / 新华书店
开　　本 /880 × 1230 毫米　1/16
字　　数 / 400 千字
印　　张 /16.75
印　　数 /1 — 2000 册
版　　别 /2005 年 11 月第 1 版
版　　次 /2005 年 11 月北京第 1 次印刷
书　　号 /ISBN 7-5037-4747-1/F · 2169
定　　价 / 88. 00 元

《中国农产品价格调查年鉴—2005》编辑委员会

CHINA YEARBOOK OF AGRICULTURAL PRICE SURVEY—2005

EDITORIAL BOARD AND STAFF

前　言

一、本书编辑目的与作用

伴随我国市场经济体制的建立与完善，农村经济运行市场化步伐加快，市场机制在农产品流通与贸易中的基础作用日益显现，宏观决策和社会公众对农产品价格信息的需求与日俱增。为了适应这一新的形势，国家统计局农村社会经济调查系统发挥自身优势，逐步建立起完整的农产品价格调查体系，对农产品生产和流通全过程进行密集跟踪调查，全方位把握农产品价格走势，深入透视农产品生产、贸易和消费环节的分配关系和利益格局。汇编这些价格数据的目的就是为了充分发挥农产品价格信息在分析研究我国农产品供给与需求、农产品市场竞争与产业结构调整、农民收入与居民消费等方面的独特作用，更好地服务于各级党政领导的“三农”决策，服务于关注农产品价格问题的研究机构和各界社会公众。

二、本书编辑的主要内容与资料调查方法

本书的内容主要包括我国农产品生产价格、集贸市场价格和国际市场农产品价格信息三部分。农产品生产价格是农产品生产者农户和农场直接出售其产品时实际获得的单位产品价格，它是农产品集贸市场价格、批发价格和消费价格形成的基础和前提。农产品生产价格调查采用随机抽样的方法抽选调查网点，实行抽样调查。全国共抽选31000个农业生产经营单位，其中农户占90.5%，农场占9.5%。调查内容涉及农林牧渔四个大类，十五个中类三十个小类600种农产品。农产品集贸市场价格调查是对全国200个农产品主产县（市）36种农产品进行的集贸市场价格调查，旨在反映我国农产品主产区大宗农产品的交易价格和价格走势。国际市场农产品价格资料主要来源于芝加哥期货交易所、纽约商品交易所主要农产品期货市场的交易信息。

三、特别说明

本书在重点收录2004年农产品价格调查资料的同时，编发了1997年以来全国主要农产品的价格数据。生产价格指数以上年或上年同期价格为100。农产品集贸市场价格单位统一为元/公斤，价格数据保留两位小数；集贸市场价格走势分为环比和同比两个系列，环比以上月或上季度价格为100，同比以上年同月或同期价格为100。

为了及时反映全国农产品价格走势，我们将定期出版《中国农产品价格调查年鉴》。由于农产品价格调查和指数编制是一项全新的工作，限于我们的经验和水平，书中疏漏在所难免，不妥之处敬请读者批评指正。

编　者

2005年8月

Preface

I. The Purpose of Editing This Book and the Role It Plays

Along with the establishment and perfection of the system of market economy in China, the market-oriented pace of the rural economic performance has been accelerated, the fundamental role of market mechanism has increasingly manifested itself in the circulation and trade of agricultural products, and the government and general public have increasingly more demand for the information on the prices of agricultural products with each passing day, so as to meet the needs of macro-economic decision-making and the public understanding.

In order to fit in with this new situation, the rural socio-economic survey system of the National Bureau of Statistics (NBS) has brought its advantages into play and gradually set up a perfect system of the survey of the prices of agricultural products, so as to conduct the intensive survey, following the track of the whole process of the production and circulation of the agricultural products, keep abreast of the change trend of the prices of agricultural products in an all-round way, and thoroughly understand the distribution relations and interest pattern among the production, trade and consumption links. The purpose in compiling these price data is to bring the unique role of the information on the prices of agricultural products into full play in analyzing and studying the supply and demand relations of the agricultural products, the market competition of agricultural products and the readjustment of industrial structure, the income of farmers and the consumption of residents, etc., thereby better serve the leaders of the communist party and government at different levels for making decisions on the issues of agriculture, rural areas and farmers, and better serve the research institutes and the general public of different circles, which pay close attention to the issues of the prices of agricultural products.

II. The Main Contents of This Book and the Survey Methods

The content of this book includes mainly the following three parts:(1)the producer prices and (2) the prices of the agricultural products at the rural market fairs (RMF) in China as well as (3)the information on the prices of the agricultural products at the international market. The producer price of the agricultural product is the price of the unit product, at which the producer of the agricultural product, i.e. the agricultural household or the farm, directly sells the product. The producer prices of agricultural products are the bases and prerequisites for the formation of the prices of the agricultural products at the RMF as well as the wholesale prices and consumers prices. The survey of the producer prices of agricultural products is conducted with the method of sample survey. The sample units are selected with random sampling method. A total of 31000 units engaged in agricultural production and management have been selected in the whole country, in which the agricultural households account for 90.5% and the farms account for 9.5%. The content of the survey covers the four categories of farming, forestry, animal husbandry and fishery, 15 divisions, 30 groups and 600 products. The survey of the prices at the RMF is the survey of the prices of 36 agricultural products in 200 major producing counties and cities. It is conducted for the purpose for reflecting the trading prices of the staple agricultural products in the major producing areas and the trend of these prices. The data on the prices of agricultural products at the international market come mainly from the trading information at the main future markets of agricultural products at Chicago Board of Trade (CBOT) and New York Board of Trade (NYBOT).

III. Special Notes

While mainly collecting the survey data on the prices of agricultural products in 2004, this book has also compiled and released the data on the prices of main agricultural products in China since 1997. The indices of the producer prices take the prices in the previous year or the prices in the same period in the previous year as 100. The unit of the prices of agricultural products at RMF is unified to be yuan/kg and two decimals are kept in the price data. The data on the trend of the prices of agricultural products at RMF are classified into two series, namely the chain indices and the fixed base indices. The chain indices take the prices of the previous month or quarter as 100 while the fixed base indices take the prices of the same month or same period in the previous year as 100.

In order to timely reflect the trend of the prices of agricultural products in China, we will publish the *China Yearbook of Agricultural Price Survey*. Because the survey of the prices of agricultural products and the compilation of the price indices is a quite new job and our experiences and knowledge are limited, there may be some slips in the book. We warmly welcome the comments or criticism from our readers.

The Editor

Beijing

Aug.2005

目 录

前　言
Preface

第一部分　2004年农产品价格走势综述
Part I　A Summary of the Trend of the Prices of Agricultural Products in 2004

第二部分　农产品生产价格指数
Part II　Indices of the Producer Prices of Agricultural Products

第三部分 农产品集贸市场价格
Part III Prices of the Agricultural Products at the Rural Market Fairs

第五部分　全国农产品价格调查方案

Part V　Programmes for the Survey of the Prices of Agricultural Products in China

1

2004 年农产品价格走势综述

A Summary of the Trend of the Prices of Agricultural Products in 2004

2004年农产品价格走势综述

2004年我国农产品市场受供求关系变化和国家实施粮食购销市场化改革的积极影响，全国农产品价格强劲回升，价格走势一举扭转持续多年的低迷徘徊局面，绝大多数农产品成交价格和价格涨幅均创2000年以来新高。全国农产品生产价格同比上涨13.1%，为1996年以来最大价格涨幅，部分产品价格接近或超过1996年历史最高价位。全国农产品市场行情和价格走势呈现以下特点：

一、2004年全国农产品生产价格上涨13.1%

据对全国27000个农业生产经营单位的生产价格调查，全国农产品生产价格总指数为113.1（上年为100，下同），比上年上涨13.1%，生产价格涨幅比上年加大8.7个百分点。分行业看，种植业、林业、畜牧业和渔业产品生产价格指数分别为115.9、104.6、111.1和110.2。

（一）种植业产品生产价格上涨15.9%

2004年谷物、豆类和油料价格回升是拉动全年种植业产品价格上涨的重要因素。

2004年全国粮食平均生产价格为1.21元/公斤，比上年上涨26.2%。谷物价格上涨28.1%，豆类价格上涨20.3%，薯类价格上涨5.8%。小麦上涨31.2%，玉米上涨16.9%。稻谷价格上涨36.3%，粳稻价格上涨37.7%，早籼稻上涨33.6%，晚籼稻价格上涨34.4%。大豆价格上涨20.2%。

棉花生产价格同比下降20.5%。棉价回落的主要原因，一是由于2004年全国棉花增产形势好于市场预期，产量达632万吨，比上年增产30.1%。二是棉花进口大量增加，2004年我国棉花净进口超过190万吨。三是国内棉花需求平稳，取消纺织品国际贸易配额限制可能对国内棉花需求增长的拉动作用并未充分显现。

油料价格上涨16.6%，花生、油菜籽和芝麻价格分别上涨17.1%、16.3%和22.3%。糖料价格上涨4.9%。

蔬菜价格上涨，水果价格小幅回落。蔬菜生产价格上涨5.2%。由于气候条件适宜，水果产量增加较多，水果价格较上年下降1.4%。烟叶价格上涨8.4%，茶叶价格上涨11.2%。

（二）林业产品生产价格上涨4.6%

近年来国家加大生态环境和林业资源保护力度，实施从木材和林产品生产为主向生态建设为主的战略转变，木材等重要林产品供给增速放缓，但随着城乡居民消费水平不断提高，市场对林产品的需求不断增加，推动林产品生产价格持续上涨。全年木材生产价格比上年上涨4.2%，竹材价格上涨8.9%，胶脂和果实类林产品价格上涨4.1%。

（三）畜牧业产品生产价格上涨11.1%

由于粮价上涨抬高生猪饲养成本的后续影响，2004年生猪出栏价格比上年上涨12.8%。肉牛价格上涨3.9%，活羊价格上涨5.7%。奶产品价格上涨3.9%，毛绒类产品价格上涨3.7%。家禽和蛋类生产价格上涨11.8%和12.6%，价格涨幅比2003年高10个百分点。

（四）渔业产品价格上涨10.2%

2004年海水产品价格比上年上涨9.0%，海水鱼类上涨9.2%，海水贝类价格上涨9.2%。淡水产品价格比上年上涨12.3%，淡水鱼类价格上涨11.5%，淡水虾蟹生产价格上涨23.0%。

二、2004年全国农产品集贸市场价格走势

（一）粮食价格大幅上涨

在主产区集贸市场上，继2003年第四季度全国粮食价格回升以来，2004年一季度粮价再度攀升，3月份稻谷价格比2月份上涨27.2%，涨幅为历年单月价格上涨之最。稻谷全年平均价格较上年上涨41.8%。籼稻1.51元/公斤，上涨40.4%；粳稻价格上涨43.3%。籼稻和粳稻价格分别比1996年上涨2.7%和6.2%。小麦全年平均价格1.52元/公斤，比上年上涨33.3%，接近1996年历史价位。玉米价格比上年上涨22.6%，比1996年上涨29.6%。大豆价格3.88元/公斤，比上年上涨0.92元，涨31%。籼米、粳米和面粉价格分别比上年上涨38.9%、40.5%和30%。

（二）棉花价格大起大落

受2003年第四季度棉花价格大幅上涨的惯性影响，2004年1～4月棉价继续上扬，4月份棉花价格比1月份上涨3.0%。5月份棉花价格开始回落，到新棉上市后，棉价加速下滑，最大单月跌幅达7.4%，四季度棉价低于上年同期价位。

（三）油料与食用油价格高位运行

受2003年油菜籽减产，全国食用油加工能力和消费需求强劲增长等诸多因素影响，2004年油料及食用油价格在上年第四季度大幅上涨的基础上高开高走。花生仁和油菜籽全年平均价格为6.75元/公斤和2.85元/公斤，比上年上涨20.7%和19%。花生油和菜籽油价格为11.15元/公斤和7.99元/公斤，分别比上年上涨18.2%和16.6%；大豆油年平均价7.71元/公斤，比上年上涨14.5%。

（四）畜产品价格大幅上扬

由于玉米、大豆等饲料用粮价格大幅上涨，2004年前三季度猪肉价格持续上涨，最高价达15.29元/公斤，接近牛肉价格。猪肉全年平均价格13.97元/公斤，比上年上涨30.6%。猪肉价格上涨激发农民养猪积极性，带动仔猪价格攀升，全年仔猪价格12.14元/公斤，比上年上涨53.6%。一至四季度牛肉价格分别比上年同期上涨7.9%、8.6%、9.8%和6.2%；全年平均价上涨8.1%。羊肉全年平均价16.98元/公斤，上涨5.1%。

受"禽流感"影响，家禽和鸡蛋价格大幅波动。2月份鸡蛋和活鸡价格比上月下降11.1%和5.8%。疫情控制后，由于家禽存栏下降，再加上饲料价格上涨，鸡蛋和活鸡价格一路攀升，9月份达年度最高价7.27元/公斤和10.85元/公斤，比上年同期上涨31.5%和22.3%，特别是鸡蛋价格连创2000年以来新高。

（五）水产品价格先扬后抑

2004年上半年鱼类价格逐月上升，下半年小幅回落。草鱼全年平均价9.1元/公斤，比上年上涨25.7%；鲤鱼平均价8.9元/公斤，上涨27%；鲢鱼平均价7.03元/公斤，比上年上涨23.3%；带鱼平均价10.13元/公斤，上涨8.5%。

（六）水果价格上涨，新鲜蔬菜价格下降

蔬菜和水果价格随季节波动较大，节日和气候因素也是影响蔬菜和水果价格波动的重要原因。苹果、香蕉和橙子年平均价3.47元/公斤、3.49元/公斤和3.55元/公斤，比上年上涨3.8%、12.2%和4.1%。大白菜、黄瓜、西红柿和菜椒价格比上年下降1.3%、1.9%、1.1%和0.8%。

三、2004年粮食价格上涨的主要特点

2004年全国粮食生产价格和流通环节价格全线上涨，并创2000年以来新高，部分品种价格接近甚至超过1996年历史最高价位。具体来说，2004年粮价走势呈现以下特点：

（一）涨价品种多

国家统计局农产品价格调查资料显示，2004年前三季度全国粮食生产价格较上年同期大幅度上涨35.1%，第四季度粮价稳中略降，但全年粮食平均生产价格仍高达1.21元/公斤，比2003年提高26.2%。谷物生产价格上涨28.1%。小麦生产价格上涨31.2%，早籼稻上涨33.6%，晚籼稻上涨34.4%，粳稻上涨37.7%，玉米上涨16.9%，大豆上涨20.2%，绿豆上涨16.7%，红小豆上涨28.3%，谷子上涨21.5%，高粱上涨27.3%，大麦上涨18.7%。薯类价格上涨5.7%。

（二）价格涨幅大

2004年全国粮食生产价格全线上涨，集贸市场价格、批发价格、进出口价格和消费价格相应上涨。在主产区的集贸市场上，籼稻价格比2000年上涨50.3%，粳稻价格上涨35%；籼稻和粳稻价格分别比1996年收购价格上涨2.7%和6.2%。小麦价格比2000年上涨48.2%，接近1996年历史价位。玉米价格比2000年上涨59.4%，比1996年收购价格高29.6%。大豆价格比2000年上涨53.6%。2004年我国谷物出口价格达174.99美元/吨，比上年上涨44.6%。2004年全国居民消费的食品价格比上年上涨9.9%，其中粮食价格上涨26.4%。

（三）涨价区域广

2004年东中西部地区全年粮食生产价格涨幅均超过20%，总体走势呈现东高西低格局，东部地区粮食生产价格上涨29.2%，中、西部地区分别上涨25.7%和20.8%。全国共有7个省市谷物生产价格涨幅超过30%，以重庆45.6%为最高；10个省区市价格涨幅介于20～30%之间；14个省区市谷物生产价格涨幅在20%以下，以宁夏9.9%为最低。粮食主产区、主销区和产销平衡区粮食价格分别比上年上涨27.4%、31.9%和20.8%。

（四）市场价格涨幅高于生产价格上涨

从谷物价格走势看，2004年稻谷、小麦和玉米生产价格上涨36.3%、31.2%和16.9%，集贸市场

价格涨幅分别为41.8%、33.3%和22.6%，集贸市场价格涨幅比生产价格高5.5、2.1和5.7个百分点。2004年我国谷物出口价格更比上年上涨44.6%。谷物生产价格涨幅低于集贸市场价格和出口价格上涨幅度，表明粮价上涨更多的是增加粮食流通环节的利润，粮食生产者农民和农场实际获利少于粮食流通经营者。

(五)市场机制成为影响价格走向的决定性因素

改革开放以来，我国粮食价格先后经历上世纪80年代中后期和90年代中期两轮较大幅度的上涨，这两轮行情的背景都是国家实施的“政策性提价”，属于政府主导的计划调控行为。2004年的粮价上涨是在粮食购销市场化改革的情况下，由粮食供求关系变化引发的市场调节行为，是市场对粮食产量连年下降、库存大幅减少导致总供给偏紧的自然反应，表现为从局部地区、个别品种价格上涨扩展到全国范围的粮价全线上涨，涨价机制的转变反映了我国市场经济体制日渐成熟。

四、粮价高位运行有利粮食增产和农民增收

粮食价格高位运行有利粮食增产。粮价上涨提高了农民的种粮效益，大大激发了农民务农种粮积极性。据调查，由于2003年四季度以来全国粮食价格持续高位运行，2004年我国粮食生产出现重要转机，粮食播种面积扭转多年下降局面，种植面积达10161万公顷，比上年增加220万公顷。粮食总产量46947万吨，增产9.0%。粮食单产308公斤/亩，提高6.6%。粮食单产和当年粮食增产量均创历史最高水平。当年秋冬播作物种植面积2638万公顷，增长4.8%。冬小麦播种面积2114万公顷，增长5.9%，种植面积扩大为2005年夏粮增产奠定了坚实基础。

2004年前三季度全国农户农业生产投入人均471元，增加86元，增长22.3%，同比增速加快19.1个百分点，农业生产投入增加额占前三季度全部生产投入增加额的88.7%。粮食主产区农户的农业生产投入人均523元，比上年增加103元，增长24.5%。事实表明，谷贱伤农，谷不贱农民的种粮积极性自然就高，实现粮食稳定增产的目标只能靠粮价在合理价位上的基本稳定。

粮价高位运行有利农民增收。粮食是国民经济重要的基础产品，1999～2003年粮食产值占我国农业总产值的36.6%。据测算，全国粮食价格每斤上涨1分钱，农民人均总收入即可增加10元钱。前些年，农民从农业中获得的收入连年下降，一个重要原因就是粮食价格长期低迷，农民把它叫做种地赔钱。2004年全国粮食生产价格1.21元/公斤，比上年回升26.2%，带动农产品生产价格整体上涨13.1%，农民收入因此呈现多年未见的增长势头，“价格高”成为2004年帮助农民增收的重要因素。

2004年全国农民人均纯收入达2936元，实际增长6.8%，是1997年以来增长最快的一年。前三季度全国农民出售农产品的现金收入人均958元，比上年同期增加191元，增长24.9%。出售粮食得到的现金收入人均257元，比上年同期增加64元，增长32.7%，因为粮食价格上涨人均增收56元，粮价上涨增加的现金收入成为农民增收的重要来源。

粮价上涨对粮食主产区农村居民的增收效应尤为显著。2004年前三季度粮食主产区农民出售农产品的现金收入人均1050元，高于全国平均水平9.6%，同比增长22.8%。由于出售粮食的生产价格提高，主产区农民出售农产品现金收入增加223元，现金收入增量全部来源于粮食价格回升。

五、2004年世界粮食市场行情与价格走势

(一)2004年世界粮食产量增长10.2%

1.世界粮食产量增幅高于市场预期。在粮食价格强劲回升的拉动下，2004年粮食生产得到较快恢复，世界粮食总产量①达22.49亿吨，比上年增产2.08亿吨，增长10.2%，产量增幅大大高于市场预期。世界市场粮食供给大幅增加，库存由降转升，扭转了1999年以来库存连续5年下降的局面。

2.世界谷物产量20.21亿吨，增产9.1%。2004年世界谷物产量创历史新高，比上年增产1.69亿吨，增长9.1%。谷物产量增长主要得益于小麦和玉米产量的大幅增加。世界小麦产量6.22

① (1)本报告的粮食口径由谷物和大豆两部分构成，不包括杂豆和薯类。(2)世界粮食产量、贸易与期末库存包括中国粮食产需量。(3)由于各国粮食生产存在季节差异，世界粮食产量、消费、贸易与期末库存数据均以各国的粮食贸易年度为准。(4)各国的粮食贸易年度和不同品种的贸易年度并不完全一致，但分国别的粮食贸易年度基本保持稳定，因而年度汇总数据具有可比性。

亿吨，增产12.6%；小麦产量增长占谷物产量增长总量的41.1%。小麦产量占世界谷物总产量的30.8%。从居民食物消费结构看，小麦是最重要的谷物产品。大米产量4.02亿吨，增长3.3%；大米产量占世界谷物总产量的19.9%。玉米产量7.02亿吨，增产7994万吨，增长12.9%；玉米产量增长占谷物产量增长总量的47.4%，玉米产量占世界谷物总产量的34.7%。

3. 美国和欧盟等贸易大国谷物产量较大幅增加，澳大利亚谷物减产。2004年美国谷物产量3.86亿吨，增长11.6%。欧盟2.87亿吨，增长24.6%。加拿大和阿根廷谷物产量分别为5239万吨和3770万吨，增长5%和20.8%。美国玉米产量比上年增产17%，欧盟小麦产量增长28.3%，越南大米产量增长0.3%。澳大利亚谷物产量3206万吨，下降21.9%。

4. 世界大豆产量2.29亿吨，增长20.5%。大豆既可用于居民的主食消费，又是重要的食用油加工原料。2004年大豆产量居世界前三位的是美国、巴西和阿根廷，它们的产量占世界大豆总产量的82%。美国大豆产量8548万吨，比上年增长28%。巴西和阿根廷大豆产量分别为6300万吨和3900万吨，增长19.8%和14.7%。

5. 世界粮食产量增长的主要原因。一是粮食价格上涨对生产者的激励作用逐步显现。2002年以来，由于国际市场粮食供给偏紧，价格止跌回升并持续走高，生产价格(PPI)相应上涨，粮食生产者收益增加较多，增产积极性提高。二是美国和中国等主要生产大国的粮食播种面积扩大。2004年美国玉米播种面积比上年增长2.9%，稻谷面积扩大10.9%。三是2004年世界粮食主产区气候条件普遍好于上年，粮食受灾面积小，单产增幅较大。

6. 粮食产量增长对市场供求关系的影响。2004年世界谷物产量20.21亿吨，谷物需求19.88亿吨，产量高于当年消费3312万吨，谷物期末库存比上年增长9.5%。大豆产量2.29亿吨，需求2.05亿吨，期末库存比上年增加2249万吨。由于谷物和大豆库存大幅增加，世界粮食期末库存较上年增加5560多万吨，库存占年度消费量的比率升至20.2%，高于18%的粮食安全线2.2个百分点。

(二)世界粮食库存恢复性增长

1. 2004年世界粮食期末库存增长14.3%。由于粮食产量大幅增长10.2%，世界粮食库存2000年以来首次实现由降转升。2004年世界粮食期末库存4.44亿吨，比上年增加5562万吨，增长14.3%，库存占年度消费量的比例达20.2%，高于18%的粮食安全线2.2个百分点，世界粮食库存持续下降的压力趋于缓解。

2. 世界谷物库存增长9.5%。小麦和玉米库存增加，大米库存下降。谷物的主要品种是小麦、稻谷和玉米，2004年世界谷物期末库存3.82亿吨，占粮食库存总量的86.2%；谷物库存为年度消费量的19.2%。小麦库存1.45亿吨，比上年增加1441万吨，增长11%；小麦库存占谷物库存的38%，占小麦年度消费量的23.9%，是居民主食消费中最重要的谷物产品。大米库存7676万吨，下降10.6%；大米库存占谷物库存总量的20.1%。玉米库存1.17亿吨，比上年增加1960万吨，增长20.1%；玉米库存占谷物库存总量的30.7%，占玉米年度消费量的17.2%。

3. 主要贸易大国谷物库存增幅高于市场预期。2004年欧盟谷物库存4057万吨，增长85.3%。小麦库存1997万吨，比上年增长1倍以上；玉米库存554万吨，增长69.9%。美国谷物库存7252万吨，增加2812万吨，增长63.3%。大米库存增长67.1%，玉米库存增长1倍多。加拿大谷物库存1271万吨，增长25.1%。澳大利亚谷物库存下降1.5%。印度大米库存增长6.4%，泰国和越南大米库存分别下降33.9%和19.8%。

4. 世界大豆库存6135万吨，增长57.9%。2004年世界大豆期末库存较上年增加2249万吨，库存增长主要得益于美国、巴西和阿根廷库存大幅增加。大豆库存居世界前四位的是巴西、阿根廷、美国和中国，它们的库存占世界大豆库存总量的93.6%。巴西和阿根廷大豆库存分别为2366万吨和1810万吨，增长40.8%和32.3%。美国大豆库存1198万吨，比上年增长近3倍。

5. 世界粮食库存止跌回升的主要原因。一是粮食总供给快速增加。受粮食价格强劲反弹和有利气候条件的共同影响，2004年世界粮食生产得到较快恢复，谷物增产1.69亿吨，大豆增产3881万吨，世界市场粮食供给总量相应增长。二是粮食消费增长平稳，消费增量小于供给增长。2004年世界小麦消费量6.08亿吨，比上年增加1830万吨；小麦供给7.53亿吨，比上年增加3271万吨。大豆消费量比上年增加1496万吨，而大豆供给增加3702万吨，消费增长明显小于供给增长。三是随着近年世界粮食库存的持续下降，粮食供给偏紧，促使许多国家从保障自身粮食安全考虑而增加政府储备，不少粮食企业的商业库存也有相应增加。

6. 世界粮食安全仍有隐忧。(1)当前的粮食库存仍然处于较低水平。与1999～2001年的历史最高库存相比，2004年世界粮食库存相当于1999年和2001年的80.6%和81.3%，只有2000年粮食库存的77.5%，表明世界粮食库存总体上仍处于较低水平。(2)粮食库存结构性矛盾突出。2004年粮食库存增加，主要增在小麦、玉米和大豆上，大米库存7676万吨，比上年下降10.6%，大米库存连续4年下跌，大米主销区特别是亚洲稻谷生产大国的大米库存下降较多。印度、泰国稻谷减产，泰国、越南大米库存分别下降33.9%和19.8%。(3)低收入缺粮国家粮食供给形势仍然严峻。据联合国粮农组织报告，全球24个国家存在粮食短缺危机，急需国际社会提供紧急粮食援助。这些国家主要分布在非洲、亚洲和拉丁美洲。

(三)2004年世界粮食贸易量增长0.8%

1. 世界粮食贸易恢复性增长。2004年由于国际市场粮食价格回升势头强劲，粮食生产得到较快恢复，产量增幅高于市场预期，世界市场粮食供给因此大幅增长。粮食国际贸易量将达2.95亿吨，比上年增加231万吨，增长0.8%。粮食贸易占粮食总产量和消费量的13.1%和13.5%。2004年中国粮食进口2998万吨，同比增长31.4%；粮食出口586万吨，下降74.8%；粮食净进口2412万吨。

2. 世界谷物贸易2.33亿吨，下降2.3%。2003年由于谷物库存大幅下降，市场供给偏紧，谷物贸易降至十年来的最低点。2004年世界谷物收成看好，谷物增产9.1%，产需缺口缩小，但世界谷物贸易量仍比上年减少544万吨，下降2.3%。谷物国际贸易占世界谷物产量的11.5%。谷物贸易减少主要是粗粮贸易减少，世界粗粮贸易9964万吨，比上年减少208万吨，下降2%；粗粮贸易占世界谷物贸易总量的42.8%。其中玉米贸易7490万吨，减少120万吨，下降1.6%；玉米贸易占世界谷物贸易总量的32.2%。大米贸易2492万吨，减少151万吨，下降7.7%；大米贸易占世界谷物贸易的10.7%。世界小麦贸易1.08亿吨，比上年减少186万吨，下降1.7%；小麦贸易占世界谷物贸易总量的46.5%。

3. 美国、澳大利亚和加拿大谷物出口下降，欧盟、阿根廷谷物出口增长。美国是世界最大谷物出口国，2004年谷物出口8431万吨，比上年下降4.9%；美国谷物出口占世界谷物贸易总量的36.2%。美国玉米出口4826万吨，增长0.2%；大米出口333万吨，与上年持平；小麦出口2790万吨，下降11.6%。阿根廷是第二大谷物出口国，2004年谷物出口2411万吨，增长20.4%；小麦出口1050万吨，增长11.6%；玉米出口1300万吨，增长26.8%。2004年欧盟小麦增产28.3%，谷物供给增长，出口达2011万吨，增长29.8%。欧盟小麦出口1500万吨，增长37.2%；玉米出口50万吨，增长25%。加拿大和澳大利亚谷物出口1895万吨和2132万吨，下降2.5%和15.4%。加拿大小麦出口1550万吨，下降1.8%。越南大米出口420万吨，与上年持平。泰国大米出口850万吨，下降16.2%。谷物进口居世界前三位的是中国、欧盟和巴西，它们的谷物进口量占世界谷物贸易的26%。欧盟谷物进口951万吨，比上年下降36.2%；巴西谷物进口560万吨，下降3.9%。

4. 世界大豆贸易6235万吨，增长14.2%。2004年大豆国际贸易占大豆产量和消费量的27.3%和30.4%。大豆出口居世界前三位的是美国、巴西和阿根廷，它们的出口量占世界大豆出口总量的91.6%。美国大豆出口量2749万吨，比上年增长14.1%。巴西和阿根廷大豆出口2230万吨和767万吨，增长12.5%和14.3%。中国、欧盟和日本是世界最大的大豆进口国，欧盟和日本大豆进口量分别为1566万吨和470万吨，增长7%和0.2%。

(四)2004年下半年世界粮食价格稳中趋降

1. 2004年下半年世界粮食期货价格持续下跌，第四季度降至年内最低点。由于世界粮食收成看好，产量增幅高于市场预期，粮食库存大幅下降的压力趋于缓解，市场对供求关系的总体判断渐趋乐观，价格也逐渐回落。从世界粮食期货行情[②]看，12月份粮食价格低位整理。与月初相比，12月底小麦价格下降8.8%，玉米下降2.6%，小麦和玉米价格降至年内最低点；12月份大米和大豆价格在11月份年内最低价的基础上略有回升，大米和

② 芝加哥商品交易所(CBOT)粮食期货价格。

大豆价格分别上涨7.4%和5%。

2.美国粮食生产价格回落。在国际市场粮价下滑带动下，美国国内粮食生产价格[3]相应走低。据美国世界农业展望委员会12月份预计，2004年度美国小麦、玉米生产价格将比上年下降1.5%和21.5%，大米和大豆价格分别下降1.2%和32.6%。该委员会2005年2月份的最新预报显示，2004年度美国小麦、玉米和大豆生产价格降幅减小，大米价格降幅加大。小麦、玉米和大豆生产价格将比上年下降0.7%、19.4%和30.5%、大米价格下降8.4%。

3.2004年12月份我国进口谷物到岸价格(CIF)比1月份下降16.6%。据海关资料测算，12月份我国进口谷物及谷物粉平均价格242.7美元/吨；大米价格399.5美元/吨，大麦价格203.6美元/吨；大豆价格280美元/吨。与1月份相比，谷物价格下降16.6%，大米价格下降14.2%，大麦价格下降0.3%，大豆价格下降18.8%。

总体上看，2004年世界粮食收成看好，产量增幅高于市场预期，世界粮食供给相应增加，库存大幅下降的压力趋于缓解，市场对供求关系的总体判断渐趋乐观，下半年粮食价格稳中趋降，这为我国从国际市场适量进口粮食以弥补国内粮食产需缺口提供了相对有利的外部环境。在政策选择上，我们必须立足当前，着眼长远，切实保护粮食生产能力，继续深化粮食流通体制改革，从根本上增强我国粮食产业的国际竞争力。

③ 指美国粮食贸易年度生产价格的加权平均价。不同品种的贸易年度起止时间各有不同。小麦贸易年度：6月1日至第二年5月31日；大米：8月1日至7月31日；玉米和大豆年度：9月1日至8月31日。

A Summary of the Trend of the Prices of Agricultural Products in 2004

Under the positive influence of the changes of the relations between supply and demand and the market-oriented reform of the grain purchase and selling carried out by the Chinese government, the prices of the agricultural products in the Chinese market rose again forcefully in 2004. The trend of the prices changing up and down at a low level in a number of past years was reversed at one stroke and new records had been set both in the prices of most agricultural products and their increase rates since 2000. The producer prices of the agricultural products in China rose by 13.1% in 2004 over the previous year. The increase rate was the highest since 1996. The prices of parts of the agricultural products were close to or had exceeded the highest historical level in 1996. The following characteristics had appeared in the market prices of agricultural products and their change trend in the whole country:

I. The producer prices of the agricultural products in China rose by 13.1% in 2004

According to the survey of the producer prices in 27000 units engaged in agricultural production and management, the general index of the producer prices of the agricultural products in the whole country was 113.1 in 2004 (the base in the previous year being 100, similarly hereinafter), a rise of 13.1% over the previous year. The increase rate of the producer prices was 8.7 percentage points higher than that in the previous year. Classified by different trades, the indices of the producer prices of the products of planting trade, forestry, animal husbandry and fishery were 115.9, 104.6, 111.1 and 110.2 respectively.

(1) The producer prices of the products of planting trade rose by 15.9%. The rise again of the prices of cereals, beans and oil-bearing crops was the important factor causing the rise of the prices of the products of planting trade in the whole year in 2004.

The average producer grain price was 1.21 yuan/kg, a rise of 26.2% over the previous year. Of the total, that of cereals rose by 28.1%, that of beans rose by 20.3%, that of potatoes rose by 5.8%, that of wheat rose by 31.2% and that of maize rose by 16.9%. The price of paddy rose by 36.3% as a whole. Of the total, the price of round-grained rice rose by 37.7%, that of early long-grained non-glutinous rice rose by 33.6% and that of late long-grained non-glutinous rice rose by 34.4%. The price of soybeans rose by 20.2%.

The producer price of cotton declined by 20.5% as compared with the previous year. The main reasons for the decline again of the cotton price were as follows: (a) The situations in increasing cotton production in China in 2004 was better than expected in the market. The yield totaled 6.32 million tons, an increase of 30.1% over the previous year. (b) The import of cotton increased greatly. The net import of cotton exceeded 1.90 million tons in 2004. (c) The domestic demand for cotton was stable. It was possible that the cancellation of the international quota restrictions on textiles had not fully shown in its role in promoting the domestic demand for cotton.

The prices of oil-bearing crops rose by 16.6% while those of groundnuts, rapeseeds and sesame seeds rose by 17.1%, 16.3% and 22.3% respectively. The prices of sugar crops rose by

4.9%.

The prices of vegetables rose while those of fruits declined again by a small extent. The prices of vegetables rose by 5.2%. Due to the proper climate, the output of fruits increased quite a lot and the prices of fruits declined by 1.4%. The prices of tobacco leaves rose by 8.4% and those of tea leaves rose by 11.2%.

(2) The producer prices of forest products rose by 4.6%. In recent years, the government had strengthened its efforts to protect the ecological environment and forest resources and implemented the change from the strategy mainly for producing timber and forest products to the strategy mainly for creating a better ecological environment. As a result, the growth rates of timber and other important forest products had slowed down. However, along with the continuously raised consumption level of the urban and rural residents, the demand of the market for the forest products increased continuously and the producer prices of forest products rose continuously as a result. The producer prices of timber rose by 4.2% in the year as compared with the previous year, those of bamboo rose by 8.9% and those of forest products like glue and fruit products rose by 4.1%.

(3) The producer prices of the products of animal husbandry rose by 11.1%. Because of the rise of the grain price and the corresponding rise of the cost for raising pigs, the prices of pigs for slaughter in 2004 rose by 12.8% over the previous year. The prices of cattle for slaughter rose by 3.9% and those of live sheep rose by 5.7%. The prices of milk products rose by 3.9%, those of hair and down rose by 3.7%. The producer prices of the poultry and eggs rose by 11.8% and 12.6% respectively, the price increase rates being 10 percentage points higher than those in 2003.

(4) The prices of fishery products rose by 10.2%. The prices of aquatic products in seawater in 2004 rose by 9.0% over the previous year, those of sea fish rose by 9.2%, those of sea shellfish rose by 9.2%. The prices of aquatic products in freshwater in 2004 rose by 12.3% over the previous year, those of freshwater fish rose by 11.5%, the producer prices of freshwater shrimps and crabs rose by 23.0%.

II. The Trend of the Prices of Agricultural Products at the Rural market Fairs in China in 2004

(1) The grain prices rose by a big margin. At the Rural Market Fairs (RMF) in the major producing areas, after the rise again of the grain prices in the fourth quarter in 2003, the grain prices rose once again in the first quarter in 2004; the paddy price rose by 27.2% in March as compared with that in Feb. the monthly increase rate being the highest in the past years. The annual average price of paddy rose by 41.8% over the previous year. The price of long-grained non-glutinous rice was 1.51 yuan/kg, a rise of 40.4%; and that of round-grained rice rose by 43.3%. As compared with 1996, the prices of long-grained non-glutinous rice and round-grained rice rose by 2.7% and 6.2% respectively. The annual average price of wheat was 1.52 yuan/kg, a rise of 33.3% over the previous year and was close to the price in 1996. The price of maize rose by 22.6% over the previous year. The price of soybeans was 3.88 yuan/kg, a rise of 0.92 yuan or 31% over the previous year. The prices of polished long-grained non-glutinous rice, polished round-grained rice and wheat flour rose by 38.9%, 40.5% and 30% respectively.

(2) The prices of cotton rose and declined sharply. Under the inertial influence of the rise of the cotton price by a big margin in the fourth quarter in 2003, the cotton price rose continuously in the period from January to April in 2004. The cotton price in April rose by 3.0% as compared with that in January. The cotton price began to decline again in May and speeded up to decline when the new cotton appeared in the market, the highest monthly decline rate being 7.4%. The cotton price in the fourth quarter of 2004 was lower than that in the same period in

the previous year.

(3) The prices of oil-bearing crops and edible oil changed at a high price level. Under the influence of the decrease of the yield of rapeseeds in 2003 and the forceful growth of the processing capacity of edible oil and the demand for it, the prices of oil-bearing crops and edible oil changed at a high level on the basis of highly rising prices in the fourth quarter in the previous year. The annual average prices of shelled peanuts and rapeseeds were 6.75 yuan/kg and 2.85 yuan/kg respectively, a rise of 20.7% and 19% over the previous year. The prices of peanut oil and rapeseed oil were 11.15 yuan/kg and 7.99 yuan/kg respectively, a rise of 18.2% and 16.6% over the previous year. The annual average price of soybean oil was 7.71 yuan/kg, a rise of 14.5% over the previous year.

(4) The prices of the products of animal husbandry rose by a big margin. Due to the rise of the prices of grains such as maize and soybeans used as forage by a big margin, the price of pork rose continuously in the first three quarters in 2004. Its highest price was 15.29 yuan/kg, close to that of beef. The annual average price of pork in 2004 was 13.97 yuan/kg, a rise of 30.6% over the previous year. The rise of pork price had encouraged the farmers to raise pigs and led to the rise of the price of piglets. The annual average price of piglets was 12.14 yuan/kg, a rise of 53.6% over the previous year. The price of beef in the four quarters in 2004 rose by 7.9%, 8.6%, 9.8% and 6.2% respectively as compared with the same period in the previous year. The annual average rise was 8.1%. The annual average price of mutton was 16.98 yuan/kg, a rise of 5.1% over the previous year.

Under the influence of bird flu, the prices of poultry and eggs fluctuated by a big margin. In February, the prices of eggs and live chicken declined by 11.1% and 5.8% respectively as compared with the previous month. When the epidemic situations were controlled, due to the decrease of the number of poultry on hand and the rise of forage price, the prices of eggs and live chicken rose continuously and were as high as 7.27 yuan/kg and 10.85 yuan/kg respectively, a rise of 31.5%% and 22.3% as compared with the same period in the previous year. Particularly, the prices of eggs had continuously set the new records since 2000.

(5) The prices of aquatic products rose in the former period and declined in the later period. The prices of fish rose month after month in the first half of 2004, but declined by a small margin in the second half of the year. The annual average price of grass carp was 9.1 yuan/kg, a rise of 25.7% over the previous year. The annual average price of carp was 8.9 yuan/kg, a rise of 27%. The annual average price of silver carp was 7.03 yuan/kg, a rise of 23.3% over the previous year. The annual average price of hairtail was 10.13 yuan/kg, a rise of 8.5%.

(6) The prices of fruits rose while the prices of fresh vegetables declined. The prices of vegetables and fruits fluctuated greatly in different seasons. Festivals and the climate factors were also the important reasons causing the changes of the prices of vegetables and fruits. The annual average prices of apples, bananas and oranges were 3.47 yuan/kg, 3.49 yuan/kg and 3.55 yuan/kg respectively, a rise of 3.8%, 12.2% and 4.1%. The prices of Chinese cabbages, cucumbers, tomatoes and sweetbells declined by 1.3%, 1.9%, 1.1% and 0.8% respectively as compared with the previous year.

III. The Main Characteristics in the Rise of Grain Prices in 2004

The producer prices of grain as well as the grain prices at the links of circulation rose in an all-round way and had set the new records since 2000. The prices of parts of the varieties had even exceeded those at the highest level in 1996. Specifically, the trend of the grain prices had the following characteristics:

(1) The prices of a good number of varieties had risen in the year. As shown in the data of the

survey of the prices of agricultural products, conducted by the National Bureau of Statistics, the producer prices of grain in the first three quarters in China in 2004 rose by 35.1%, a big margin and declined a little while remaining stable as a whole in the fourth quarter. The annual average producer grain price was still as high as 1.21 yuan/kg, a rise of 26.2% over 2003. The producer price of cereals rose by 28.1%. The producer price of wheat rose by 31.2%. The prices of early and late long-grained non-glutinous rice rose by 33.6% and 34.4% respectively and the price of round-grained rice rose by 37.7%. The prices of maize, soybeans rose by 16.9% and 20.2% respectively. The prices of mung beans and red beans rose by 16.7% and 28.3% respectively. The prices of millet, Chinese sorghum, barley and potatoes rose by 21.5%, 27.3%, 18.7% and 5.7% respectively.

(2) The price increase rates were big. The producer prices of grain rose in an all-round way in China in 2004 while the grain prices at the RMF, wholesale prices, import and export prices as well as the consumer price rose correspondingly. At the RMF in the major producing areas, the price of long-grained non-glutinous rice rose by 50.3% while the price of round-grained rice rose by 35% as compared with 2000. The prices of long-grained non-glutinous rice and round-grained rice rose by 2.7% and 6.2% respectively as compared with their purchasing prices in 1996. The price of wheat rose by 48.2% as compared with 2000 and was close to the price level in 1996. The price of maize rose by 59.4% as compared with 2000, 29.6% higher than the purchasing price in 1996. The price of soybeans rose by 53.6% as compared with 2000. The export price of China's cereals in 2004 was as high as 174.99 US dollars per ton, an increase of 44.6%. The price of food consumed by the residents in the whole country rose by 9.9% over the previous year. Of the total, the grain price rose by 26.4%.

(3) The rise of prices covered wide areas. The producer prices of grain in the eastern, central and western regions in China all exceeded 20%. A overall pattern of high rise in the eastern region and low rise in the western region had appeared. The producer prices of grain in the eastern region rose by 29.2% while those in the central and western regions rose by 25.7% and 20.8% respectively. The increase rates of the producer prices of grain in 7 provinces and municipalities had exceeded 30%, the increase rate in Chongqing Municipality being the highest. The increase rates of the producer prices of grain in 10 provinces and autonomous regions were in the range between 20% and 30%. The increase rates of the producer prices of grain in 14 provinces, autonomous regions and municipalities were lower than 20%. The grain prices in the major producing areas, in the major selling areas and in the areas where the yield was basically the same with the sales, rose by 27.4%, 31.9% and 20.8% respectively over the previous year.

(4) The increase rate of grain prices at the market was higher than that of the producer prices. Judging by the change trend of cereal prices, the producer prices of paddy, wheat and maize rose by 36.3%, 31.2% and 16.9% respectively while their prices at the RMF rose by 41.8%, 33.3% and 22.6% respectively. The increase rates of the prices at the RMF were 5.5, 2.1 and 5.7 percentage points higher than the increase rate of the producer prices respectively. The export price of cereals rose by 44.6% in 2004 as compared with the previous year. As shown in the fact that the increase rates of the producer prices of grain were lower than those of the prices at the RMF and the export price, the rise of grain price had led to the profit more gained at the circulating links and the profit gained by the farmers and farms were less than those gained by the managers of grain circulation.

(5) Market mechanism had become the decisive factor affecting the trend of price changes. Since the policy of reform and opening to the outside world was implemented, two rises of grain prices by a quite big margin occurred in the mid-

dle and later eighties and in the middle nineties in the previous century. The two rises of prices were made under the policy of the government. They were the behaviour of planned regulation and control guided by the government. The rise of grain prices in 2004 was the behaviour of market regulation caused by the changes of the relations between the supply of and the demand for grain under the circumstances of the market-oriented reform of the purchase and selling of grain. It was the natural reaction of the market under the condition that the grain yield had decreased year after year, the grain storage had declined by a big margin and, as a result, the total supply of grain was on the tight side. The rise of grain prices had started from a part of regions and expanded to the whole country and had started from individual varieties and expanded to all varieties. The changes of the price rising mechanism had reflected the gradual maturity of the system of market economy in China.

IV. The changes of grain prices at a high level were favourable to the increase of grain yield and the increase of farmer income.

The changes of grain prices at a high level were favourable to the increase of grain yield. The rise of grain prices had increased the economic benefit of farmers in growing grain crops and had greatly encouraged farmers to grow grain crops. According to the data collected from surveys, because the grain prices had changed at a high level since the fourth quarter of 2003, an important change had happened in the grain production in China in 2004. The situation of decreasing sown areas of grain crops in a number of past years had been reversed. The grain growing areas totaled 101.61 million hectares in 2004, an increase of 2.20 million hectares over the previous year. The grain yield totaled 469.47 million tons, an increase of 9.0%. The grain yield per unit area was 308 kg/ mu (1 hectare equals to 15 mu), an increase of 6.6%. Both the grain yield per unit area and the increase of grain yield in the year had set a new record in the history. The areas of grain crops sown in autumn and winter in the year totaled 26.38 million hectares, an increase of 4.8%. The sown areas of winter wheat totaled 21.14 million hectares, an increase of 5.9%. The enlarged growing areas had laid a solid foundation for the increase of the yield of summer grain crops in 2005.

The per capita input of the rural households in agricultural production was 471 yuan in the first three quarters in 2004, an increase of 86 yuan or 22.3%. The increase rate was 19.1 percentage points higher as compared with the same period in the previous year. The increase of the input in agricultural production accounted for 88.7% of the increase of the input in total production in the first three quarters. The per capita input of the rural households in agricultural production in major grain producing areas was 523 yuan, an increase of 103 yuan or 24.5%. As shown in the facts, cheap grain prices were unfavourable to farmers and reasonable grain prices had encouraged them to grow grain crops. The target of stably increasing the grain yield can be achieved only when the grain prices change basically stably at a reasonable level.

The changes of grain prices at a high level were favourable to the increase of farmers. Grain was the important basic product in the national economy. The grain output value in the period from 1999 to 2003 accounted for 36.6% of the agricultural gross output value in China. According to the estimation, a rise of 0.01 yuan/kg in grain price resulted in 10 yuan in the per capita income of farmers. In the previous years, the income of farmers obtained from agriculture decreased year after year. One of the important reasons was the grain price at a low level for a long time. As the farmers said, they lost money in growing grain crops. The producer prices of grain was 1.21 yuan/kg in China in 2004, a rise again of 26.2%, which led to a rise of 13.1% in the overall producer prices of agricultural products. As a result, a growing trend had appeared in farmer income, which was unseen in a number of past years. High price had become an important factor causing the increase of farmer income.

The per capita net income of farmers in China was 2936 yuan in 2004, a real increase of 6.8%. The growth rate of farmer income was the highest since 1997. The per capita cash income of farmers from selling agricultural products was 958 yuan in the first three quarters, an increase of 191 yuan or 24.9% as compared with the same period in the previous year. The per capita cash income of farmers from selling grain was 257 yuan, a year-on-year increase of 64 yuan or 32.7%. The per capita increase of income due to the increase of grain price was 56 yuan. The increase of cash income due to the increase of grain price had become the important source for increasing farmer income.

It was particularly noticeable that the rise of grain price had a good result in increasing the income of rural residents in the major grain producing areas. The per capita cash income of farmers in the major grain producing areas from selling agricultural products was 1050 yuan in the first three quarters of 2004, an increase of 22.8% as compared with the same period in the previous year. It was 9.6% higher than the national average income. Because of the rise of the producer price of grain, the per capita cash income of farmers in the major grain producing areas from selling agricultural products increased by 223 yuan. All the increase of the cash income came from the rise again of grain price.

V. The situations of grain markets and the trend of grain prices in the world in 2004

(1) The grain yield increased by 10.2% in the world in 2004.

(a) The increase rate of grain yield in the world was higher than expected at the market. Under the influence of the forceful rise again of grain price, there was a quite rapid recovery in the grain production in 2004. The grain yield totaled 2.249 billion tons in the world in 2004, an increase of 208 million tons or 10.2% over the previous year. The increase rate of grain yield was much higher than expected at the market. The grain supply at the world market increased by a big margin and the grain storage had changed from the decreasing situation to an increasing one. The situation of decreasing grain storage in the successive five years since 1999 had been reversed.

(b) The cereal yield totaled 2.021 billion tons in the world in 2004, an increase of 9.1%. In the year of 2004, the cereal yield set a new record in the world, an increase of 169 million tons or 9.1% over the previous year. The increase of cereal yield came mainly from the increase of the yields of wheat and maize by a big margin. The wheat yield totaled 622 million tons in the world in 2004, an increase of 12.6%. The increase of wheat yield accounted for 41.1% of the total increase of cereal yield. The wheat yield accounted for 30.8% of the total cereal yield in the world. Judging from the composition of resident food consumption, wheat is the most important product among cereals. The rice yield totaled 402 million tons in the world in 2004, an increase of 3.3%. The rice yield accounted for 19.9% of the total cereal yield in the world. The maize yield totaled 702 million tons in the world in 2004, an increase of 79.94 million tons or 12.9%. The increase of maize yield accounted for 47.4% of the total increase of cereal yield. The maize yield accounted for 34.7% of the total cereal yield in the world.

(c) The cereal yields in major trading countries such as USA and European Union (EU) increased by a quite big margin, but it decreased in Australia. In 2004, the cereal yield in USA totaled 386 million tons, an increase of 11.6%; that in EU totaled 287 million tons, an increase of 24.6%. The cereal yields in Canada and Argentina totaled 52.39 million tons and 37.70 million tons respectively, an increase of 5% and 20.8%.

The maize yield in USA increased by 17% over the previous year. The wheat yield in EU increased by 28.3%. The rice yield in Vietnam increased by 0.3%. The cereal yield in Australia totaled 32.06 million tons, a decrease of 21.96%.

(d) The soybean yield totaled 229 million tons in the world in 2004, an increase of 20.5%. The soybeans can be used as the resident staple food and the important materials for processing edible oil. The soybean yields in USA, Brazil and Argentina ranked in first three places in the world in 2004 and accounted for 82% of the total yield in the world. The soybean yield in USA totaled 85.48 million tons in 2004, an increase of 28% over the previous year. The soybean yields in Brazil and Argentina were 63.00 million tons and 39.00 million tons respectively, an increase of 19.8% and 14.7%.

(e) The main reasons for the increase of grain yield in the world: (i) The role of rising grain prices in encouraging the producers to grow grain had gradually manifested itself. Since 2002, due to the quite tight grain supply in the international market, the grain prices ceased to decline but rose again and continuously changed at a high level, the producer prices rose correspondingly. As a result, the economic benefit of the grain producers increased quite a lot and their enthusiasm in increasing the yield was enhanced. (ii) The sown areas of grain crops in major producing countries such as USA and China were enlarged. The sown area of maize increased by 2.9% and that of paddy increased by 10.9% in USA in 2004. (iii) The climate conditions in the major grain producing areas were generally better as compared with the previous year. The stricken areas of grain crops were relatively small. The increase rate of per unit area yield was quite high.

(f) The increase of grain yield had the influence over the relations between the supply and demand at the grain market: In 2004, the cereal yield was 2.021 billion tons in the world while the demand for cereals was 1.988 billion tons. The cereal yield exceeded the cereal consumption in the year by 33.12 million tons. The cereal storage at the end of the period increased by 9.5% over the previous year. The soybean yield was 229 million tons while the demand for soybeans was 205 million tons. The soybean storage at the end of the period increased by 22.49 million tons over the previous year. Because of the increase of the cereal and soybean storage by a big margin, the grain storage at the end of the period increased by more than 55.60 million tons over the previous year in the world. The ratio of grain storage to the annual grain consumption rose to 20.2%, 2.2 percentage points higher than 18%, the ratio for safety.

(2) The recovery in the increase of the grain storage in the world.

(a) The grain storage at the end of the period increased by 14.3% in the world in 2004. Due to the increase of grain yield by 10.2%, a big margin, in 2004, the grain storage in the world had changed from decline to rise for the first time since 2000. The grain storage at the end of the period totaled 444 million tons, an increase of 55.62 million tons or 14.3%. The ratio of grain storage to the annual grain consumption was as high as 20.2%, 2.2 percentage points higher than 18%, the ratio for safety. The pressure due to the continuous decline of the grain storage in the world tended to be alleviated.

(b) The cereal storage increased by 9.5% in the world in 2004. The wheat and maize storages increased while the rice storage decreased. The main products of cereals are wheat, paddy and maize. The cereal storage at the end of the period totaled 382 million tons in the world in 2004, accounting for 86.2% of the total grain storage. The cereal storage accounted for 19.2% of the annual consumption. The wheat storage totaled 145 million tons, an increase of 14.41 million tons or 11%. The wheat storage accounted for 38% of the cereal storage or 23.9% of the annual wheat consumption. Therefore wheat was the most important staple food for the residents in their consumption. The rice storage totaled 76.76 million tons, a decrease of 10.6%. The rice storage accounted for 20.1% of the total cereal storage. The maize storage totaled 117 million tons, an increase of 19.60 million tons or 20.1% over the previous year. The maize storage accounted for 30.7% of the total cereal storage or 17.2% of the annual maize consumption.

(c) The increase rates of the cereal storage in main trading countries were higher than expected at the market. In EU in 2004, the cereal storage totaled 40.57 million tons, an increase of 85.3%; the wheat storage totaled 19.97 million tons, an increase of more than 1 fold over the previous year while the maize storage totaled 5.54 million tons, an increase of 69.9%. In USA in 2004, the cereal storage totaled 72.52 million tons, an increase of 28.12 million tons or 63.3%; the rice storage rose by 67.1% while the maize storage increased more than 1 fold. In Canada, the cereal storage totaled 12.71 million tons, an increase of 25.1%. In Australia, the cereal storage declined by 1.5%. In India, the rice storage increased by 6.4%. In Thailand and Vietnam, the rice storages decreased by 33.9% and 19.8% respectively.

(d) The soybean storage totaled 61.35 million tons in the world, an increase of 57.9%. The storage of soybeans at the end of period in the world in 2004 increased by 22.49 million tons over the previous year. The increase in the storage in the world was caused mainly by the increase in the storage in USA, Brazil and Argentina by a big margin. The soybean storage in Brazil, Argentina, USA and China ranked in the first four places in the world. The soybean storage of these four countries counted for 93.6% of the total storage in the world. The soybean storages in Brazil and Argentina were 23.66 million tons and 18.10 million tons respectively, an increase of 40.8% and 32.3%. The soybean storage in USA was 11.98 million tons, an increase of nearly 3 folds over the previous year.

(e) The main reasons for no longer declining but rising again of the grain storage in the world were as follows: (i) The total grain supply increased rapidly. Under the influence of the forceful rise again of grain price and the favourable climate conditions, a quite rapid recovery in the grain production was achieved in the world in 2004. The cereal yield increased by 169 million tons. The soybean yield increased by 38.81 million tons. The total grain supply in the world market increased correspondingly. (ii) The grain consumption increased smoothly and steadily. The increase in grain consumption was less than the increase in grain supply. The wheat consumption totaled 608 million tons in the world in 2004, an increase of 18.30 million tons while the wheat supply totaled 753 million tons, an increase of 32.71 million tons over the previous year. The soybean consumption increased by 14.96 million tons in the world in 2004 while the soybean supply increased by 37.02 million tons, the increase in consumption being noticeably less than the increase in supply. (iii) Along with the continuous decline of the grain storage in the world in recent years, the grain supply was on the tight side. As a result, a lot of countries had increased the government storage to ensure their own grain safety and the commercial storages of a number of grain enterprises increased correspondingly.

(f) There are still hidden troubles in the grain safety in the world: (i) The grain storage in the world is still at a comparatively low level at present. As compared with the highest storage level in 1999 — 2001, the grain storage in the world in 2004 was equivalent to 80.6% and 81.3% of the grain storage in the world in 1999 and 2001 respectively. It was equivalent to 77.5% of the grain storage in the world in 2000. It shows that the grain storage in the world as a whole is still at a comparatively low level. (ii) There are striking structural contradictions in the grain storage in the world. The increase of the grain storage in 2004 was caused mainly by the increase of the storage of wheat, maize and soybeans. The rice storage totaled 76.76 million tons in 2004, a decline of 10.6% as compared with the previous year. The rice storage had declined in successive four years. The rice storage in the major rice selling areas, particularly in the major rice producing countries in Asia had declined quite a lot. The rice yield decreased in India and Thailand. The rice storages in Thailand and Vietnam declined by 33. 9% and 19. 8% respectively. (iii) The situations of grain supply in low-income countries short of grain supply are still stern. According to the report of Food and Agriculture Organization (FAO), the crisis of grain deficiency exists in 24 countries in the world, where the international community is necessary to render the urgent grain assistance. These countries are distributed mainly in Africa, Asia and Latin America.

(3) The trading volume of grain increased by 0. 8% in the world in 2004.

(a) There was a recovery in the growth of grain trade in the world in 2004: Because of the forceful trend of the rise again of grain prices at the international market in 2004, a quite rapid recovery was achieved in grain production, the growth rate of grain yield was higher than expected at the market and the grain supply grew by a big margin at the world market correspondingly. The international trading volume of grain would total 295 million tons in 2004, an increase of 2. 31million tons or 0. 8% over the previous year. The trading volume of grain accounted for 13. 1% and 13. 5% of the total grain yield and grain consumption respectively. 29. 98 million tons of grain had been imported to China in 2004, an increase of 31. 4% while 5. 86 million tons of grain had been exported from China, a decline of 74. 8%. China's net import of grain were 24. 12 million tons in 2004.

(b) The trading volume of cereals totaled 233 million tons in the world in 2004, a decline of 2. 3%. In the year of 2003, because the cereal storage declined by a big margin and the cereal supply at the market was on the tight side, the cereal trading volume declined to the lowest level in the past ten years in the world. In the year of 2004, the harvest of cereals was good, the cereal yield increased by 9. 1%, the shortage between the yield and the demand was reduced, but the trading volume of cereals still decreased by 5. 44 million tons or 2. 3% as compared with the previous year. The international trading volume of cereals accounted for 11. 5% of the cereal yield in the world. The decrease of the trading volume of cereals was caused mainly by the decrease of the trading volume of the coarse food grain. The trading volume of the coarse food grain totaled 99. 64 million tons in the world in 2004, a decrease of 2. 08 million tons or 2% as compared with the previous year. The trading volume of coarse food grain accounted for 42. 8% of the total trading volume of cereals in the world. The trading volume of maize totaled 74. 90 million tons in the world in 2004, a decrease of 1. 20 million tons or 1. 6 %as compared with the previous year. The trading volume of maize accounted for 32. 2% of the total trading volume of cereals in the world. The trading volume of rice totaled 24. 92 million tons in the world in 2004, a decrease of 1. 51 million tons or 7. 7% as compared with the previous year. The trading volume of rice accounted for 10. 7% of the total trading volume of cereals in the world. The trading volume of wheat totaled 108 million tons in the world in 2004, a decrease of 1. 86 million tons or 1. 7% as compared with the previous year. The trading volume of wheat accounted for 46. 5% of the total trading volume of cereals in the world.

(c) The export of cereals from USA, Australia and Canada declined while the export of cereals from EU and Argentina increased. USA is the largest country in exporting cereals. Its cereal export was 84. 31 million tons in 2004, a decrease of 4. 9% as compared with the previous year. The export of cereals from USA accounted for 36. 2% of the total trading volume of cereals in the world. Its maize export totaled 48. 26 million tons in 2004, an increase of 0. 2%. Its rice export totaled 3. 33 million tons in 2004, at the same level as the previous year. Its wheat export totaled

27.90 million tons in 2004, a decrease of 11.6%. Argentina is the second largest country in exporting cereals. Its cereal export was 24.11 million tons in 2004, an increase of 20.4% as compared with the previous year. Its wheat export was 10.50 million tons, an increase of 11.6%. Its maize export was 13.00 million tons, an increase of 26.8%. The wheat yield increased by 28.3% in EU in 2004. As a result, the cereal supply in EU increased and the cereal export from EU totaled 20.11 million tons, an increase of 29.8%. The wheat export from EU totaled 15.00 million tons, an increase of 37.2%. The maize export from EU totaled 0.5 million tons, an increase of 25%. The cereal export from Canada and Australia totaled 18.95 million tons and 21.32 million tons respectively, a decline of 2.5% and 15.4%. The wheat export from Canada totaled 15.50 million tons, a decline of 1.8%. The rice export from Vietnam totaled 4.20 million tons, at the same level as the previous year. The rice export from Thailand totaled 8.50 million tons, a decline of 16.2%. China, EU and Brazil ranked in the first three places in the world in cereal import. Their cereal import accounted for 26% of the trading volume of cereals in the world. The cereal import in EU totaled 9.51 million tons, a decline of 36.2% as compared with the previous year. The cereal import in Brazil totaled 5.60 million tons, a decline of 3.9%.

(d) The trading volume of soybeans totaled 62.35 million tons in the world in 2004, an increase of 14.2%. The international trading volume of soybeans accounted for 27.3% and 30.4% of the soybean yield and soybean consumption in the world. USA, Brazil and Argentina ranked in the first three places in the world in exporting soybeans. Their export accounted for 91.6% of the total export of soybeans in the world. The soybean export from USA totaled 27.49 million tons, an increase of 14.1%. The soybean export from Brazil and Argentina totaled 22.30 million tons and 7.67 million tons respectively, an increase of 12.5% and 14.3%. China, EU and Japan were the three largest countries in importing soybeans. The soybean import in EU and Japan totaled 15.66 million tons and 4.70 million tons respectively, an increase of 7% and 0.2%.

(4) The grain prices tended to decline while remaining stable as a whole in 2004.

(a) The future prices of grain declined continuously in the second half of 2004 and declined to the lowest level in the year in the fourth quarter. Because the grain harvest was good in the world, the increase rate of the grain yield was higher than expected at the market, the pressure caused by the decline of grain storage by a big margin had the trend to be alleviated, the overall judgment at the market on the relations between supply and demand gradually tended to be optimistic, the grain prices gradually declined. As shown in the future quotations of grains, the grain prices in December had the trend of decline. As compared with the beginning of the month, the wheat price declined by 8.8% while the maize price declined by 2.6% at the end of December. The prices of wheat and maize had declined to the lowest level in the year. On the basis of the lowest level in the year in November, the prices of rice and soybeans rose again a little in December. The prices of rice and soybeans rose by 7.4% and 5% respectively.

(b) The producer prices of grain declined again in USA. Under the influence of the decreasing grain prices at the international market, the producer prices of grain declined correspondingly at the domestic market in USA. A predicted by the World Agricultural Outlook Board in USA in December, the producer prices of wheat and maize in 2004 would decline by 1.5% and 21.5% respectively as compared with the previous year while the rice and soybean prices would decline by 1.2% and 32.6% respectively. As shown in the latest prediction made in February of 2005, the decrease rates of the producer prices of wheat, maize and soybeans were reduced while the decrease rate of the producer price of rice was enlarged. The producer prices of wheat, maize and soybeans would decline by 0.7%, 19.4% and 30.5% respectively as compared with the previous year while the rice price would decline by 8.4%.

(c) The CIF (cost, insurance and freight) of the imported cereals in China declined in December by 16.6% as compared with January. As estimated on the basis of the data of the customs, in December, the average price of cereals and cereal powder was 242.7 US dollars/ton, the price of imported rice was 399.5 US dollars/ton, the price of imported barley was 203.6 US dollars/ton and the price of imported soybeans was 280 US dollars/ton. As compared with January, the cereal price declined by 16.6%, the rice price declined by 14.2%, the barley price declined by 0.3% and the soybean price declined by 18.8%.

Generally speaking, in the year of 2004, the grain harvest was good in the world, the increase rate of the grain yield was higher than expected at the market, the grain supply in the world increased correspondingly, the pressure caused by the decline of grain storage by a big margin had the trend to be alleviated, the overall judgment at the market on the relations between supply and demand gradually tended to be optimistic, the grain prices tended to decline while remaining stable as a whole. This situation had provided a relatively favourable international environment for China to import grain in a proper volume from the international market so as to make up the grain shortage in the country. In choice of policies, we should base ourselves upon the present time, have a long-term prospect in mind, effectively protect the grain production capability, continuously deepen the reform of the system of grain circulation, so as to thoroughly strengthen the international competitive power of our grain industry.

世界粮食库存持续下降的压力趋于缓解
World Supply And Use for Grains and Soybean

单位：百万吨 millions ton

粮食品种 Commodity	产量 Output	总供给 Total supply	国际贸易 Trade	总需求 Total use	期末库存 Ending stocks
谷物合计 Total grains					
2000/01	1,839.67	2,401.88	232.95	1,860.16	541.72
2001/02	1,870.46	2,414.35	238.68	1,900.71	513.64
2002/03	1,817.28	2,353.39	241.21	1,909.80	443.60
2003/04	1,852.14	2,295.74	238.40	1,946.67	349.07
2004/05	2,020.87	2,369.95	232.96	1,987.75	382.20
小麦 Wheat					
2000/01	582.05	788.69	102.78	584.41	204.29
2001/02	581.01	787.72	108.12	586.34	201.38
2002/03	566.96	769.03	108.48	601.41	167.62
2003/04	552.83	720.45	110.25	589.48	130.97
2004/05	622.19	753.16	108.39	607.78	145.38
大米 Rice,milled					
2000/01	397.96	543.59	24.17	395.56	148.03
2001/02	398.42	547.47	26.90	410.41	137.05
2002/03	377.89	517.32	28.62	407.05	119.27
2003/04	389.27	499.53	26.43	413.7	85.83
2004/05	402.13	487.96	24.92	411.19	76.76
粗粮 Coarse grains					
2000/01	859.67	1069.60	106.00	880.19	189.41
2001/02	891.02	1,079.17	103.66	903.96	175.21
2002/03	872.43	1,067.05	104.11	901.34	165.71
2003/04	910.05	1,075.76	101.72	943.48	132.28
2004/05	996.55	1,128.83	99.64	968.77	160.05
大豆 Soybean					
2000/01	175.06	202.82	55.33	171.82	30.64
2001/02	184.87	215.58	53.92	183.99	32.19
2002/03	197.12	230.31	62.18	190.64	40.65
2003/04	189.81	230.46	54.61	190.45	38.86
2004/05	228.62	267.48	62.35	205.41	61.35

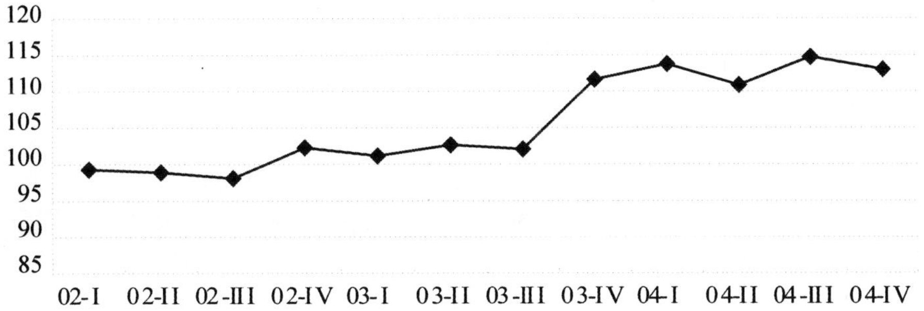

2002—2004 年农产品生产价格总指数

Indices of the Producer Prices of Agricultural Products(**2002—2004**)

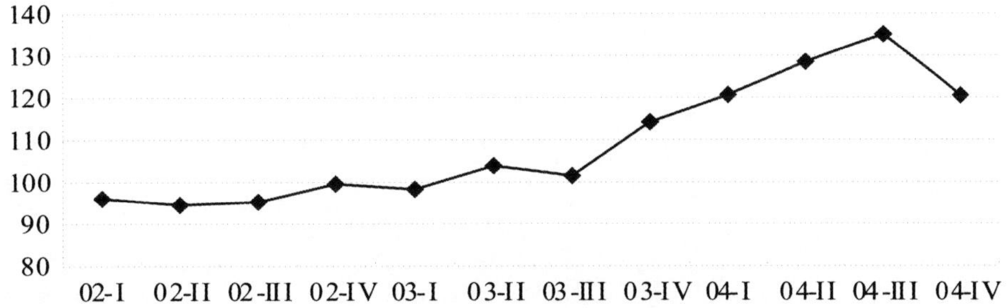

2002—2004 年种植业产品生产价格指数

Indices of the Producer Prices of Farming Products(**2002—2004**)

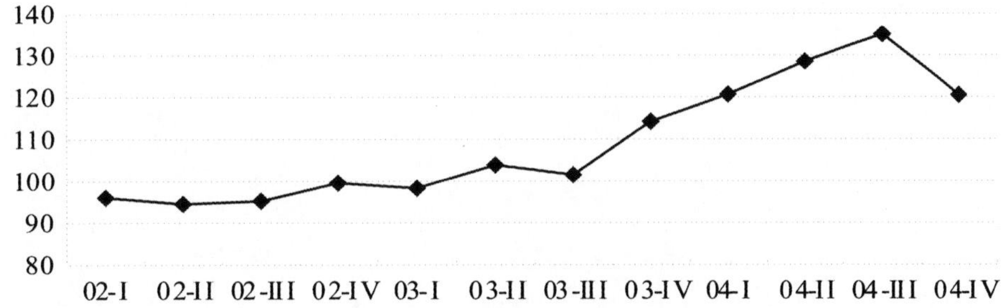

2002—2004 粮食生产价格指数

Indices of the Producer Prices of Grain(**2002—2004**)

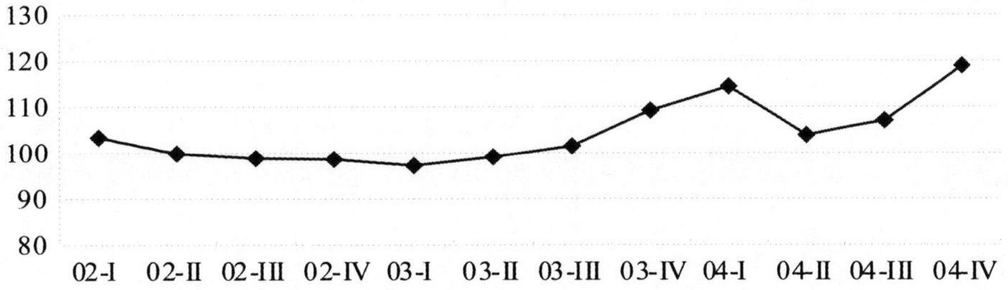

2002—2004 畜牧业产品生产价格指数

Indices of of the Producer Prices of Animal Products(**2002—2004**)

2

农产品生产价格指数

Indices of the Producer Prices of Agricultural Products

2—1 全国农产品生产价格总指数

National Gross Indices of the Producer Prices of Agricultural Products

（上年＝100） (preceding year＝100)

年份 Year	农产品生产价格总指数 Indices of Producer Prices of Agricultural Products				
	总指数 Gross Index	种植业产品 Crop products	林业产品 Forest products	畜牧业产品 Livestock products	渔业产品 Fishery products
1978	103. 90				
1980	107. 10				
1985	108. 60				
1990	97. 40				
1991	98. 00				
1992	103. 40				
1993	113. 40				
1994	139. 90				
1995	119. 90				
1996	104. 20				
1997	95. 50				
1998	92. 00				
1999	87. 80				
2000	96. 40				
2001	103. 10				
2002	99. 70	100. 04	98. 31	100. 15	95. 89
2003	104. 37	107. 42	107. 01	101. 76	100. 34
2004	113. 09	115. 86	104. 62	111. 08	110. 19

注：2000 年以前农产品生产价格总指数为农产品收购价格指数。

Note: The gross indices of producer prices of agricultural products before 2000 were the indices of purchase prices of agricultural products.

2—2 全国分品种农产品生产价格指数
National Indices of the Producer Prices of Agricultural Products

（上年=100） （Year） （preceding year=100）

农产品名称	Categories of agricultural products	2002	2003	2004
总指数	Gross Index	99.70	104.37	113.09
一、种植业产品	I. Crop products	100.04	107.42	115.86
粮食	Grain	96.16	104.48	126.21
谷物（原粮）	Cereal (unprocessed food grains)	95.83	102.34	128.06
小麦	Wheat	98.14	102.99	131.16
硬粒小麦	Hard-grained wheat	99.70	103.96	132.28
软粒小麦	Soft-grained wheat	87.66	103.12	130.97
混合小麦	Mixed wheat	98.76	101.84	132.88
稻谷	Paddy rice	97.17	99.89	136.30
早籼稻	Early long-grained nonglutinous rice	99.39	101.69	133.57
晚籼稻	Late long-grained nonglutinous rice	100.79	103.70	134.39
粳稻	Round-grained rice	94.71	97.85	137.68
玉米	Maize (corn)	91.50	104.58	116.92
黄玉米	Yellow maize	91.25	104.59	116.89
白玉米	White maize	102.89	101.33	117.43
混合玉米	Mixed maize	109.95	104.66	117.48
薯类	Potato	93.71	92.87	105.75
红薯	Sweet potato	142.94	94.54	108.97
马铃薯	White potato	75.42	92.21	104.89
豆类	Beans	98.11	119.33	120.29
大豆	Soybeans	98.95	120.62	120.17
绿豆	Mung beans	86.11	100.45	116.73
红小豆	Red beans	99.30	103.60	128.26
油料	Oil-bearing crops	104.82	119.40	116.58
花生	Peanut	102.71	124.19	117.07
油菜籽	Rapeseeds	103.14	119.15	116.33
芝麻	Sesame	88.64	128.92	122.34
胡麻籽	Flaxseeds	118.53	116.34	115.44
棉花	Cotton (unginned cotton)	103.35	135.33	79.54
细绒棉（籽棉）	Thin-staple cotton	103.83	135.81	79.80
长绒棉（籽棉）	Long-staple cotton	94.40	121.21	83.50
麻类	Fiber crops	93.84	111.11	124.99
黄红麻	Jute and blueish dogbane	96.63	107.67	116.59

2—2 续表 1 continued 1

农产品名称	Categories of agricultural products	2002	2003	2004
苎麻	Ramie	86.27	113.83	131.10
糖料	Sugar crops	86.01	90.50	104.86
甘蔗	Sugarcane	86.57	90.49	104.86
甜菜	Beet	97.14	106.56	106.10
烟叶	Tobacco	132.78	97.21	108.42
烤烟叶	Flue-cured tobacco	153.69	94.94	106.42
晒烟叶	Sun-cured tobacco	99.09	112.40	113.45
蔬菜	Vegetable	95.06	110.44	105.17
叶菜类	Leaf vegetable	98.09	113.21	101.85
菠菜	Spinach	85.62	113.94	101.57
芹菜	Celery	81.62	127.10	99.28
大白菜	Chinese cabbage	81.37	115.76	102.10
元白菜	Cabbage	90.32	99.55	106.45
甘蓝	Wild cabbage	146.08	97.81	100.78
花椰菜	Cauliflower	89.66	112.08	101.29
莴笋	Asparagus lettuce	119.20	102.77	107.36
油菜	Rape	155.50	109.50	101.61
瓜菜类	Gourd vegetable	98.01	110.71	101.10
黄瓜	Cucumber	96.97	113.37	103.66
冬瓜	White gourd	93.21	122.81	92.92
西葫芦	Summer squash	146.05	107.46	99.41
块根、块茎菜类	Root and tuber vegetable	85.86	111.62	103.59
萝卜	Radish	86.33	110.46	103.08
胡萝卜	Carrot	99.17	115.09	102.90
生姜	Ginger	67.06	95.91	145.13
茄果菜类	Eggplant, tomato and chili, etc.	86.18	108.55	103.18
茄子	Eggplant	101.74	117.82	108.01
西红柿	Tomato	79.20	103.82	104.06
辣椒	Chili	87.87	111.06	103.62
青椒	Sweetbell	109.39	109.38	96.48
葱蒜类	Onion and Garlic	96.39	105.98	115.91
大葱	Scallion	173.41	110.21	111.81
蒜苔	Garlic stalk	109.81	115.60	115.10

2－2 续表 2 continued 2

农产品名称	Categories of agricultural products	2002	2003	2004
蒜头	Garlic head	84.59	94.67	117.72
菜用豆类	Garden beans	100.38	109.98	104.96
四季豆	Kidney beans	98.54	104.16	108.45
豇豆	Cowpeas	103.14	117.49	101.77
水生菜类	Water vegetable	129.38	112.41	113.37
莲藕	Lotus root	112.73	114.53	108.84
茭白	Wild ruice stem	143.37	102.64	106.81
荸荠	Water chestnut	85.94	99.69	122.09
水果	Garden fruits	109.91	102.04	97.44
苹果	Apple	106.53	103.51	102.50
红富士苹果	Hongfushi apple	120.67	103.84	102.48
国光苹果	Guoguang apple	94.63	91.60	98.21
秦冠苹果	Qinguan apple	88.92	107.81	108.62
香蕉苹果	Banana apple	49.18	110.85	105.10
梨	Pear	112.35	102.91	95.31
雪花梨	Snowflake pear	125.20	109.54	93.96
鸭梨	Ya-pear	103.04	103.56	98.29
酥梨	Soft-pear	90.75	106.64	95.31
香梨	Bergamot pear	146.51	142.19	108.04
柑桔类	Citrus	103.02	100.50	94.73
柑	Mandarin orange	109.41	99.24	95.73
桔	Tangerine	107.11	106.19	91.83
橙	Orange	93.44	109.41	102.14
柚	Shaddock	79.90	93.89	99.23
热带亚热带水果	Tropical and subtropics area fruits	104.50	114.98	101.61
香蕉	Banana	143.80	111.31	114.25
荔枝	Litchi	76.89	125.03	64.76
龙眼	Longan	49.66	115.09	79.61
果用瓜	Melon	168.06	88.59	109.63
西瓜	Watermelon	287.81	88.54	110.00
甜瓜	Muskmelon	90.94	91.83	107.34
桃	Peach	113.45	89.42	96.66
杏	Apricot	91.66	98.72	99.61

2—2 续表 3 continued 3

农产品名称	Categories of agricultural products	2002	2003	2004
杨梅	Red bayberry	277.56	81.29	106.76
草莓	Strawberry	95.65	110.38	105.37
猕猴桃	Yangtao	101.85	87.77	113.20
葡萄	Grape	136.62	99.14	95.36
红枣	Chinese date	101.96	91.62	108.02
柿子	Persimmon	113.64	97.86	92.29
红毛茶	Black tea	105.33	83.22	109.41
绿毛茶	Green tea	180.71	100.56	110.48
乌龙茶	Oolong tea	106.26	94.56	107.50
二、林业产品	II. Forest products	98.31	107.01	104.62
工业用原料	Products of natural and artificial forest	110.48	121.49	104.05
橡胶	Rubber	110.48	121.49	117.47
油桐籽	Seeds of tung oil tree	84.93	180.53	114.47
油茶籽	Seeds of tea-oil tree	75.08	113.54	115.56
坚果	Nuts	142.89	96.39	108.36
核桃	Walnut	142.89	96.39	102.66
花椒	Chinese prickly ash	101.11	98.68	93.49
八角	Anise	82.52	74.93	77.36
桂皮	Cassia bark	81.44	92.07	96.73
三、畜牧业产品	III. Livestock products	100.15	101.76	111.08
猪	Hog (gross weight)	97.96	102.86	112.84
肉牛	Live cattle (gross weight)	91.44	101.68	103.93
家禽(毛重)	Poultry (gross weight)	106.09	101.00	111.25
鸡	Chicken	105.94	101.02	111.22
鸭	Duck	100.69	95.81	116.32
鹅	Goose	115.09	101.83	113.47
蛋类	Eggs	102.80	101.06	112.58
鸡蛋	Chicken's eggs	102.58	101.06	112.54
鸭蛋	Duck's eggs	110.74	101.61	113.95
鹅蛋	Goose's eggs	79.36	100.35	105.95
奶类	Milk products	99.71	103.68	103.73
牛奶	Cow milk	99.76	103.67	103.73
羊奶	Sheep milk	62.67	105.90	105.30

2—2 续表 4　　continued 4

农产品名称	Categories of agricultural products	2002	2003	2004
毛绒类	Hair and down products	80.11	102.23	103.10
山羊毛	Goat's wool	175.45	85.72	98.98
山羊绒	Cashmere	67.54	104.92	104.71
蚕茧	Silkworm cocoon	64.38	106.29	125.01
蜂蜜	Honey	137.68	106.87	99.07
四、渔业产品	IV. Fishery products	95.89	100.34	110.19
海水水产品	Seawater aquatic products	98.09	101.13	109.00
海水鱼类	Seawater Fish	104.87	103.98	109.16
大黄鱼	Large yellow croaker	76.64	94.01	108.66
小黄鱼	Small yellow croaker	91.57	97.68	110.53
带鱼	Hairtail	94.92	102.75	107.29
石斑鱼	Grouper	468.10	84.24	116.27
海水虾蟹类	Seawater shrimp and crab	149.68	110.19	108.80
海水贝类	Seawater shellfish	106.68	97.80	109.17
贻贝	Mussel	89.10	99.63	136.84
扇贝	Scallop	101.40	102.41	134.07
牡蛎	Oyster	107.78	96.65	102.39
鲍鱼	Abalone	99.20	111.12	117.06
蛤	Clam	107.05	98.35	106.35
蚶	Blood clam	93.05	138.03	94.30
藻类	Seaweeds	118.13	102.66	120.68
海带	Kelp	108.75	103.98	114.47
紫菜	Laver	132.98	103.19	95.60
内陆水域水产品	Aquatic products in inland water areas	93.07	98.83	112.30
淡水鱼类	Freshwater fish	93.07	98.65	111.52
青鱼	Black carp	59.97	99.28	106.65
草鱼	Grass carp	90.97	97.33	115.47
鲤鱼	Carp	93.92	101.06	112.06
鲢鱼	Silver carp	89.03	97.28	113.29
鲫鱼	Crucian carp	85.06	98.06	109.33
罗非鱼	Tilapia	104.73	96.57	104.88
淡水虾蟹类	Freshwater shrimps and crabs	91.72	104.13	122.97

2—3 全国农产品生产价格指数(第一季度)
National Indices of the Producer Prices of Agricultural Products

(上年同期=100) (1st quarter) (the same period of the preceding year=100)

农产品名称	Categories of agricultural products	2002	2003	2004
		第一季度 1st quarter		
合 计	Gross Index	99.30	101.15	113.75
一、农业产品	I. Crop products	95.13	105.01	114.82
1. 谷物及其他作物	1. Cereal and other crops			119.93
#粮食	Grain	96.06	98.33	120.69
谷物(原粮)	Cereal (unprocessed food grains)	98.21	95.92	121.00
小麦	Wheat	103.79	96.00	124.36
硬粒小麦	Hard-grained wheat	112.72	98.69	130.45
软粒小麦	Soft-grained wheat	97.43	94.69	117.34
混合小麦	Mixed wheat	101.00	94.95	123.38
其他小麦	Other wheat			120.71
稻谷	Paddy rice	98.21	94.12	129.55
早籼稻	Early long-grained nonglutinous rice	102.68	99.11	124.73
晚籼稻	Late long-grained nonglutinous rice	101.33	99.93	127.20
粳稻	Round-grained rice	96.67	92.02	130.67
其他稻谷	Other paddy			119.22
玉米	Maize (corn)	97.21	97.48	112.86
黄玉米	Yellow maize	97.20	97.48	112.86
白玉米	White maize	111.68	96.15	113.63
混合玉米	Mixed maize	90.97	98.53	112.09
其他玉米	Other maize		87.83	114.42
杂粮	Coarse cereals		116.43	0.00
谷子	Millet		117.82	117.63
高粱	Chinese sorghum		97.47	116.19
大麦	Barley		102.79	108.25
荞麦	Buckwheat		109.02	103.52
元麦	poulard wheat		129.34	0.00
青稞	Highland barley		107.74	103.02
莜麦	Naked oats		103.86	109.55
燕麦	Oats		130.85	
其他杂粮	Other coarse cereals			109.48
谷物副产品	By-products of cereals			
小麦秸	Wheat straw		96.57	123.29
稻草	Rice straw		95.07	117.98
玉米秆	Corn stover		92.23	111.45

2—3 续表 1 continued 1

农产品名称	Categories of agricultural products	2002	2003	2004
		第一季度 1st quarter		
谷子秆	Millet stalk		107.56	123.63
高粱秆	Chinese sorghum stalk		113.10	
薯类	Potato	90.81	89.44	100.65
红薯	Sweet potato	120.60	92.27	100.86
马铃薯	White potato	73.93	87.83	100.53
其他薯类	Other potatoes			101.79
薯藤	Potato vines		99.15	94.07
油料	Oil-bearing crops	108.55	109.02	120.27
花生	Peanut	80.98	129.34	120.47
油菜籽	Rapeseeds	110.09	107.74	120.06
芝麻	Sesame	92.55	103.86	148.68
向日葵	Sunflower		100.74	109.87
胡麻籽	Flaxseeds	153.38	123.78	111.23
苏籽	Perillaseeds		112.32	105.77
其他油料作物	Other oil-bearing crops			112.77
花生蔓	Peanut vine		106.67	125.00
豆类	Beans	82.87	116.43	123.15
大豆	Soybeans	83.15	117.82	123.92
绿豆	Mung beans	76.05	97.47	108.89
红小豆	Red beans	107.91	102.79	150.78
蚕豆	Broad beans		91.97	117.80
豌豆	Peas		112.72	109.02
芸豆	Kidney beans		126.87	108.85
其他杂豆	Other beans			113.32
豆秸	Beanstalk		100.00	85.71
棉花(籽棉)	Cotton (unginned cotton)	77.20	130.85	136.52
细绒棉	Thin-staple cotton	77.30	131.16	136.93
长绒棉	Long-staple cotton	73.76	119.36	121.51
棉籽	Cottonseeds		94.44	110.89
麻类	Fiber crops	106.71	95.45	118.04
黄红麻	Jute and blueish dogbane	115.14	93.92	114.18
亚麻	Flax		98.03	
苎麻	Ramie	82.74	99.80	129.00
线麻	Thread hemp		106.06	0.00

2—3 续表 2 continued 2

农产品名称	Categories of agricultural products	2002	2003	2004
		第一季度 1st quarter		
苘麻	Piemarker		105.08	0.00
剑麻	Steel hemp		81.57	
其他麻类	Other fiber crops			102.37
麻秆	Stalks of fiber crops			
糖料	Sugar crops	81.41	88.38	101.75
甘蔗	Sugarcane	81.39	88.38	101.77
甜菜	Beet	98.20	99.68	86.90
烟草	Tobacco	83.23	95.10	101.21
烤烟叶	Flue-cured tobacco	86.05	91.97	96.75
晒烟叶	Sun-cured tobacco	67.32	112.72	126.41
白肋烟	Whiteerib tobacco		95.44	91.01
香料烟	Perfume tobacco		124.75	0.00
其他烟叶	Other tobacco			106.94
青饲料	Greenfeed		130.73	108.73
牧草	Herbage		130.73	98.57
绿肥	Green manure		97.03	
桑叶	Mulberry leaves		109.04	
席草	Stems or leaves of cattail		95.65	62.39
蓖麻籽	Castor beans		110.30	99.48
除虫菊	Pyrethrum		102.29	0.00
薄荷油	Peppermint oil		102.87	0.00
野生植物的采集	Gathering of wild plants			102.41
未列明的其他农作物	Other agricultural crops			110.31
2.蔬菜、园艺作物	2. Vegetable and Horticulture crops		126.87	98.73
蔬菜	Vegetable	77.48	126.87	98.73
叶菜类	Leaf vegetable	77.05	131.15	96.09
菠菜	Spinach	95.47	142.97	101.47
芹菜	Celery	68.07	152.13	94.25
大白菜	Chinese cabbage	53.29	124.52	108.26
元白菜	Cabbage	63.48	100.74	100.36
甘蓝	Wild cabbage	21.03	123.78	97.17
花椰菜	Cauliflower	87.03	112.32	88.86
莴笋	Asparagus lettuce	120.53	106.48	102.77
油菜	Rape	87.83	119.23	91.36

2—3 续表 3 continued 3

农产品名称	Categories of agricultural products	2002	2003	2004
		第一季度 1st quarter		
其他叶菜	Other leaf vegetable			96.29
瓜菜类	Gourd vegetable	85.70	128.78	94.11
黄瓜	Cucumber	86.82	147.41	94.37
冬瓜	White gourd	55.66	158.76	92.77
西葫芦	Summer squash	67.51	107.56	91.97
苦瓜	Balsam pear		126.68	127.24
丝瓜	Towed gourd		98.03	96.34
南瓜	Pumpkin		74.03	103.46
打瓜	Seeded watermelon		108.65	
瓠子	Bottle gourd		108.65	83.33
其他瓜菜	Other gourd vegetable			71.49
块根、块茎菜类	Root and tuber vegetable	75.21	105.33	107.69
萝卜	Radish	75.63	106.06	105.48
胡萝卜	Carrot	134.46	105.08	109.96
生姜	Ginger	52.12	81.57	150.92
芋头	Taro		119.88	112.94
苔干	Dried bryophyte		71.74	89.44
百合(根)	Lily (root)		97.63	97.64
芋艿	Taro		63.45	124.81
山药	Chinese yam		97.23	116.56
其他块根、块茎菜	Other root and tuber vegetable			91.51
茄果菜类	Eggplant, tomato and chili, etc.	58.98	128.74	97.98
茄子	Eggplant	79.65	152.02	104.87
西红柿	Tomato	56.46	116.87	103.41
辣椒	Chili	59.23	116.70	100.37
青椒	Sweetbell	88.31	139.46	75.16
其他茄果菜类	Others			111.71
葱蒜类	Onion and Garlic	135.35	111.64	110.24
大葱	Scallion	171.63	107.40	125.90
蒜苔	Garlic stalk	177.80	122.06	111.24
蒜头	Garlic head	116.54	95.44	101.06
洋葱	Onion		98.24	98.40
蒜苗	Garlic bolt		98.21	106.30
小葱	Shallot		99.33	99.92

2—3 续表 4 continued 4

农产品名称	Categories of agricultural products	2002	2003	2004
		第一季度 1st quarter		
韭菜	Fragrant-flowered garlic		89.15	107.79
其他葱蒜类	Others			102.34
菜用豆类	Garden beans	46.54	124.75	95.90
四季豆	Kidney beans	47.51	106.21	102.73
豇豆	Cowpeas	35.24	150.18	86.53
其他菜用豆	Other garden beans			102.18
水生菜类	Water vegetable	99.47	130.73	110.67
莲藕	Lotus root	100.24	130.73	111.28
茭白	Wild ruice stem	100.00	96.32	100.00
荸荠	Water chestnut	85.94	99.83	120.52
其他水生菜	Other water vegetable			109.98
食用菌(干鲜混合)	Mushroom		97.03	103.91
香菇(干品)	Mushroom (dried)		109.04	98.64
蘑菇(鲜品)	Mushroom (fresh)		95.65	104.12
黑木耳(干品)	Black edible fungus (dried)		110.30	106.26
白木耳(干品)	Tremella (dried)		79.50	
金针菇(鲜品)	Golden mushroom		90.49	110.54
猴头菌(干品)	Bearded tooth(dried)		100.00	0.00
平菇(鲜品)	Oyster mushroom		100.00	112.67
花菇(干品)	Black forest mushroom		97.34	100.15
其他食用菌	Other edible mushrooms			98.58
椿芽	Chinese cedrela sprouts		95.15	126.49
未列明的其他蔬菜	Other vegetable			104.45
花卉	Flowers		96.63	0.00
鲜切花	Fresh flowers		97.29	0.00
百合花	Lily		99.46	54.49
康乃馨	Carnation		100.00	98.33
满天星	June snow (serissa)		95.65	117.10
勿忘我	Forgetmenot		78.22	70.08
非洲菊	Flameray Gerbera		100.00	98.00
玫瑰	Rugosa rose		78.70	130.25
郁金香	Tulip			83.33
情人草	Evans begonia		100.00	96.20
其他鲜切花	Other fresh flowers			121.36

2—3 续表 5 continued 5

农产品名称	Categories of agricultural products	2002	2003	2004
		第一季度 1st quarter		
盆栽植物	Potted plants		102.08	0.00
观赏苗木	Ornamental plants		91.71	0.00
草坪草皮	Sod for lawn		98.46	87.40
其他园艺作物	Other horticulture crops			104.58
3. 水果、坚果、饮料和香料	3. Fruits, beverages and perfume		102.29	104.97
水果、坚果	Fruits and nuts		102.87	104.80
园林水果	Garden fruits	125.09		104.78
苹果	Apple	141.53	111.26	96.42
红富士苹果	Hongfushi apple	143.08	111.05	95.76
国光苹果	Guoguang apple	111.80	84.29	99.07
秦冠苹果	Qinguan apple	115.87	124.80	101.70
香蕉苹果	Banana apple	100.00	96.68	113.79
元帅苹果	Yuanshuai (Marshal) apple		95.24	112.78
新红星苹果	New Hongxing apple		111.11	98.62
其他苹果	Other apples			112.04
梨	Pear	104.56	98.26	107.33
雪花梨	Snowflake pear	149.65	118.98	113.26
鸭梨	Ya-pear	104.33	98.21	107.48
酥梨	Soft-pear	110.92	95.40	86.39
香梨	Bergamot pear	100.00	100.00	
苹果梨	Apple pear		103.45	91.66
其他梨	Other pears			79.37
柑桔	Citrus	89.67	101.97	102.38
柑	Mandarin orange	90.04	98.62	104.68
桔	Tangerine	89.29	117.80	89.82
橙	Orange	81.64	119.23	98.79
柚	Shaddock	85.49	95.58	95.50
其他柑桔	Others			96.32
其他水果	Other fruits			125.77
香蕉	Banana	267.44	103.51	125.77
菠萝	Pineapple		60.58	71.79
芒果	Mango		202.51	
木瓜	Papaya		60.83	89.44
桃	Peach	100.00	100.00	98.57

2－3 续表 6 continued 6

农产品名称	Categories of agricultural products	2002	2003	2004
		第一季度 1st quarter		
猕猴桃	Yangtao	100.00	100.00	101.67
葡萄	Grape	191.12	75.65	89.99
红枣	Chinese date	115.16	97.87	108.36
柿子	Persimmon	139.41	89.51	105.66
其他园林水果	Other garden fruits			114.08
瓜果类	Melon	420.22	52.79	119.18
西瓜	Watermelon	900.54	53.28	121.15
甜瓜	Muskmelon	100.00	52.46	117.87
草莓	Strawberry	93.48	109.25	106.24
其他瓜果	Others			100.22
坚果类	Nuts			
椰子	Coconut			128.96
槟榔	Areca			78.30
其他坚果	Other nuts			106.27
茶及其他饮料(干品)	Tea and other beverages			112.02
茶	Tea	114.40		112.02
红毛茶	Black tea	100.00	74.03	102.37
绿毛茶	Green tea	114.40	103.20	112.02
乌龙茶	Oolong tea	100.00	103.48	94.33
其他茶	Others			81.16
咖啡豆	Coffee bean		102.79	92.46
茴香	Fennel			101.89
其他	Others			179.31
4. 中药材	4. Traditional Chinese medicinal materials			
茯苓	Fuling (poris cocos)		100.00	108.01
党参	Tangshen (pilose asiabell)		208.82	92.20
当归	Chinese angelica		119.06	142.01
黄芪	Root of membranous milk vetch		125.00	106.26
金银花	Honeysuckle		100.00	111.55
黄连	Rhizome of Chinese goldthread		100.00	118.42
甘草	Licorice root		112.34	100.00
贝母	Bulb of fritillary		212.45	143.94
元胡	Amur corydalis		119.65	
枸杞	Fruit of Chinese wolfberry		119.09	156.00

2—3 续表 7 continued 7

农产品名称	Categories of agricultural products	2002	2003	2004
		第一季度 1st quarter		
菊花	Chrysanthemum		92.09	145.97
白术	Largehead atractyldes		88.34	116.45
半夏	Tuber of pinelia		94.63	100.00
麦冬	Tuber of dwarf lilyturf			105.26
生地	Dried rhizome of rehmannia		101.14	83.33
杜仲	Bark of eucommia		100.00	100.54
板蓝根	Root of common baphicacanthus		100.00	71.39
苦丁茶	Kudin crotoxylum (bitter tea tree)		41.65	173.84
天麻	Tuber of elevated gastrodia		102.82	78.25
灵芝	Glossy ganoderma			96.00
穿心莲	Creat		100.00	147.73
桔梗	Rampion		169.97	107.33
丹参	Root of red-rooted salvia		82.97	193.01
大青叶	Common conehead		125.00	
二、林业产品	II. Forest products	86.42	108.65	107.04
1. 竹木采运	1. Felling and transport of bamboo and wood			108.79
木材采运	Felling and transport of wood	96.40		106.97
原木	Log	94.80		106.97
红松	Korean pine		93.04	107.55
落叶松	Larch		82.72	111.93
马尾松	Masson pine		99.75	109.10
杉木	China fir		99.67	105.29
云南松	Yunnan pine		100.12	94.30
薪材	Firewood	211.21	99.27	104.53
竹材采运	Felling and transport of bamboo	71.42		112.90
水竹	Water bamboo		90.98	109.39
斑竹	Mottled bamboo		89.93	108.11
毛竹(楠竹)	Mao bamboo		102.39	117.53
蒿竹	Hao bamboo		83.12	105.25
淡竹	Henon bamboo		140.00	99.34
其他竹材	Other bamboo		102.56	103.87
2. 林产品的采集	2. Gathering of forest products	79.97	108.65	105.34
天然和人工林的果实	Products of natural and artificial forest			105.34
橡胶	Rubber	76.05	127.31	127.89

2—3 续表 8 continued 8

农产品名称	Categories of agricultural products	2002	2003	2004
		第一季度 1st quarter		
生漆	Raw lacquer			96.43
油桐籽	Seeds of tung oil tree	84.93	164.07	113.44
乌桕籽	Seeds of Chinese tallow tree		100.39	110.87
油茶籽	Seeds of tea-oil tree	75.08	101.65	120.39
棕片	Palm fibre		96.99	102.95
松脂	Rosin		97.28	94.18
核桃	Walnut	124.96	119.88	95.31
板栗	Chinese chestnut		100.04	103.35
白果	Ginkgo		104.50	95.98
花椒	Chinese prickly ash	197.96	97.63	86.04
八角	Anise	52.20	63.45	71.17
胡椒	Pepper		81.18	107.39
其他果实	Other products			90.67
柳条	Willow twigs		96.00	117.63
藤条	Rattan		99.39	107.72
竹笋干	Dried bamboo shoots		101.76	101.07
未列明的其他林产品采集	Gathering of other wild plants			107.28
三、牧业(畜产品)	III. Livestock products	103.42	97.23	114.47
1. 牲畜的饲养	1. Livestock raising			102.06
牛的饲养	Cattle raising	92.22		101.88
活牛(毛重)	Live cattle (gross weight)	92.22	100.39	101.88
牛肉	Beef		101.56	111.49
羊的饲养	Sheep raising			101.21
活羊(毛重)	Live sheep		92.96	101.21
羊肉	Mutton		96.51	97.16
马	Horse		100.43	100.31
驴	Donkey		104.74	62.23
骡	Mule		99.10	102.64
其他未列牲畜的饲养	Other livestock raising			111.34
奶产品	Milk products	97.09	98.99	107.64
牛奶	Cow milk	97.12	98.99	107.63
羊奶	Sheep milk	77.49	100.85	111.52
其他奶类	Other milk			100.64
毛绒产品	Hair and down products	120.24	103.99	92.44

2—3 续表 9 continued 9

农产品名称	Categories of agricultural products	2002	2003	2004
		第一季度 1st quarter		
山羊毛	Goat's wool	419.69	67.95	100.00
绵羊毛	Sheep's wool		96.00	108.21
山羊绒	Cashmere	82.81	108.49	91.50
牦牛毛	Yak hair		63.63	160.00
骆驼绒	Camel hair cloth		103.33	
其他毛绒产品	Other Hair and down products			107.75
其他牲畜产品	Other animal products			111.76
2. 猪的饲养	2. Hog raising	97.67		119.96
活猪(毛重)	Hog (gross weight)	97.67	96.51	119.96
猪肉	Pork		99.99	120.07
猪鬃	Bristles			96.51
3. 家禽	3. Poultry	127.93	99.20	106.02
肉禽(毛重)	Poultry (gross weight)	127.93		105.53
鸡	Chicken	127.96	99.20	105.53
鸭	Duck	105.74	97.57	106.41
鹅	Goose	100.00	106.01	104.54
鹌鹑	Furs			100.00
其他家禽	Other poultry			103.95
禽蛋	Eggs	108.18	98.24	106.72
鸡蛋	Chicken's eggs	108.09	98.21	106.68
鸭蛋	Duck's eggs	111.78	99.33	108.15
鹅蛋	Goose's eggs	60.59	89.15	102.87
其他蛋	Other eggs			98.92
羽绒	Eider down		94.03	0.00
鸭绒	Duck's down			113.33
其他羽绒	Other down			99.78
4. 狩猎和捕捉动物	4. Hunting and catching animals			
兽皮	Furs		96.72	107.21
未列明的动物皮张	Furs not identified			115.25
5. 其他畜牧业	5. Other animal husbandry			
鸽子	Pigeon		109.23	105.40
兔	Rabbit		110.72	99.89
狗	Dog		100.69	94.61
猫	Cat			96.72

2—3 续表 10 continued 10

农产品名称	Categories of agricultural products	2002	2003	2004
		第一季度 1st quarter		
兔毛	Rabbit hair		96.05	119.07
其他家养动物	Other domestic animals			97.81
蛇	Snake		97.28	
蚯蚓	Earthworm			110.00
蚕茧	Silkworm cocoon	75.41	86.82	114.14
蜂蜜	Honey	115.91	128.72	89.25
动物皮张	Animal furs		99.99	120.94
四、渔业	IV. Fishery products	106.00	96.88	106.95
1. 海水水产品	1. Seawater aquatic products	114.64	96.32	106.72
鱼类	Seawater fish	148.51	99.83	105.47
大黄鱼	Large yellow croaker	110.68	72.42	120.01
小黄鱼	Small yellow croaker	98.03	111.81	102.88
带鱼	Hairtail	122.27	90.11	107.93
鲈鱼	Perch			101.81
沙丁鱼	Sardine		100.00	101.31
鳕鱼	Cod	164.65		93.92
石斑鱼	Grouper	100.00	91.98	108.99
醍鱼	Anchovy		100.24	105.81
梭鱼	Mullet		100.00	105.40
鲳鱼	Silvery pomfret		106.16	121.69
海鳗	Conger pike		94.77	99.63
鲅鱼	Spanish mackerel		103.93	103.62
鲐鱼	Chub mackerel		100.37	103.34
马面鱼	Black scraper		94.88	108.56
鳓鱼	Chinese herring			103.45
马鲛	Japanese Spanish mackerel		87.94	125.25
梅童鱼	Baby croaker		95.59	99.79
梭参	Barrachuda		101.46	0.00
鲷鱼	Porgy			101.70
蓝圆	Blue scad		101.38	103.39
远东拟沙丁鱼	Far East imitation sardine			109.09
鲆鲽	Left-eyed flounder		100.00	111.11
其他海水鱼类	Other seawater fish			103.29
海水虾蟹类	Seawater shrimp and crab	276.24	100.00	113.85

2—3 续表 11 continued 11

农产品名称	Categories of agricultural products	2002	2003	2004
		第一季度 1st quarter		
对虾	Prawn		99.88	116.78
毛虾	Shrimp		93.42	105.04
爬虾	Hypplyte		96.01	
鹰爪虾	Trachypemaeus curvirostris		124.49	103.45
梭子蟹	Swimming crab		106.54	118.74
其他海水虾蟹类	Other seawater shrimps and crabs			104.53
海水贝类	Seawater shellfish	59.02	90.40	106.52
贻贝	Mussel	100.00	100.00	104.00
扇贝	Scallop	100.00	100.00	103.45
牡蛎	Oyster	156.00	79.50	102.71
鲍鱼	Abalone	35.29	113.31	110.37
蛤	Clam	58.96	90.49	106.55
蚶	Blood clam	93.05	160.05	94.58
海螺	Conch		85.95	106.67
蛏	Razor clam		90.77	102.54
其他海水贝类	Other seawater shellfish			84.53
藻类	Seaweeds	114.41	100.00	100.24
海带	Kelp	76.87	100.00	81.63
紫菜	Laver	121.44	100.00	103.73
其他藻类	Other seaweeds			101.91
其他海水产品	Other seawater products			
墨鱼	Inkfish		114.97	115.92
鱿鱼	Squid		100.00	108.01
章鱼	Octopus		114.51	64.49
海蜇	Jellyfish		131.67	
未列明的其他海水产品	Other seawater products			105.51
2. 内陆水域水产品	2. Aquatic products in inland water areas	93.62	97.34	107.15
淡水鱼类	Freshwater fish	93.62	97.34	105.41
青鱼	Black carp	69.60	98.66	108.12
草鱼	Grass carp	94.33	95.15	108.40
鲤鱼	Carp	101.84	99.63	103.85
鲢鱼	Silver carp	101.03	96.63	105.28
鲫鱼	Crucian carp	79.73	97.29	104.71
罗非鱼	Tilapia	68.20	99.46	100.27

2—3 续表 12 continued 12

农产品名称 Categories of agricultural products		2002 第一季度 1st quarter	2003	2004
虹鳟鱼	Rainbow trout	83.89		100.00
白鱼	Whitefish		86.36	96.19
鳜鱼	Mandarin fish		110.41	82.93
白昌鱼	Round spadefish		80.76	95.47
黑鱼	Snakeheaded fish		105.48	110.00
鲶鱼	Oriental sheatfish		97.94	103.73
武昌鱼	Blunt-snout bream		96.36	89.37
鳙鱼	Variegated carp		100.36	109.34
鲮鱼	Dace		93.45	109.96
鳊	Bream		92.56	102.20
黄颡鱼	Yellowcat fish			106.67
银鱼	Whitebait		90.91	66.67
淡水鲈	Freshwater perch		85.36	104.17
其他淡水鱼类	Other freshwater fish			93.11
淡水虾蟹类	Freshwater shrimps and crabs	89.48	100.00	120.96
龙虾	Lobster		111.80	107.24
罗氏沼虾	M. rosenbergii		100.00	106.38
青虾	Black shrimps		97.90	131.96
基围虾	Exopalaemom carinicauda			103.45
红螯螯虾	Shrimps with red chelas		100.00	128.24
大闸蟹	Dazha crab		88.50	99.67
其他淡水虾蟹类	Other freshwater shrimp and crab			106.05
淡水贝类	Freshwater shellfish			
淡水珍珠	Freshwater pearl			5.67
螺丝	Spiral shell		97.33	98.23
其他淡水贝类	Other freshwater shellfish			116.03
其他淡水养殖产品	Other freshwater breeding products			
河鳗	River eel		92.69	
牛蛙	Bullfrog		104.11	
甲鱼	Soft-shelled turtle		98.56	102.54
黄鳝	Ricefield eel		104.51	112.17
泥鳅	Loach		103.87	103.88
蛙	Frog		93.75	
未列明的其他淡水养殖产品	Other freshwater breeding products			90.54

2－4 全国农产品生产价格指数(第二季度)

National Indices of the Producer Prices of Agricultural Products

(上年同期＝100)　　(2nd quarter)　　(the same period of the preceding year＝100)

农产品名称	Categories of agricultural products	2002	2003	2004
		第二季度 2nd quarter		
合　计	Gross Index	98.90	102.65	110.89
一、农业产品	I. Crop products	99.70	106.73	117.37
1. 谷物及其他作物	1. Cereal and other crops			126.63
＃粮食	Grain	94.60	103.89	128.55
谷物(原粮)	Cereal (unprocessed food grains)	95.60	101.51	129.98
小麦	Wheat	93.20	103.20	138.13
硬粒小麦	Hard-grained wheat	90.20	104.22	137.97
软粒小麦	Soft-grained wheat	81.30	103.40	142.73
混合小麦	Mixed wheat	100.60	100.76	138.39
其他小麦	Other wheat			139.14
稻谷	Paddy rice	101.20	97.29	141.42
早籼稻	Early long-grained nonglutinous rice	101.60	98.04	135.86
晚籼稻	Late long-grained nonglutinous rice	103.50	101.26	140.71
粳稻	Round-grained rice	98.20	93.23	144.72
其他稻谷	Other paddy			132.91
玉米	Maize (corn)	93.30	103.44	118.97
黄玉米	Yellow maize	93.10	103.45	118.96
白玉米	White maize	115.50	99.63	120.55
混合玉米	Mixed maize	165.00	102.26	120.81
其他玉米	Other maize		94.15	112.21
杂粮	Coarse cereals		120.92	0.00
谷子	Millet		121.54	122.12
高粱	Chinese sorghum		95.74	133.14
大麦	Barley		98.48	116.95
荞麦	Buckwheat		125.83	121.55
元麦	poulard wheat		124.75	0.00
青稞	Highland barley		126.29	119.55
莜麦	Naked oats		113.88	102.10
燕麦	Oats		131.67	66.67
其他杂粮	Other coarse cereals			107.86
谷物副产品	By-products of cereals			0.00
小麦秸	Wheat straw		99.26	127.46
稻草	Rice straw		93.12	125.17
玉米秆	Corn stover		132.80	108.47

2—4 续表 1 continued 1

农产品名称	Categories of agricultural products	2002	2003	2004
		第二季度 2nd quarter		
大麦秸	Barley straw			101.10
谷子秆	Millet stalk		162.54	107.74
高粱秆	Chinese sorghum stalk		100.00	122.79
薯类	Potato	88.30	94.88	101.94
红薯	Sweet potato	139.00	97.87	112.87
马铃薯	White potato	76.00	94.15	99.27
其他薯类	Other potatoes			110.59
薯藤	Potato vines		103.20	122.17
油料	Oil-bearing crops	103.20	125.83	121.61
花生	Peanut	104.70	124.75	120.45
油菜籽	Rapeseeds	102.80	126.29	121.80
芝麻	Sesame	88.20	113.88	129.58
向日葵	Sunflower		93.83	114.70
胡麻籽	Flaxseeds	112.50	112.70	106.54
苏籽	Perillaseeds		114.76	99.01
其他油料作物	Other oil-bearing crops			101.14
花生蔓	Peanut vine		103.08	125.00
豆类	Beans	90.20	120.92	127.09
大豆	Soybeans	90.40	121.54	127.48
绿豆	Mung beans	77.10	95.74	110.61
红小豆	Red beans	117.20	98.48	117.48
蚕豆	Broad beans		112.03	140.84
豌豆	Peas		108.47	112.75
芸豆	Kidney beans		108.47	123.52
其他杂豆	Other beans			114.62
豆秸	Beanstalk		101.03	79.06
棉花(籽棉)	Cotton (unginned cotton)	88.00	131.67	122.61
细绒棉	Thin-staple cotton	88.00	131.67	122.61
长绒棉	Long-staple cotton	100.00	125.04	141.71
棉籽	Cottonseeds		97.56	121.00
棉花秆	Cotton stalk			87.50
麻类	Fiber crops	85.20	90.68	135.33
黄红麻	Jute and blueish dogbane	95.70	78.56	115.39
亚麻	Flax		108.75	98.71

2－4 续表 2 continued 2

农产品名称	Categories of agricultural products	2002	2003	2004
		第二季度 2nd quarter		
苎麻	Ramie	77.90	99.14	149.25
线麻	Thread hemp		108.16	0.00
苘麻	Piemarker		100.94	0.00
剑麻	Steel hemp		74.47	
麻秆	Stalks of fiber crops			104.43
糖料	Sugar crops	105.20	87.14	104.59
甘蔗	Sugarcane	105.20	87.09	104.59
甜菜	Beet	96.10	120.00	
其他糖料	Other sugar crops			104.94
烟草	Tobacco	183.30	105.99	107.00
烤烟叶	Flue-cured tobacco	263.90	100.29	103.41
晒烟叶	Sun-cured tobacco	97.80	112.03	110.80
白肋烟	Whiteerib tobacco		99.20	
香料烟	Perfume tobacco		107.15	0.00
其他烟叶	Other tobacco			104.64
其他农作物	Other agricultural crops			
青饲料	Greenfeed		110.68	102.60
牧草	Herbage		113.13	105.00
绿肥	Green manure		106.16	81.65
桑叶	Mulberry leaves		97.70	111.80
席草	Stems or leaves of cattail		102.34	113.89
蓖麻籽	Castor beans		96.45	119.69
除虫菊	Pyrethrum		103.74	0.00
薄荷油	Peppermint oil		98.01	0.00
野生植物的采集	Gathering of wild plants			175.51
未列明的其他农作物	Other agricultural crops			115.94
2.蔬菜、园艺作物	2. Vegetable and Horticulture crops		108.47	102.56
蔬菜	Vegetable	95.90	108.47	102.56
叶菜类	Leaf vegetable	86.80	110.54	100.34
菠菜	Spinach	94.10	109.35	103.13
芹菜	Celery	78.60	114.03	101.01
大白菜	Chinese cabbage	50.70	120.44	101.08
元白菜	Cabbage	73.90	102.59	102.30
甘蓝	Wild cabbage	38.70	93.83	99.41

2—4 续表 3 continued 3

农产品名称	Categories of agricultural products	2002	2003	2004
		第二季度 2nd quarter		
花椰菜	Cauliflower	72.10	112.70	94.97
莴笋	Asparagus lettuce	105.80	114.76	97.94
油菜	Rape	107.30	111.19	98.64
其他叶菜	Other leaf vegetable			101.89
瓜菜类	Gourd vegetable	86.80	107.80	100.47
黄瓜	Cucumber	86.90	100.16	108.94
冬瓜	White gourd	63.60	125.04	73.55
西葫芦	Summer squash	99.90	96.55	102.06
苦瓜	Balsam pear		120.04	110.64
丝瓜	Towed gourd		108.75	111.39
南瓜	Pumpkin		93.35	109.93
打瓜	Seeded watermelon		96.87	100.00
瓠子	Bottle gourd		96.87	109.17
其他瓜菜	Other gourd vegetable			109.00
块根、块茎菜类	Root and tuber vegetable	82.30	104.98	103.68
萝卜	Radish	81.40	108.16	99.07
胡萝卜	Carrot	144.50	100.94	110.33
生姜	Ginger	92.90	74.47	133.12
芋头	Taro		117.29	95.05
苔干	Dried bryophyte		117.29	113.01
百合(根)	Lily (root)		78.37	89.57
芋艿	Taro		78.37	114.34
山药	Chinese yam		76.76	104.03
其他块根、块茎菜	Other root and tuber vegetable			102.92
茄果菜类	Eggplant, tomato and chili, etc.	108.80	107.64	102.80
茄子	Eggplant	123.70	112.51	112.44
西红柿	Tomato	105.50	108.75	98.41
辣椒	Chili	87.50	115.41	113.30
青椒	Sweetbell	106.60	98.31	100.20
其他茄果菜类	Others			109.15
葱蒜类	Onion and Garlic	60.90	114.85	110.87
大葱	Scallion	250.10	109.17	109.05
蒜苔	Garlic stalk	81.40	118.58	110.14
蒜头	Garlic head	50.30	99.20	114.08

2—4 续表 4 continued 4

农产品名称	Categories of agricultural products	2002	2003	2004
		第二季度 2nd quarter		
洋葱	Onion		94.17	90.55
蒜苗	Garlic bolt		94.19	103.70
小葱	Shallot		83.86	99.11
韭菜	Fragrant-flowered garlic		98.74	106.87
其他葱蒜类	Others			97.59
菜用豆类	Garden beans	111.40	107.15	110.19
四季豆	Kidney beans	97.60	101.55	110.87
豇豆	Cowpeas	136.90	112.51	109.55
其他菜用豆	Other garden beans			102.57
水生菜类	Water vegetable	105.10	110.68	105.07
莲藕	Lotus root	98.60	113.13	114.07
茭白	Wild ruice stem	115.30	106.16	88.51
荸荠	Water chestnut	100.00	94.62	121.04
其他水生菜	Other water vegetable			110.22
食用菌(干鲜混合)	Mushroom		97.70	101.73
香菇(干品)	Mushroom (dried)		102.34	99.70
蘑菇(鲜品)	Mushroom (fresh)		96.45	100.05
黑木耳(干品)	Black edible fungus (dried)		103.74	124.89
白木耳(干品)	Tremella (dried)		112.20	87.43
金针菇(鲜品)	Golden mushroom		89.64	108.47
猴头菌(干品)	Bearded tooth(dried)		100.67	0.00
平菇(鲜品)	Oyster mushroom		105.42	104.08
花菇(干品)	Black forest mushroom		89.59	81.47
其他食用菌	Other edible mushrooms			112.29
椿芽	Chinese cedrela sprouts		98.23	107.42
未列明的其他蔬菜	Other vegetable			103.20
花卉	Flowers		96.18	0.00
鲜切花	Fresh flowers		97.55	0.00
百合花	Lily		98.55	100.29
康乃馨	Carnation		94.56	125.36
满天星	June snow (serissa)		99.75	89.37
勿忘我	Forgetmenot		87.43	92.64
非洲菊	Flameray Gerbera		100.00	86.58
玫瑰	Rugosa rose		113.18	74.49

2—4 续表 5 continued 5

农产品名称 Categories of agricultural products		2002	2003	2004
		第二季度 2nd quarter		
郁金香	Tulip			83.33
情人草	Evans begonia		59.54	71.21
其他鲜切花	Other fresh flowers			106.84
其他园艺作物	Other horticulture crops			
盆栽植物	Potted plants		101.21	0.00
观赏苗木	Ornamental plants		85.66	0.00
草坪草皮	Sod for lawn		90.72	97.49
其他园艺作物	Other horticulture crops			96.27
3.水果、坚果、饮料和香料	3. Fruits, beverages and perfume		98.01	106.93
水果、坚果	Fruits and nuts			101.09
园林水果	Garden fruits	117.90	98.69	98.16
苹果	Apple	100.50	100.74	111.25
红富士苹果	Hongfushi apple	93.10	103.47	108.83
国光苹果	Guoguang apple	117.30	78.56	109.29
秦冠苹果	Qinguan apple	107.30	99.50	115.42
香蕉苹果	Banana apple	100.00	103.36	
金冠苹果	Jinguan apple			
元帅苹果	Yuanshuai (Marshal) apple		100.00	175.28
新红星苹果	New Hongxing apple		93.94	
梨	Pear	95.60	107.84	93.38
雪花梨	Snowflake pear	99.90	114.22	82.53
鸭梨	Ya-pear	102.00	100.00	99.99
酥梨	Soft-pear	69.60	104.34	102.08
香梨	Bergamot pear	100.00	100.00	
其他梨	Other pears			101.00
柑桔	Citrus	96.20	96.96	81.05
柑	Mandarin orange	94.30	95.72	83.81
桔	Tangerine	101.00	100.05	78.63
橙	Orange	100.00	103.74	93.99
柚	Shaddock	100.00	75.00	107.78
其他水果	Other fruits			96.20
香蕉	Banana	186.10	104.79	122.34
菠萝	Pineapple		74.48	105.72
荔枝	Litchi		138.03	74.52

2—4 续表 6 continued 6

农产品名称	Categories of agricultural products	2002	2003	2004
		第二季度 2nd quarter		
芒果	Mango		71.56	118.37
木瓜	Papaya		98.04	107.17
橄榄	Chinese olive		80.00	
桃	Peach	161.80	93.35	95.31
杏	Apricot	90.60	99.15	103.29
杨梅	Red bayberry	133.40	91.01	120.27
猕猴桃	Yangtao	100.00	87.50	
葡萄	Grape	196.70	113.52	97.47
红枣	Chinese date	100.90	78.72	108.81
柿子	Persimmon	100.00	100.00	73.68
其他园林水果	Other garden fruits			93.35
瓜果类	Melon	44.00	93.61	104.04
西瓜	Watermelon	38.40	93.62	102.73
甜瓜	Muskmelon	140.60	93.36	111.73
哈蜜瓜	Hami melon	100.00		100.00
香瓜	Musk melon		116.82	111.05
伊利沙白瓜	Elizabeth melon		98.52	120.00
草莓	Strawberry	77.70	104.81	107.14
其他瓜果	Others			109.23
坚果类	Nuts			
椰子	Coconut			106.25
杏仁	Apricot kernel			
槟榔	Areca			113.24
沙棘果	Seabuck thorn			0.00
其他坚果	Other nuts			125.00
茶及其他饮料(干品)	Tea and other beverages			116.86
茶	Tea	144.40		116.86
红毛茶	Black tea	135.30	91.14	106.34
绿毛茶	Green tea	145.30	97.19	117.38
乌龙茶	Oolong tea	109.00	90.31	110.16
其他茶	Others			104.41
可可和咖啡	Cocoa and Coffee			
咖啡豆	Coffee bean	88.00	99.68	86.57
香料作物	Perfume crops			

2—4 续表 7 continued 7

农产品名称	Categories of agricultural products	2002	2003	2004
		第二季度 2nd quarter		
茴香	Fennel			100.95
4. 中药材	4. Traditional Chinese medicinal materials			
茯苓	Fuling (poris cocos)		104.39	121.82
党参	Tangshen (pilose asiabell)		311.35	88.04
当归	Chinese angelica		164.20	81.55
黄芪	Root of membranous milk vetch		113.21	105.64
金银花	Honeysuckle		120.02	85.56
人参	Ginseng			85.00
黄连	Rhizome of Chinese goldthread		100.00	100.78
甘草	Licorice root		98.55	85.00
贝母	Bulb of fritillary		186.21	90.91
红花	Safflower		95.35	109.54
元胡	Amur corydalis		100.00	83.08
枸杞	Fruit of Chinese wolfberry		100.00	83.77
砂仁	Villous amomum			90.00
菊花	Chrysanthemum		104.20	139.48
白术	Largehead atractyldes		92.31	89.82
半夏	Tuber of pinelia		117.08	106.90
麦冬	Tuber of dwarf lilyturf			90.91
三七	Pseudo-ginseng			111.11
麻黄草	Chinese ephedra			90.91
玄参	Root of Zhejiang figwort			87.50
肉桂	Cinnamon			102.25
生地	Dried rhizome of rehmannia		100.00	86.07
厚朴	Bark of official magnolia			130.00
杜仲	Bark of eucommia		99.41	100.36
薄荷	Peppermint			80.00
田七	Notoginseng			80.00
板蓝根	Root of common baphicacanthus		137.92	72.13
苦丁茶	Kudin crotoxylum (bitter tea tree)		54.70	103.84
霍香	Wrinkled giant hyssop			90.00
天麻	Tuber of elevated gastrodia		107.92	99.69
穿心莲	Creat		98.33	127.44
桔 梗	Rampion		137.07	102.58
干 姜	Dried ginger			111.11

2—4 续表 8　　continued 8

农产品名称	Categories of agricultural products	2002	2003	2004
		第二季度 2nd quarter		
丹参	Root of red-rooted salvia		99.75	84.81
大青叶	Common conehead		100.00	50.00
白芷	Root of Dahurian angelica			90.91
川芎	Ligusticum wallichii			97.56
虫草	Chinese caterpillar fungus			112.19
其他药材	Other medicinal materials			109.96
二、林业产品	II. Forest products	88.40	101.24	108.91
1. 竹木采运	1. Felling and transport of bamboo and wood			
木材采运	Felling and transport of wood	104.50		
原木	Log	104.40		
红松	Korean pine		105.93	103.28
落叶松	Larch		89.69	97.94
马尾松	Masson pine		102.32	100.70
杉木	China fir		101.82	102.22
云南松	Yunnan pine		101.43	104.98
薪材	Firewood	165.20	98.41	105.57
竹材采运	Felling and transport of bamboo	149.90		
水竹	Water bamboo		64.03	118.89
斑竹	Mottled bamboo		100.00	99.02
毛竹(楠竹)	Mao bamboo		99.02	101.50
蒿竹	Hao bamboo		89.63	97.93
淡竹	Henon bamboo		113.14	183.40
其他竹材	Other bamboo		91.00	112.16
2. 林产品的采集	2. Gathering of forest products	83.30	101.24	108.91
天然和人工林的果实	Products of natural and artificial forest			108.91
橡胶	Rubber	92.00	117.29	123.43
油桐籽	Seeds of tung oil tree	100.00	214.46	98.17
油茶籽	Seeds of tea-oil tree	100.00	118.48	129.73
棕片	Palm fibre		104.99	93.45
松脂	Rosin		105.39	110.32
核桃	Walnut	184.60	78.37	103.19
板栗	Chinese chestnut		81.23	
花椒	Chinese prickly ash	72.60	93.73	98.30
八角	Anise	57.70	77.76	73.64
桂皮	Cassia bark	90.60	67.35	111.73

2—4 续表 9　　continued 9

农产品名称	Categories of agricultural products	2002	2003	2004
		第二季度 2nd quarter		
胡椒	Pepper		112.23	110.13
茴油	Fennel oil			0.00
桂油	Cassia oil			0.00
其他果实	Other products			99.78
其他林产品采集	Gathering of other wild plants			
柳条	Willow twigs		100.27	133.33
藤条	Rattan		100.00	83.33
竹笋干	Dried bamboo shoots		94.36	109.70
桉树叶	Eucalyptus leaves			81.89
黄柏	Chinese weeping cypress			104.65
未列明的其他林产品采集	Gathering of other wild plants			100.91
三、牧业(畜产品)	III. Livestock products	99.80	99.08	103.87
1.牲畜的饲养	1. Livestock raising			105.80
牛的饲养	Cattle raising			103.77
活牛(毛重)	Live cattle (gross weight)	78.70	103.49	103.77
牛肉	Beef		113.47	91.91
羊的饲养	Sheep raising			104.30
活羊(毛重)	Live sheep		100.29	104.30
羊肉	Mutton		127.38	110.11
其他牲畜饲养	Other livestock raising			
马	Horse		101.20	104.99
驴	Donkey		96.75	103.12
骡	Mule		106.70	100.00
奶产品	Milk products	98.50	99.97	102.13
牛奶	Cow milk	98.50	99.97	102.12
羊奶	Sheep milk	60.50	102.21	104.41
其他奶类	Other milk			100.08
毛绒产品	Hair and down products	80.70	92.92	112.29
山羊毛	Goat's wool	139.90	77.49	104.29
绵羊毛	Sheep's wool		94.71	108.46
山羊绒	Cashmere	74.20	94.62	113.17
绵羊绒	Sheep's down		100.00	106.93
牦牛毛	Yak hair		100.00	76.55
骆驼绒	Camel hair cloth		103.67	160.00
2.猪的饲养	2. Hog raising			100.76

2—4 续表 10 continued 10

农产品名称	Categories of agricultural products	2002	2003	2004
		第二季度 2nd quarter		
活猪(毛重)	Hog (gross weight)	97.50	99.88	100.76
猪肉	Pork		100.62	122.46
猪鬃	Bristles			109.54
3. 家禽	3. Poultry	107.90	94.17	110.62
肉禽(毛重)	Poultry (gross weight)			109.76
鸡	Chicken	107.90	94.19	109.74
鸭	Duck	103.50	83.86	116.63
鹅	Goose	100.00	90.70	114.43
其他家禽	Other poultry			111.77
禽蛋	Eggs	104.80	98.74	111.77
鸡蛋	Chicken's eggs	104.50		111.73
鸭蛋	Duck's eggs	119.90		113.48
鹅蛋	Goose's eggs	98.10		109.12
鹌鹑蛋	Quail's eggs			98.89
其他蛋	Other eggs			93.99
羽绒	Eider down		76.83	0.00
鸭绒	Duck's down			107.08
其他羽绒	Other down			105.69
4. 狩猎和捕捉动物	4. Hunting and catching animals			
兽皮	Furs		100.00	108.57
未列明的动物皮张	Furs not identified			112.47
5. 其他畜牧业	5. Other animal husbandry			
各种鸟类	Birds			
鸽子	Pigeon		112.75	101.62
其他鸟类	Other birds			118.18
家养动物	Domestic animals			
兔	Rabbit		112.22	111.30
狗	Dog		90.86	105.62
猫	Cat			104.05
兔毛	Rabbit hair		99.06	139.95
珍贵动物	Rare animals			
狐狸	Fox		100.00	125.00
蛇	Snake		101.25	109.21
虫类	Worms			
蚯蚓	Earthworm			112.14

2—4 续表 11 continued 11

农产品名称	Categories of agricultural products	2002	2003	2004
		第二季度 2nd quarter		
蝎子	Scorpion			94.28
其他虫类	Other Worms			109.16
活的家畜产品	Domestic animal products			0.00
蚕茧	Silkworm cocoon	65.90	98.39	149.73
蜂蜜	Honey	223.80	104.29	107.54
蜂蜡	Beeswax			100.90
鹿茸	Pilose antler			70.18
其他活的家畜产品	Other domestic animal products			118.71
毛皮的生产	Production of furs			
动物皮张	Animal furs		99.35	117.36
四、渔业	IV. Fishery products	93.40	98.99	111.91
1. 海水水产品	1. Seawater aquatic products	98.60	99.29	111.44
鱼类	Seawater fish	94.50	108.65	113.27
大黄鱼	Large yellow croaker	61.10	105.63	103.88
小黄鱼	Small yellow croaker	63.00	88.16	119.53
带鱼	Hairtail	59.30	112.20	112.24
鲈鱼	Perch			106.14
沙丁鱼	Sardine		100.00	105.72
石斑鱼	Grouper	100.00	66.28	98.36
醍鱼	Anchovy		105.86	109.72
梭鱼	Mullet		99.98	105.94
鲳鱼	Silvery pomfret		93.51	114.91
海鳗	Conger pike		103.71	96.77
鲅鱼	Spanish mackerel		114.38	106.98
鲐鱼	Chub mackerel		149.69	113.07
马面鱼	Black scraper		75.81	126.75
黄姑鱼	Spotted maigre			0.00
鳓鱼	Chinese herring			114.59
马鲛	Japanese Spanish mackerel		92.91	115.95
梅童鱼	Baby croaker		151.72	
梭参	Barrachuda		100.01	0.00
鲷鱼	Porgy			115.22
蓝圆	Blue scad		113.09	98.85
鲆鲽	Left-eyed flounder		109.59	116.95
舌鳎	Tonguefish			123.08

2—4 续表 12 continued 12

农产品名称	Categories of agricultural products	2002	2003	2004
		第二季度 2nd quarter		
其他海水鱼类	Other seawater fish			105.75
海水虾蟹类	Seawater shrimp and crab	164.50	100.00	
对虾	Prawn		103.22	97.50
毛虾	Shrimp		125.25	108.71
爬虾	Hypplyte		87.82	121.11
脊尾白虾	Exopataemom carimicauda		100.00	104.17
鹰爪虾	Trachypemaeus curvirostris		151.32	113.13
梭子蟹	Swimming crab		91.65	108.93
其他海水虾蟹类	Other seawater shrimps and crabs			115.63
海水贝类	Seawater shellfish	111.30	89.64	108.49
贻贝	Mussel	87.50	100.67	104.66
扇贝	Scallop	101.40	100.00	111.11
牡蛎	Oyster	97.10	105.42	104.92
鲍鱼	Abalone	51.80	102.76	124.95
蛤	Clam	111.60	89.59	108.50
蚶	Blood clam	100.00	116.82	101.03
海螺	Conch		107.56	114.13
蛏	Razor clam		86.00	106.45
其他海水贝类	Other seawater shellfish			107.29
藻类	Seaweeds	144.80	101.04	129.88
海带	Kelp	144.80	100.00	129.88
紫菜	Laver	144.50	100.00	
其他藻类	Other seaweeds			96.38
其他海水产品	Other seawater products			0.00
墨鱼	Inkfish		70.64	132.21
鱿鱼	Squid		100.00	125.24
章鱼	Octopus		115.52	104.42
海参	Sea cucumber			112.50
未列明的其他海水产品	Other seawater products			178.05
2. 内陆水域水产品	2. Aquatic products in inland water areas	85.90	98.23	113.10
淡水鱼类	Freshwater fish	85.90	97.71	112.57
青鱼	Black carp	61.60	96.18	99.37
草鱼	Grass carp	88.40	97.55	117.92
鲤鱼	Carp	82.60	98.55	114.44
鲢鱼	Silver carp	75.70	94.56	110.30

2-4 续表 13 continued 13

农产品名称 Categories of agricultural products		2002	2003	2004
		第二季度 2nd quarter		
鲫鱼	Crucian carp	91.50	99.75	109.55
罗非鱼	Tilapia	66.90	87.43	105.30
虹鳟鱼	Rainbow trout	115.40		100.00
白鱼	Whitefish		97.59	115.94
鳜鱼	Mandarin fish		100.00	106.77
黑鱼	Snakeheaded fish		100.08	98.14
鲶鱼	Oriental sheatfish		101.82	110.51
武昌鱼	Blunt-snout bream		95.39	126.75
鳙鱼	Variegated carp		102.04	116.55
鲮鱼	Dace		83.91	128.02
鳊	Bream		88.92	97.12
黄颡鱼	Yellowcat fish			101.83
银鱼	Whitebait		80.00	
淡水鲈	Freshwater perch		79.55	87.87
其他淡水鱼类	Other freshwater fish			106.84
淡水虾蟹类	Freshwater shrimps and crabs	99.90	113.18	128.35
龙虾	Lobster		113.18	128.35
罗氏沼虾	M. rosenbergii		99.24	99.72
青虾	Black shrimps		103.28	104.79
基围虾	Exopalaemom carinicauda			120.00
红螯螯虾	Shrimps with red chelas		179.64	123.87
大闸蟹	Dazha crab		81.44	113.71
其他淡水虾蟹类	Other freshwater shrimp and crab			107.67
淡水贝类	Freshwater shellfish			
螺丝	Spiral shell		105.51	108.08
河蚌	Freshwater mussel		68.04	104.17
其他淡水贝类	Other freshwater shellfish			84.58
其他淡水养殖产品	Other freshwater breeding products			0.00
河鳗	River eel			111.11
牛蛙	Bullfrog		215.38	104.46
甲鱼	Soft-shelled turtle		111.57	93.63
黄鳝	Ricefield eel		102.88	107.94
泥鳅	Loach		102.41	123.87
蛙	Frog		92.78	107.16
未列明的其他淡水养殖产品	Other freshwater breeding products			94.35

2—5 全国农产品生产价格指数(第三季度)

National Indices of the Producers Prices of Agricultural Products

(上年同期=100)　　(3rd quarter)　　(the same period of the preceding year=100)

农产品名称	Categories of agricultural products	2002	2003	2004
		第三季度 3rd quarter		
合　计	Gross Index	98.10	102.05	114.71
一、农业产品	I. Crop products	98.10	102.91	122.26
1.谷物及其他作物	1.Cereal and other crops			129.07
＃粮食	Grain	95.30	101.47	135.09
谷物(原粮)	Cereal (unprocessed food grains)	93.00	100.15	137.26
小麦	Wheat	98.00	100.69	137.74
硬粒小麦	Hard-grained wheat	97.90	100.81	136.48
软粒小麦	Soft-grained wheat	82.30	103.99	134.38
混合小麦	Mixed wheat	100.20	99.86	143.52
其他小麦	Other wheat			136.36
稻谷	Paddy rice	93.10	97.81	143.12
早籼稻	Early long-grained nonglutinous rice	95.10	102.73	140.82
晚籼稻	Late long-grained nonglutinous rice	97.80	102.99	139.68
粳稻	Round-grained rice	90.60	93.10	145.47
其他稻谷	Other paddy			134.27
玉米	Maize (corn)	79.40	103.27	124.49
黄玉米	Yellow maize	78.20	103.06	124.57
白玉米	White maize	91.10	104.10	117.90
混合玉米	Mixed maize	92.40	105.60	124.25
其他玉米	Other maize		103.99	112.63
杂粮	Coarse cereals			
谷子	Millet		105.98	119.90
高粱	Chinese sorghum		106.17	131.30
大麦	Barley		101.33	132.26
荞麦	Buckwheat		95.31	110.87
青稞	Highland barley		102.55	108.20
莜麦	Naked oats		101.36	110.08
燕麦	Oats		92.61	151.05
其他杂粮	Other coarse cereals			111.32
谷物副产品	By-products of cereals			
小麦秸	Wheat straw			115.87
稻草	Rice straw			114.65
玉米秆	Corn stover			107.68

2—5 续表 1 continued 1

农产品名称 Categories of agricultural products		2002	2003	2004
		第三季度 3rd quarter		
大麦秸	Barley straw			117.14
高粱秆	Chinese sorghum stalk			111.11
薯类	Potato	118.70	84.92	111.10
红薯	Sweet potato	223.20	91.29	110.71
马铃薯	White potato	79.30	82.52	111.24
其他薯类	Other potatoes			120.18
薯藤	Potato vines			139.27
油料	Oil-bearing crops	102.10	120.55	115.20
花生	Peanut	110.90	115.13	116.91
油菜籽	Rapeseeds	97.90	123.27	114.50
芝麻	Sesame	89.20	110.12	111.07
向日葵	Sunflower		99.65	110.30
胡麻籽	Flaxseeds	112.10	110.16	125.67
其他油料作物	Other oil-bearing crops			102.05
油菜籽秆	Rapeseed stalk			115.39
豆类	Beans	109.50	114.80	121.86
大豆	Soybeans	110.60	116.77	122.66
绿豆	Mung beans	99.10	95.18	113.72
红小豆	Red beans	62.40	86.94	120.20
蚕豆	Broad beans		105.58	126.59
豌豆	Peas		99.99	115.68
芸豆	Kidney beans		100.42	94.57
其他杂豆	Other beans			108.47
豆秸	Beanstalk			109.71
棉花(籽棉)	Cotton (unginned cotton)	110.10	127.91	95.55
细绒棉	Thin-staple cotton	110.80	128.83	95.14
长绒棉	Long-staple cotton	89.00	100.00	107.95
麻类	Fiber crops	92.50	120.28	136.75
黄红麻	Jute and blueish dogbane	90.50	140.33	123.38
亚麻	Flax		92.93	137.53
苎麻	Ramie	92.70	115.89	139.68
其他麻类	Other fiber crops			101.01
糖料	Sugar crops	70.90	87.56	103.20

2—5 续表 2 continued 2

农产品名称 Categories of agricultural products		2002	2003	2004
		第三季度 3rd quarter		
甘蔗	Sugarcane	73.20	87.56	103.20
甜菜	Beet	100.00	104.00	
其他糖料	Other sugar crops			
烟草	Tobacco	111.40	92.26	112.91
烤烟叶	Flue-cured tobacco	111.60	92.08	112.96
晒烟叶	Sun-cured tobacco	80.30	117.43	105.13
其他烟叶	Other tobacco			104.10
其他农作物	Other agricultural crops			
青饲料	Greenfeed		104.45	102.31
牧草	Herbage		94.65	129.82
绿肥	Green manure		100.00	105.41
桑叶	Mulberry leaves		123.38	100.00
席草	Stems or leaves of cattail		75.69	111.07
薄荷油	Peppermint oil		108.11	0.00
野生植物的采集	Gathering of wild plants			141.54
未列明的其他农作物	Other agricultural crops			104.24
2.蔬菜、园艺作物	2. Vegetable and Horticulture crops		99.22	116.33
蔬菜	Vegetable	84.70	99.22	116.33
叶菜类	Leaf vegetable	77.20	100.19	115.60
菠菜	Spinach	87.20	94.08	107.15
芹菜	Celery	89.50	130.12	112.07
大白菜	Chinese cabbage		101.80	112.23
元白菜	Cabbage	84.20	91.36	120.19
甘蓝	Wild cabbage	52.50	60.80	106.21
花椰菜	Cauliflower	61.60	110.32	114.44
莴笋	Asparagus lettuce	118.50	75.84	125.35
油菜	Rape	105.30	101.61	116.55
其他叶菜	Other leaf vegetable			109.55
瓜菜类	Gourd vegetable	102.90	102.03	111.30
黄瓜	Cucumber	99.60	102.72	111.84
冬瓜	White gourd	122.20	97.34	112.86
西葫芦	Summer squash	283.30	105.09	104.42
苦瓜	Balsam pear		106.57	103.26

2—5 续表 3 continued 3

农产品名称	Categories of agricultural products	2002	2003	2004
		第三季度 3rd quarter		
丝瓜	Towed gourd		94.98	103.70
南瓜	Pumpkin		99.52	106.26
打瓜	Seeded watermelon		104.90	96.25
瓠子	Bottle gourd		86.78	119.39
其他瓜菜	Other gourd vegetable			109.40
块根、块茎菜类	Root and tuber vegetable	60.40	122.40	106.54
萝卜	Radish	60.70	116.21	109.76
胡萝卜	Carrot	54.90	136.40	98.25
生姜	Ginger		104.68	160.91
芋头	Taro		107.43	115.49
苔干	Dried bryophyte		100.00	133.34
百合(根)	Lily (root)		115.31	116.83
芋艿	Taro		146.66	124.67
山药	Chinese yam		113.87	112.13
其他块根、块茎菜	Other root and tuber vegetable			107.79
茄果菜类	Eggplant, tomato and chili, etc.	82.10	99.11	110.15
茄子	Eggplant	97.00	106.79	113.52
西红柿	Tomato	67.40	89.70	112.06
辣椒	Chili	74.80	106.93	100.82
青椒	Sweetbell	133.10	104.31	108.65
其他茄果菜类	Others			108.91
葱蒜类	Onion and Garlic	84.70	89.35	127.40
大葱	Scallion	182.70	106.61	106.79
蒜苔	Garlic stalk	54.30	106.00	136.38
蒜头	Garlic head	55.60	83.32	133.18
洋葱	Onion		106.02	117.30
蒜苗	Garlic bolt		145.57	102.88
小葱	Shallot		90.94	96.44
韭菜	Fragrant-flowered garlic		107.00	109.39
菜用豆类	Garden beans	105.90	98.49	112.12
四季豆	Kidney beans	124.90	95.82	114.58
豇豆	Cowpeas	95.20	99.40	111.28
水生菜类	Water vegetable	129.70	109.45	131.62

2—5 续表 4 continued 4

农产品名称 Categories of agricultural products		2002	2003	2004
		第三季度 3rd quarter		
莲藕	Lotus root	153.90	106.13	108.84
茭白	Wild ruice stem	128.80	109.57	132.45
荸荠	Water chestnut	100.00	99.73	
其他水生菜	Other water vegetable			99.52
食用菌(干鲜混合)	Mushroom		98.00	105.24
香菇(干品)	Mushroom (dried)		87.17	111.82
蘑菇(鲜品)	Mushroom (fresh)		97.76	104.33
黑木耳(干品)	Black edible fungus (dried)		114.20	125.29
白木耳(干品)	Tremella (dried)		89.09	103.33
金针菇(鲜品)	Golden mushroom		113.04	134.62
猴头菌(干品)	Bearded tooth(dried)		100.00	0.00
平菇(鲜品)	Oyster mushroom		105.69	109.61
花菇(干品)	Black forest mushroom		99.98	94.86
其他食用菌	Other edible mushrooms			110.09
椿芽	Chinese cedrela sprouts		106.07	115.47
花卉	Flowers			
鲜切花	Fresh flowers			
百合花	Lily		62.43	94.28
康乃馨	Carnation		296.79	59.77
满天星	June snow (serissa)		128.51	87.05
勿忘我	Forgetmenot		100.00	78.36
非洲菊	Flameray Gerbera		109.99	121.12
玫瑰	Rugosa rose		92.81	84.74
郁金香	Tulip			42.82
情人草	Evans begonia		57.15	40.00
其他鲜切花	Other fresh flowers			91.49
其他园艺作物	Other horticulture crops			
盆栽植物	Potted plants		134.83	0.00
观赏苗木	Ornamental plants		100.09	0.00
草坪草皮	Sod for lawn		91.84	93.38
其他园艺作物	Other horticulture crops			133.63
3.水果、坚果、饮料和香料	3. Fruits, beverages and perfume			98.16
水果、坚果	Fruits and nuts			97.18

2—5 续表 5 continued 5

农产品名称 Categories of agricultural products		2002	2003	2004
		第三季度 3rd quarter		
园林水果	Garden fruits	103.00	104.91	96.47
苹果	Apple	124.40	107.19	104.18
红富士苹果	Hongfushi apple	181.40	107.25	104.40
国光苹果	Guoguang apple	60.00	107.15	97.47
秦冠苹果	Qinguan apple	73.70	106.83	110.10
香蕉苹果	Banana apple	60.80	124.57	102.31
金冠苹果	Jinguan apple			108.46
元帅苹果	Yuanshuai (Marshal) apple		104.73	103.34
新红星苹果	New Hongxing apple		116.12	98.11
其他苹果	Other apples			88.06
梨	Pear	123.40	95.79	95.42
雪花梨	Snowflake pear	125.50	95.29	94.90
鸭梨	Ya-pear	103.50	118.26	96.81
酥梨	Soft-pear		108.75	111.38
香梨	Bergamot pear	181.90	142.19	108.04
苹果梨	Apple pear		99.79	103.01
其他梨	Other pears			105.68
柑桔	Citrus	91.70	99.37	96.48
柑	Mandarin orange	90.40	98.62	95.16
桔	Tangerine	120.10	109.85	97.07
橙	Orange	100.00	100.00	119.19
柚	Shaddock	83.50	108.00	100.77
其他柑桔	Others			108.79
其他水果	Other fruits			89.46
香蕉	Banana		113.74	105.71
菠萝	Pineapple		116.67	109.12
荔枝	Litchi	104.60	170.40	42.08
龙眼	Longan	33.90	138.64	75.69
芒果	Mango		115.81	106.38
橄榄	Chinese olive		96.17	90.50
桃	Peach	88.30	94.75	94.39
杏	Apricot	103.70	97.02	93.34
杨梅	Red bayberry	100.00	69.53	93.26

2—5 续表 6 continued 6

农产品名称 Categories of agricultural products		2002	2003	2004
		第三季度 3rd quarter		
猕猴桃	Yangtao	101.50	91.37	125.00
葡萄	Grape	96.20	93.52	98.57
红枣	Chinese date	101.20	84.02	115.21
柿子	Persimmon	70.60	103.91	91.54
其他园林水果	Other garden fruits			101.97
瓜果类	Melon	135.40	105.01	106.38
西瓜	Watermelon	138.00	104.47	106.84
甜瓜	Muskmelon	88.20	115.16	97.92
哈蜜瓜	Hami melon	135.20		
香瓜	Musk melon		100.06	110.67
草莓	Strawberry			97.77
其他瓜果	Others			107.49
坚果类	Nuts			
椰子	Coconut			107.00
杏仁	Apricot kernel			117.47
沙棘果	Seabuck thorn			0.00
其他坚果	Other nuts			136.84
茶及其他饮料(干品)	Tea and other beverages			108.14
茶	Tea	255.20		108.14
红毛茶	Black tea	119.80	83.83	112.52
绿毛茶	Green tea	320.00	103.61	105.70
乌龙茶	Oolong tea	70.70	75.66	115.12
紧压茶原料	Raw material for pressed tea	81.00		0.00
其他茶	Others			102.60
可可和咖啡	Cocoa and Coffee			
咖啡豆	Coffee bean		215.48	102.86
香料作物	Perfume crops			
茴香	Fennel			150.36
香茅草	Lemon grass			0.00
留兰香	Spearmint			76.87
百里香	Chinese thyme			112.35
其他	Others			108.58
4.中药材	4. Traditional Chinese medicinal materials			

2—5 续表 7 continued 7

农产品名称	Categories of agricultural products	2002	2003	2004
		第三季度 3rd quarter		
茯苓	Fuling (poris cocos)		107.99	126.49
当归	Chinese angelica		200.00	93.66
黄芪	Root of membranous milk vetch		104.66	105.98
金银花	Honeysuckle		148.85	99.41
人参	Ginseng			83.69
黄连	Rhizome of Chinese goldthread		100.90	124.24
甘草	Licorice root		103.79	100.00
贝母	Bulb of fritillary		141.28	50.71
红花	Safflower		164.10	98.01
元胡	Amur corydalis		100.30	104.03
枸杞	Fruit of Chinese wolfberry		133.59	106.91
砂仁	Villous amomum			101.38
菊花	Chrysanthemum		100.00	
白术	Largehead atractyldes		100.00	107.21
半夏	Tuber of pinelia		116.46	122.77
三七	Pseudo-ginseng			108.29
玄参	Root of Zhejiang figwort			113.44
生地	Dried rhizome of rehmannia		103.07	
杜仲	Bark of eucommia		105.39	72.94
枳壳	Trifoliate-orange			100.07
板蓝根	Root of common baphicacanthus		111.11	87.71
苦丁茶	Kudin crotoxylum (bitter tea tree)		39.80	113.36
天麻	Tuber of elevated gastrodia		157.89	120.59
灵芝	Glossy ganoderma			121.97
白芍	Root of herbaceous peony			108.83
虫草	Chinese caterpillar fungus			121.96
其他药材	Other medicinal materials			104.56
二、林业产品	II. Forest products	106.90	112.79	103.84
1. 竹木采运	1. Felling and transport of bamboo and wood			102.91
木材采运	Felling and transport of wood	95.60		102.90
原木	Log	95.50		102.90
红松	Korean pine		98.35	
落叶松	Larch		100.17	100.00

2—5 续表 8 continued 8

农产品名称	Categories of agricultural products	2002	2003	2004
		第三季度 3rd quarter		
马尾松	Masson pine		96.96	105.49
杉木	China fir		101.21	102.91
云南松	Yunnan pine		101.72	104.71
薪材	Firewood		100.69	107.43
竹材采运	Felling and transport of bamboo			106.06
水竹	Water bamboo		175.28	91.01
斑竹	Mottled bamboo		100.00	113.76
毛竹(楠竹)	Mao bamboo		93.24	106.06
蒿竹	Hao bamboo		82.33	112.34
淡竹	Henon bamboo		93.75	116.71
其他竹材	Other bamboo		98.74	96.61
2. 林产品的采集	2. Gathering of forest products		112.79	104.02
天然和人工林的果实	Products of natural and artificial forest			104.02
橡胶	Rubber	116.30	124.41	113.92
生漆	Raw lacquer			105.00
山苍籽	Seeds of mountain spicy tree			117.63
五倍籽	Chinese gall (gall nut)		137.32	108.01
油茶籽	Seeds of tea-oil tree	100.00	124.61	103.46
棕片	Palm fibre		77.20	113.54
松脂	Rosin		101.80	112.25
核桃	Walnut	179.00	78.37	98.60
板栗	Chinese chestnut		81.23	87.03
白果	Ginkgo		100.00	81.29
花椒	Chinese prickly ash	84.30	93.73	93.82
八角	Anise	139.90	91.37	80.17
桂皮	Cassia bark	66.40	88.00	102.15
胡椒	Pepper		109.88	94.71
其他果实	Other products			96.02
其他林产品采集	Gathering of other wild plants			
柳 条	Willow twigs		110.06	
竹笋干	Dried bamboo shoots		96.50	104.32
黄柏	Chinese weeping cypress			109.49
未列明的其他林产品采集	Gathering of other wild plants			86.90

2—5 续表 9 continued 9

农产品名称 Categories of agricultural products		2002	2003	2004
		第三季度 3rd quarter		
三、牧业(畜产品)	III. Livestock products	98.80	101.49	107.05
1. 牲畜的饲养	1. Livestock raising	99.50		105.21
牛的饲养	Cattle raising			106.10
活牛(毛重)	Live cattle (gross weight)	96.80	98.92	106.10
牛肉	Beef		103.05	106.61
羊的饲养	Sheep raising			105.74
活羊(毛重)	Live sheep		94.01	105.74
羊肉	Mutton		89.76	99.22
其他牲畜饲养	Other livestock raising			
马	Horse		103.19	123.88
驴	Donkey		90.07	102.89
骡	Mule		100.00	101.19
奶产品	Milk products	99.20	104.69	103.87
牛奶	Cow milk	99.30	104.69	103.88
羊奶	Sheep milk	58.20	107.27	101.01
其他奶类	Other milk			100.19
毛绒产品	Hair and down products	62.30	98.13	103.99
山羊毛	Goat's wool	86.80	97.45	87.99
绵羊毛	Sheep's wool		114.62	107.49
山羊绒	Cashmere	55.40	98.33	108.50
绵羊绒	Sheep's down		101.02	102.17
牦牛毛	Yak hair		100.00	125.17
牦牛绒	Yak down			0.00
骆驼绒	Camel hair cloth		100.00	107.95
其他毛绒产品	Other Hair and down products			88.37
其他牲畜产品	Other animal products			117.33
2. 猪的饲养	2. Hog raising			104.28
活猪(毛重)	Hog (gross weight)	97.20	102.09	104.28
猪肉	Pork		103.51	128.08
猪鬃	Bristles			114.25
3. 家禽	3. Poultry			116.81
肉禽(毛重)	Poultry (gross weight)	93.90	104.59	115.97
鸡	Chicken	93.30	104.67	115.88

2—5 续表 10 continued 10

农产品名称	Categories of agricultural products	2002	2003	2004
		第三季度 3rd quarter		
鸭	Duck	97.10	98.41	123.86
鹅	Goose	115.10	101.42	119.10
鹌鹑	Furs			139.40
其他家禽	Other poultry			116.26
禽蛋	Eggs	98.60	102.27	118.07
鸡蛋	Chicken's eggs	98.50	102.34	118.04
鸭蛋	Duck's eggs	102.70	99.94	118.93
鹅蛋	Goose's eggs	100.00	96.79	107.99
其他蛋	Other eggs			103.09
羽绒	Eider down		96.75	0.00
鸭绒	Duck's down			109.40
其他羽绒	Other down			109.35
4. 狩猎和捕捉动物	4. Hunting and catching animals			
兽皮	Furs			92.77
未列明的动物皮张	Furs not identified			102.93
5. 其他畜牧业	5. Other animal husbandry			
各种鸟类	Birds			
鸽子	Pigeon		112.53	98.66
山鸡	Pheasant			103.28
家养动物	Domestic animals			
兔	Rabbit		94.06	114.59
狗	Dog		91.44	104.70
猫	Cat			98.25
兔毛	Rabbit hair			167.40
珍贵动物	Rare animals			
鹿	Deer			79.29
狐狸	Fox		102.65	
水貂	Marten			128.42
蛇	Snake		72.07	117.62
虫类	Worms			
蚯蚓	Earthworm			122.75
蝎子	Scorpion			88.95
其他虫类	Other Worms			134.16

2—5 续表 11 continued 11

农产品名称	Categories of agricultural products	2002	2003	2004
		第三季度 3rd quarter		
活的家畜产品	Domestic animal products			
蚕茧	Silkworm cocoon	69.30	94.87	135.42
蜂蜜	Honey	152.70	93.59	98.45
鹿茸	Pilose antler			76.66
其他活的家畜产品	Other domestic animal products			134.46
毛皮的生产	Production of furs			
动物皮张	Animal furs		100.61	98.95
其他毛皮的生产	Production of other furs			110.00
四、渔业	IV. Fishery products	93.30	99.37	112.08
1. 海水水产品	1. Seawater aquatic products	92.30	99.37	109.57
鱼类	Seawater fish	93.10	97.28	109.91
大黄鱼	Large yellow croaker	80.60	85.18	109.19
小黄鱼	Small yellow croaker	120.40	88.09	115.20
带鱼	Hairtail	93.50	98.53	100.48
沙丁鱼	Sardine		100.98	121.61
鳕鱼	Cod	224.60		
石斑鱼	Grouper	110.60	94.46	138.19
鳀鱼	Anchovy		117.59	110.85
梭鱼	Mullet		100.00	116.18
鲳鱼	Silvery pomfret		86.56	106.60
海鳗	Conger pike		89.33	101.36
鲅鱼	Spanish mackerel		118.89	112.84
鲐鱼	Chub mackerel		102.13	100.00
马面鱼	Black scraper		102.12	113.26
马鲛	Japanese Spanish mackerel		88.18	108.38
梭参	Barrachuda		100.82	0.00
鲷鱼	Porgy			106.67
蓝圆	Blue scad		102.74	
鲆鲽	Left-eyed flounder		112.27	94.71
舌鳎	Tonguefish			123.06
其他海水鱼类	Other seawater fish			105.25
海水虾蟹类	Seawater shrimp and crab		110.19	95.83
对虾	Prawn		110.15	95.44

2—5 续表 12 continued 12

农产品名称	Categories of agricultural products	2002	2003	2004
		第三季度 3rd quarter		
毛虾	Shrimp		111.81	105.10
爬虾	Hypplyte		108.67	106.01
脊尾白虾	Exopataemom carimicauda		100.29	102.72
鹰爪虾	Trachypemaeus curvirostris		69.93	162.87
梭子蟹	Swimming crab		135.34	92.55
其他海水虾蟹类	Other seawater shrimps and crabs			98.55
海水贝类	Seawater shellfish		108.99	122.73
贻贝	Mussel		84.43	201.86
扇贝	Scallop		103.66	176.49
牡蛎	Oyster		102.90	94.13
鲍鱼	Abalone		101.55	120.12
蛤	Clam		112.81	111.61
蚶	Blood clam		100.00	90.00
海螺	Conch		112.90	112.00
蛏	Razor clam		106.94	98.35
其他海水贝类	Other seawater shellfish			117.36
藻类	Seaweeds		100.00	131.91
海带	Kelp		100.00	131.91
其他藻类	Other seaweeds			125.65
其他海水产品	Other seawater products			0.00
墨鱼	Inkfish		106.16	92.16
鱿鱼	Squid		108.60	137.64
章鱼	Octopus		107.60	110.28
海蜇	Jellyfish		105.25	100.39
2.内陆水域水产品	2. Aquatic products in inland water areas	95.10	99.60	116.46
淡水鱼类	Freshwater fish	95.10	99.37	115.82
青鱼	Black carp	60.90	99.25	107.66
草鱼	Grass carp	89.80	95.42	120.06
鲤鱼	Carp	94.70	105.45	117.91
鲢鱼	Silver carp	88.00	96.62	120.99
鲫鱼	Crucian carp	90.80	96.95	109.59
罗非鱼	Tilapia	122.00	99.19	113.27

2—5 续表 13 continued 13

农产品名称 Categories of agricultural products		2002	2003	2004
		第三季度 3rd quarter		
虹鳟鱼	Rainbow trout	125.10		100.00
白鱼	Whitefish		101.26	117.74
鳜鱼	Mandarin fish		100.00	108.94
白昌鱼	Round spadefish		97.51	131.64
黑鱼	Snakeheaded fish		104.49	108.56
鲶鱼	Oriental sheatfish		91.30	112.43
武昌鱼	Blunt-snout bream		99.23	114.91
鳙鱼	Variegated carp		106.26	114.99
鲮鱼	Dace		100.85	128.19
鳊	Bream		108.80	115.47
银鱼	Whitebait		93.25	111.11
淡水鲈	Freshwater perch		94.59	106.73
其他淡水鱼类	Other freshwater fish			104.08
淡水虾蟹类	Freshwater shrimps and crabs	91.30	103.47	126.76
龙虾	Lobster		103.47	130.33
罗氏沼虾	M. rosenbergii		94.27	96.93
青虾	Black shrimps		98.80	113.60
红螯螯虾	Shrimps with red chelas		110.76	127.99
大闸蟹	Dazha crab		86.43	98.15
其他淡水虾蟹类	Other freshwater shrimp and crab			90.74
淡水贝类	Freshwater shellfish			
淡水珍珠	Freshwater pearl			97.48
螺丝	Spiral shell		97.62	109.57
其他淡水养殖产品	Other freshwater breeding products			
河鳗	River eel		102.79	
甲鱼	Soft-shelled turtle		100.37	104.62
黄鳝	Ricefield eel		105.77	112.74
泥鳅	Loach		102.46	112.26
龟	Tortoise			86.44
蛙	Frog		129.23	134.27
未列明的其他淡水养殖产品	Other freshwater breeding products			88.68

2－6　全国农产品生产价格指数(第四季度)

National Indices of the Producer Prices of Agricultural Products

(上年同期＝100)　　(4th quarter)　　(the same period of the preceding year＝100)

农产品名称	Categories of agricultural products	2002 第四季度 4th quarter	2003	2004
合　计	Gross Index	102.29	111.64	113.02
一、农业产品	I. Crop products	107.25	115.03	108.98
1.谷物及其他作物	1. Cereal and other crops			112.77
#粮食	Grain	98.60	114.21	120.50
谷物(原粮)	Cereal (unprocessed food grains)	96.43	111.79	124.01
小麦	Wheat	97.56	114.21	124.43
硬粒小麦	Hard-grained wheat	98.03	111.79	124.22
软粒小麦	Soft-grained wheat	89.67	114.21	129.42
混合小麦	Mixed wheat	93.20	111.79	126.21
其他小麦	Other wheat			131.80
稻谷	Paddy rice	96.17	110.35	131.09
早籼稻	Early long-grained nonglutinous rice	98.15	106.87	132.88
晚籼稻	Late long-grained nonglutinous rice	100.54	110.64	129.98
粳稻	Round-grained rice	93.40	113.04	129.87
其他稻谷	Other paddy			125.04
玉米	Maize (corn)	96.11	114.12	111.35
黄玉米	Yellow maize	96.53	114.36	111.17
白玉米	White maize	93.31	105.43	117.66
混合玉米	Mixed maize	91.35	112.24	112.76
其他玉米	Other maize		111.58	108.87
杂粮	Coarse cereals		100.00	0.00
谷子	Millet		105.41	126.30
高粱	Chinese sorghum		106.22	128.62
大麦	Barley		106.72	117.54
荞麦	Buckwheat		109.39	108.30
元麦	poulard wheat		100.00	0.00
青稞	Highland barley		105.35	102.47
莜麦	Naked oats		101.88	104.03
燕麦	Oats		100.00	100.00
其他杂粮	Other coarse cereals			117.78
谷物副产品	By-products of cereals			
小麦秸	Wheat straw			122.69
稻草	Rice straw			103.04
玉米秆	Corn stover			107.63
谷子秆	Millet stalk			177.80

2－6 续表 1 continued 1

农产品名称	Categories of agricultural products	2002	2003	2004
		第四季度 4th quarter		
高粱秆	Chinese sorghum stalk			100.00
薯类	Potato	76.97	102.25	109.31
红薯	Sweet potato	88.97	96.73	111.44
马铃薯	White potato	72.45	104.33	108.51
其他薯类	Other potatoes			108.02
薯藤	Potato vines			100.00
油料	Oil-bearing crops	105.47	122.22	109.25
花生	Peanut	114.21	127.54	110.46
油菜籽	Rapeseeds	101.75	119.31	108.96
芝麻	Sesame	84.58	187.81	100.04
向日葵	Sunflower		105.66	119.35
胡麻籽	Flaxseeds	96.12	118.73	118.33
苏籽	Perillaseeds		123.26	108.81
其他油料作物	Other oil-bearing crops			107.41
花生蔓	Peanut vine			79.95
豆类	Beans	109.90	125.17	109.07
大豆	Soybeans	111.65	126.33	106.63
绿豆	Mung beans	92.22	113.41	133.69
红小豆	Red beans	109.68	126.18	124.58
蚕豆	Broad beans		115.13	125.23
豌豆	Peas		99.90	120.00
芸豆	Kidney beans		105.58	103.48
其他杂豆	Other beans			117.08
豆秸	Beanstalk			99.55
棉花(籽棉)	Cotton (unginned cotton)	138.13	150.90	76.09
细绒棉	Thin-staple cotton	139.27	151.57	75.61
长绒棉	Long-staple cotton	120.46	140.45	83.47
棉籽	Cottonseeds			85.15
麻类	Fiber crops	90.95	138.03	109.85
黄红麻	Jute and blueish dogbane	85.27	117.89	113.40
亚麻	Flax		100.00	121.77
苎麻	Ramie	91.64	140.50	106.50
剑麻	Steel hemp		112.42	110.49
麻秆	Stalks of fiber crops			208.16
糖料	Sugar crops	86.51	98.93	109.89

2—6 续表 2 continued 2

农产品名称	Categories of agricultural products	2002	2003	2004
		第四季度 4th quarter		
甘蔗	Sugarcane	86.51	98.93	109.89
甜菜	Beet	100.00	102.55	125.30
其他糖料	Other sugar crops			
烟草	Tobacco	86.51	95.51	112.56
烤烟叶	Flue-cured tobacco	86.51	95.42	112.57
晒烟叶	Sun-cured tobacco	100.00	107.44	111.44
白肋烟	Whiteerib tobacco		109.62	98.95
其他烟叶	Other tobacco			105.60
其他农作物	Other agricultural crops			
青饲料	Greenfeed		101.33	113.31
牧草	Herbage		102.96	112.59
桑叶	Mulberry leaves		100.00	154.20
席草	Stems or leaves of cattail		69.46	86.52
蓖麻籽	Castor beans		111.11	106.58
野生植物的采集	Gathering of wild plants			107.93
未列明的其他农作物	Other agricultural crops			77.33
2. 蔬菜、园艺作物	2. Vegetable and Horticulture crops		107.20	103.05
蔬菜	Vegetable	122.21	107.20	103.05
叶菜类	Leaf vegetable	151.35	110.95	95.36
菠菜	Spinach	65.66	109.35	94.52
芹菜	Celery	90.29	112.12	89.79
大白菜	Chinese cabbage	179.29	116.29	86.84
元白菜	Cabbage	139.64	103.49	102.94
甘蓝	Wild cabbage		112.81	100.34
花椰菜	Cauliflower	137.90	113.00	106.90
莴笋	Asparagus lettuce	132.01	114.01	103.38
油菜	Rape	321.62	105.99	99.89
其他叶菜	Other leaf vegetable			102.25
瓜菜类	Gourd vegetable	116.64	104.23	98.53
黄瓜	Cucumber	114.62	103.20	99.50
冬瓜	White gourd	131.46	110.09	92.49
西葫芦	Summer squash	133.52	120.64	99.19
苦瓜	Balsam pear		89.64	111.64
丝瓜	Towed gourd		103.95	103.75
南瓜	Pumpkin		107.08	108.91

2—6 续表 3 continued 3

农产品名称	Categories of agricultural products	2002	2003	2004
		第四季度 4th quarter		
打瓜	Seeded watermelon		104.28	113.51
瓠子	Bottle gourd		105.80	100.33
其他瓜菜	Other gourd vegetable			97.39
块根、块茎菜类	Root and tuber vegetable	125.50	113.77	96.45
萝卜	Radish	127.59	111.42	98.02
胡萝卜	Carrot	62.79	117.95	93.07
生姜	Ginger	73.31	122.94	135.59
芋头	Taro		101.54	106.04
苔干	Dried bryophyte		119.29	77.36
百合(根)	Lily (root)		113.49	94.45
芋艿	Taro		122.03	112.76
山药	Chinese yam		112.17	119.19
其他块根、块茎菜	Other root and tuber vegetable			104.43
茄果菜类	Eggplant, tomato and chili, etc.	94.88	98.71	101.79
茄子	Eggplant	106.62	99.94	101.19
西红柿	Tomato	87.35	99.94	102.35
辣椒	Chili	129.96	105.20	100.00
青椒	Sweetbell	109.55	95.43	101.90
其他茄果菜类	Others			110.96
葱蒜类	Onion and Garlic	104.59	108.08	115.11
大葱	Scallion	89.26	117.67	105.50
蒜苔	Garlic stalk	125.74	115.76	102.64
蒜头	Garlic head	115.92	100.70	122.57
洋葱	Onion		98.11	98.36
蒜苗	Garlic bolt		114.95	106.37
小葱	Shallot		108.83	97.25
韭菜	Fragrant-flowered garlic		101.46	107.01
其他葱蒜类	Others			99.61
菜用豆类	Garden beans	137.59	109.55	101.62
四季豆	Kidney beans	124.18	113.07	105.61
豇豆	Cowpeas	145.18	107.88	99.72
其他菜用豆	Other garden beans			104.52
水生菜类	Water vegetable	183.24	98.80	106.14
莲藕	Lotus root	98.13	108.12	101.16
茭白	Wild ruice stem	185.99	98.50	106.30

2—6 续表 4 continued 4

农产品名称	Categories of agricultural products	2002	2003	2004
		第四季度 4th quarter		
荸荠	Water chestnut	100.00	104.58	124.73
其他水生菜	Other water vegetable			111.92
食用菌(干鲜混合)	Mushroom		104.15	94.76
香菇(干品)	Mushroom (dried)		89.19	91.17
蘑菇(鲜品)	Mushroom (fresh)		102.54	93.51
黑木耳(干品)	Black edible fungus (dried)		123.33	105.46
白木耳(干品)	Tremella (dried)		102.50	91.34
金针菇(鲜品)	Golden mushroom		99.07	100.00
猴头菌(干品)	Bearded tooth(dried)		100.00	0.00
平菇(鲜品)	Oyster mushroom		110.90	94.83
花菇(干品)	Black forest mushroom		100.00	92.68
其他食用菌	Other edible mushrooms			106.33
未列明的其他蔬菜	Other vegetable			104.41
花卉	Flowers			
鲜切花	Fresh flowers			
百合花	Lily		87.89	115.95
康乃馨	Carnation		210.94	166.42
满天星	June snow (serissa)		388.07	81.76
勿忘我	Forgetmenot		135.23	143.98
非洲菊	Flameray Gerbera		100.00	78.81
玫瑰	Rugosa rose		108.57	94.11
情人草	Evans begonia		100.00	90.33
其他鲜切花	Other fresh flowers			101.08
其他园艺作物	Other horticulture crops			
盆栽植物	Potted plants		107.76	0.00
观赏苗木	Ornamental plants		108.62	0.00
草坪草皮	Sod for lawn		85.94	91.72
3.水果、坚果、饮料和香料	3. Fruits, beverages and perfume			92.14
水果、坚果	Fruits and nuts			91.44
园林水果	Garden fruits	93.65	101.70	90.37
苹果	Apple	59.71	94.83	98.15
红富士苹果	Hongfushi apple	65.11	93.60	100.94
国光苹果	Guoguang apple	89.38	96.39	87.00
秦冠苹果	Qinguan apple	58.90	100.10	107.24
香蕉苹果	Banana apple		118.78	99.18

2—6 续表 5 continued 5

农产品名称 Categories of agricultural products		2002	2003	2004
		第四季度 4th quarter		
元帅苹果	Yuanshuai (Marshal) apple		95.58	104.11
新红星苹果	New Hongxing apple		107.36	110.03
其他苹果	Other apples			96.94
梨	Pear	125.84	109.76	85.10
雪花梨	Snowflake pear	125.71	109.67	85.15
鸭梨	Ya-pear	102.32	97.75	88.89
酥梨	Soft-pear	139.24	118.05	81.40
香梨	Bergamot pear	111.11	100.00	
苹果梨	Apple pear		108.09	105.08
冬果梨	Dongguo pear			100.00
其他梨	Other pears			100.21
柑桔	Citrus	134.56	103.71	99.01
柑	Mandarin orange	162.88	103.99	99.26
桔	Tangerine	118.07	97.07	101.79
橙	Orange	98.68	105.25	96.60
柚	Shaddock	70.70	96.98	92.88
其他柑桔	Others			108.50
其他水果	Other fruits			95.00
香蕉	Banana	74.57	123.20	103.18
菠萝	Pineapple		100.00	114.82
荔枝	Litchi	100.00	66.67	77.69
龙眼	Longan	15.04	91.55	83.53
芒果	Mango		98.06	
木瓜	Papaya		92.02	119.35
橄榄	Chinese olive		101.56	126.07
桃	Peach	103.72	80.14	98.38
杏	Apricot	80.65	100.00	102.20
杨梅	Red bayberry	100.00	83.33	
猕猴桃	Yangtao	105.88	72.23	112.93
葡萄	Grape	62.50	113.87	95.43
红枣	Chinese date	90.54	105.85	99.71
柿子	Persimmon	130.97	100.17	98.27
其他园林水果	Other garden fruits			98.82
瓜果类	Melon	72.64	102.96	108.91
西瓜	Watermelon	74.30	102.79	109.28

2—6 续表 6　　continued 6

农产品名称	Categories of agricultural products	2002	2003	2004
		第四季度 4th quarter		
甜瓜	Muskmelon	34.96	106.33	101.83
香瓜	Musk melon		108.89	
草莓	Strawberry			110.34
其他瓜果	Others			103.13
坚果类	Nuts			108.36
椰子	Coconut			108.36
杏仁	Apricot kernel			446.43
槟榔	Areca			120.04
其他坚果	Other nuts			117.93
茶及其他饮料(干品)	Tea and other beverages			107.85
茶	Tea	140.89		107.85
红毛茶	Black tea	60.84	83.86	116.41
绿毛茶	Green tea	143.11	98.23	106.84
乌龙茶	Oolong tea	139.09	108.80	110.38
其他茶	Others			99.01
可可和咖啡	Cocoa and Coffee			
咖啡豆	Coffee bean		106.46	110.38
香料作物	Perfume crops			
茴香	Fennel			138.82
留兰香	Spearmint			97.78
其他	Others			90.82
4. 中药材	4. Traditional Chinese medicinal materials			
茯苓	Fuling (poris cocos)		112.28	123.37
党参	Tangshen (pilose asiabell)		107.97	94.62
当归	Chinese angelica		100.00	103.52
黄芪	Root of membranous milk vetch		113.03	88.08
金银花	Honeysuckle		103.04	79.73
黄连	Rhizome of Chinese goldthread		91.64	
甘草	Licorice root		100.00	207.12
贝母	Bulb of fritillary		153.54	104.76
红花	Safflower		100.17	104.00
元胡	Amur corydalis		111.87	
枸杞	Fruit of Chinese wolfberry		107.19	89.00
菊花	Chrysanthemum		201.98	31.07
白术	Largehead atractyldes		137.56	84.86

2—6 续表 7 continued 7

农产品名称	Categories of agricultural products	2002	2003	2004
		第四季度 4th quarter		
半夏	Tuber of pinelia		100.00	99.82
西洋参	American ginseng			100.47
生地	Dried rhizome of rehmannia		105.80	121.55
杜仲	Bark of eucommia		101.35	96.00
板蓝根	Root of common baphicacanthus		101.85	90.38
苦丁茶	Kudin crotoxylum (bitter tea tree)		68.66	130.98
天麻	Tuber of elevated gastrodia		94.21	93.46
穿心莲	Creat		181.29	101.78
桔梗	Rampion		118.27	100.26
其他药材	Other medicinal materials			93.00
二、林业产品	II. Forest products	111.49	105.36	98.69
1. 竹木采运	1. Felling and transport of bamboo and wood			102.74
木材采运	Felling and transport of wood	105.26		102.71
原木	Log	105.54		102.71
红松	Korean pine		100.90	
落叶松	Larch		101.69	93.95
马尾松	Masson pine		103.32	103.74
杉木	China fir		101.73	108.40
云南松	Yunnan pine		93.63	111.11
薪材	Firewood		99.49	99.72
竹材采运	Felling and transport of bamboo			107.69
水竹	Water bamboo		101.63	106.27
斑竹	Mottled bamboo		101.29	
毛竹(楠竹)	Mao bamboo		104.05	107.69
蒿竹	Hao bamboo		97.44	117.66
淡竹	Henon bamboo		104.48	107.28
其他竹材	Other bamboo		113.63	106.32
2. 林产品的采集	2. Gathering of forest products		105.36	97.93
天然和人工林的果实	Products of natural and artificial forest			97.93
橡胶	Rubber	157.52	116.94	104.62
生漆	Raw lacquer			99.80
油桐籽	Seeds of tung oil tree	100.00	163.07	131.79
乌桕籽	Seeds of Chinese tallow tree		183.15	101.39
五倍籽	Chinese gall (gall nut)		177.86	105.27
油茶籽	Seeds of tea-oil tree	100.00	109.41	108.66

2—6 续表 8 continued 8

农产品名称	Categories of agricultural products	2002	2003	2004
		第四季度 4th quarter		
棕片	Palm fibre		97.24	99.26
松脂	Rosin		106.94	114.19
核桃	Walnut	83.02	98.46	113.53
板栗	Chinese chestnut		97.77	98.72
白果	Ginkgo		76.75	83.73
松子	Pine nut		113.27	127.72
花椒	Chinese prickly ash	49.58	100.47	95.82
八角	Anise	80.28	67.15	84.46
桂皮	Cassia bark	87.27	120.86	73.04
胡椒	Pepper		106.70	79.61
其他果实	Other products			106.20
其他林产品采集	Gathering of other wild plants			
藤条	Rattan		100.00	113.71
竹笋干	Dried bamboo shoots		97.71	112.70
桉树叶	Eucalyptus leaves			96.00
黄柏	Chinese weeping cypress			104.17
未列明的其他林产品采集	Gathering of other wild plants			103.20
三、牧业(畜产品)	III. Livestock products	98.59	109.25	118.92
1. 牲畜的饲养	1. Livestock raising	102.03		103.57
牛的饲养	Cattle raising			103.96
活牛(毛重)	Live cattle (gross weight)	98.04	103.92	103.96
牛肉	Beef		102.73	99.11
羊的饲养	Sheep raising			103.61
活羊(毛重)	Live sheep		98.11	103.61
羊肉	Mutton		106.06	106.02
其他牲畜饲养	Other livestock raising			
马	Horse		105.27	105.31
驴	Donkey		108.50	94.22
骆驼	Camel		130.01	0.00
其他未列牲畜的饲养	Other livestock raising			100.08
奶产品	Milk products	104.09	111.06	101.29
牛奶	Cow milk	104.16	111.06	101.28
羊奶	Sheep milk	54.49	113.28	104.25
毛绒产品	Hair and down products	57.25	113.89	103.67
山羊毛	Goat's wool	55.39	100.00	103.67

2—6 续表 9　　continued 9

农产品名称	Categories of agricultural products	2002	2003	2004
		第四季度 4th quarter		
绵羊毛	Sheep's wool		98.16	97.72
山羊绒	Cashmere	57.83	118.24	105.66
绵羊绒	Sheep's down		146.25	
骆驼绒	Camel hair cloth		106.38	
其他毛绒产品	Other Hair and down products			113.03
2. 猪的饲养	2. Hog raising			126.36
活猪(毛重)	Hog (gross weight)	99.46	112.97	126.36
猪肉	Pork		109.54	117.34
猪鬃	Bristles			121.27
3. 家禽	3. Poultry			113.74
肉禽(毛重)	Poultry (gross weight)	94.59	106.03	113.73
鸡	Chicken	94.58	106.03	113.72
鸭	Duck	96.36	103.40	118.39
鹅	Goose	100.00	109.18	115.80
其他家禽	Other poultry			115.38
禽蛋	Eggs	99.57	104.99	113.75
鸡蛋	Chicken's eggs	99.27	105.09	113.70
鸭蛋	Duck's eggs	108.56	101.65	115.24
鹅蛋	Goose's eggs	100.00	102.79	103.83
其他蛋	Other eggs			90.61
羽绒	Eider down		111.60	0.00
鸭绒	Duck's down			117.84
其他羽绒	Other down			115.54
4. 狩猎和捕捉动物	4. Hunting and catching animals			
兽皮	Furs			96.89
未列明的动物皮张	Furs not identified			108.06
5. 其他畜牧业	5. Other animal husbandry			0.00
各种鸟类	Birds			0.00
鸽子	Pigeon		104.36	122.04
家养动物	Domestic animals			
兔	Rabbit		95.10	112.25
狗	Dog		100.91	103.93
猫	Cat			102.61
兔毛	Rabbit hair			163.91
其他家养动物	Other domestic animals			120.00

2—6 续表 10 continued 10

农产品名称	Categories of agricultural products	2002	2003	2004
		第四季度 4th quarter		
珍贵动物	Rare animals			0.00
水貂	Marten			76.65
蛇	Snake		100.33	95.64
活的家畜产品	Domestic animal products			
蚕茧	Silkworm cocoon		145.09	100.76
蜂蜜	Honey	58.30	100.90	101.03
鹿茸	Pilose antler			15.50
其他活的家畜产品	Other domestic animal products			128.38
毛皮的生产	Production of furs			
动物皮张	Animal furs		105.93	97.02
四、渔业	IV. Fishery products	90.87	106.12	109.82
1. 海水水产品	1. Seawater aquatic products	86.81	109.53	108.30
鱼类	Seawater fish	83.38	110.15	107.99
大黄鱼	Large yellow croaker	54.21	112.79	101.55
小黄鱼	Small yellow croaker	84.82	102.64	104.51
带鱼	Hairtail	104.61	110.15	108.49
鲈鱼	Perch			92.01
沙丁鱼	Sardine		107.49	111.88
鳕鱼	Cod	83.15		
石斑鱼	Grouper	100.00	100.00	119.55
醍鱼	Anchovy		106.62	111.74
梭鱼	Mullet		89.29	117.01
鲳鱼	Silvery pomfret		101.56	111.31
海鳗	Conger pike		95.49	107.65
鲅鱼	Spanish mackerel		91.51	115.60
鲐鱼	Chub mackerel		102.12	113.99
马面鱼	Black scraper		87.50	100.77
马鲛	Japanese Spanish mackerel		108.72	105.19
梅童鱼	Baby croaker		104.85	
梭参	Barrachuda		103.55	0.00
鲷鱼	Porgy			105.62
蓝圆	Blue scad		111.29	166.67
鲆鲽	Left-eyed flounder		116.14	
舌鳎	Tonguefish			145.20
其他海水鱼类	Other seawater fish			112.23

2—6 续表 11 continued 11

农产品名称	Categories of agricultural products	2002	2003	2004
		第四季度 4th quarter		
海水虾蟹类	Seawater shrimp and crab	88.76	100.00	116.72
对虾	Prawn		94.47	103.56
毛虾	Shrimp		109.89	103.77
爬虾	Hypplyte		98.87	133.30
脊尾白虾	Exopataemom carimicauda		100.00	104.88
鹰爪虾	Trachypemaeus curvirostris		129.70	
梭子蟹	Swimming crab		105.16	114.24
其他海水虾蟹类	Other seawater shrimps and crabs			97.22
海水贝类	Seawater shellfish		102.17	98.93
贻贝	Mussel		113.79	
扇贝	Scallop		101.17	145.22
牡蛎	Oyster		98.81	107.79
鲍鱼	Abalone		126.87	112.81
蛤	Clam		100.52	98.73
蚶	Blood clam		137.23	91.60
海螺	Conch		117.14	115.57
蛏	Razor clam		109.44	106.13
其他海水贝类	Other seawater shellfish			80.12
藻类	Seaweeds		106.93	
海带	Kelp		106.93	
紫菜	Laver		106.38	87.46
其他藻类	Other seaweeds			133.06
其他海水产品	Other seawater products			0.00
墨鱼	Inkfish		107.22	94.39
鱿鱼	Squid		133.65	136.84
章鱼	Octopus		103.01	84.22
海蜇	Jellyfish		110.68	43.78
未列明的其他海水产品	Other seawater products			98.53
2.内陆水域水产品	2. Aquatic products in inland water areas	97.64	100.16	112.49
淡水鱼类	Freshwater fish	97.64	100.18	112.29
青鱼	Black carp	47.77	103.04	111.47
草鱼	Grass carp	91.35	101.20	115.51
鲤鱼	Carp	96.56	100.63	112.04
鲢鱼	Silver carp	91.39	101.30	116.61
鲫鱼	Crucian carp	78.25	98.25	113.50

2—6 续表 12 continued 12

农产品名称	Categories of agricultural products	2002	2003	2004
		第四季度 4th quarter		
罗非鱼	Tilapia	161.80	100.20	100.67
虹鳟鱼	Rainbow trout	111.09		103.34
白鱼	Whitefish		90.72	104.34
鳜鱼	Mandarin fish		107.73	102.29
白昌鱼	Round spadefish		104.36	118.51
黑鱼	Snakeheaded fish		99.69	99.97
鲶鱼	Oriental sheatfish		101.01	107.82
武昌鱼	Blunt-snout bream		106.77	107.24
鳙鱼	Variegated carp		103.43	110.21
鲮鱼	Dace		96.50	112.92
鳊	Bream		93.15	107.41
黄颡鱼	Yellowcat fish			110.00
淡水鲈	Freshwater perch		110.64	123.53
其他淡水鱼类	Other freshwater fish			103.91
淡水虾蟹类	Freshwater shrimps and crabs	86.23	99.87	115.82
龙虾	Lobster		99.87	128.76
罗氏沼虾	M. rosenbergii		93.82	100.72
青虾	Black shrimps		98.74	103.43
基围虾	Exopalaemom carinicauda			102.33
红螯螯虾	Shrimps with red chelas		113.96	145.61
大闸蟹	Dazha crab		91.20	101.69
其他淡水虾蟹类	Other freshwater shrimp and crab			103.84
淡水贝类	Freshwater shellfish			
螺丝	Spiral shell		114.07	
其他淡水贝类	Other freshwater shellfish			104.76
其他淡水养殖产品	Other freshwater breeding products			
河鳗	River eel		94.57	114.29
牛蛙	Bullfrog		120.00	107.77
甲鱼	Soft-shelled turtle		101.95	85.76
黄鳝	Ricefield eel		104.10	105.30
泥鳅	Loach		109.18	117.56
龟	Tortoise			86.52
蛙	Frog		104.17	

2—7 各地区农产品生产价格总指数

Gross Indices of the Producer Prices of Agricultural Products by Region

（上年=100） (the preceding year=100)

地　区 Region	2002	2003	2004
全　国 National Total	**99.70**	**104.37**	**113.09**
北　京 Beijing	104.10	102.46	105.76
天　津 Tianjin	104.17	104.44	108.06
河　北 Hebei	97.70	107.48	110.09
山　西 Shanxi	94.74	103.94	110.61
内蒙古 Inner Mongolia	99.34	106.45	112.00
辽　宁 Liaoning	99.41	103.33	120.41
吉　林 Jilin	98.60	136.86	118.11
黑龙江 Heilongjiang	102.39	110.23	117.27
上　海 Shanghai	100.00	102.15	110.84
江　苏 Jiangsu	97.28	107.21	122.68
浙　江 Zhejiang	101.22	101.88	116.77
安　徽 Anhui	99.85	106.42	117.78
福　建 Fujian	99.10	101.72	106.80
江　西 Jiangxi	100.00	105.09	119.48
山　东 Shandong	102.15	108.55	112.31
河　南 Henan	99.70	111.84	121.95
湖　北 Hubei	100.90	106.94	121.66
湖　南 Hunan	99.91	111.69	127.31
广　东 Guangdong	98.45	101.30	110.70
广　西 Guangxi	100.00	104.51	118.93
海　南 Hainan	100.00	104.26	106.36
重　庆 Chongqing	101.10	103.80	125.53
四　川 Sichuan	101.82	103.54	120.38
贵　州 Guizhou	103.89	101.93	111.14
云　南 Yunnan	108.12	100.33	112.91
陕　西 Shaanxi	101.12	105.48	111.66
甘　肃 Gansu	97.81	103.36	113.06
青　海 Qinghai	101.16	105.75	108.75
宁　夏 Ningxia	93.40	104.40	114.23
新　疆 Xinjiang	100.91	126.16	100.80

2—8 各地区农林牧渔业产品生产价格指数
Indices of the Producer Prices of Agricultural Products by Region

（上年=100） (the preceding year=100)

地区 Region	总指数 Gross Index		种植业产品 Crop products		林业产品 Forest products	
	2003	2004	2003	2004	2003	2004
全国 National Total	**104.37**	**113.09**	**107.42**	**115.86**	**107.01**	**104.62**
北京 Beijing	102.46	105.76	101.92	103.21	100.85	111.40
天津 Tianjin	104.44	108.06	110.75	103.11	98.75	98.80
河北 Hebei	107.48	110.09	111.76	107.10	95.00	112.34
山西 Shanxi	103.94	110.61	105.49	109.14	98.63	106.33
内蒙古 Inner Mongolia	106.45	112.00	107.23	112.26	97.21	98.97
辽宁 Liaoning	103.33	120.41	105.61	117.73	104.90	95.05
吉林 Jilin	136.86	118.11	148.11	119.78	100.00	250.55
黑龙江 Heilongjiang	110.23	117.27	116.36	117.14	100.00	83.75
上海 Shanghai	102.15	110.84	113.75	108.12	100.00	0.00
江苏 Jiangsu	107.21	122.68	110.79	124.96	101.40	99.36
浙江 Zhejiang	101.88	116.77	97.66	116.98	116.57	98.75
安徽 Anhui	106.42	117.78	108.40	117.73	97.65	102.78
福建 Fujian	101.72	106.80	101.30	104.70	101.50	102.30
江西 Jiangxi	105.09	119.48	106.23	122.60	103.35	109.06
山东 Shandong	108.55	112.31	110.23	111.40	90.09	110.24
河南 Henan	111.84	121.95	116.30	118.43	103.52	103.81
湖北 Hubei	106.94	121.66	109.71	119.58	141.73	100.09
湖南 Hunan	111.69	127.31	113.16	118.13	107.55	111.10
广东 Guangdong	101.30	110.70	103.15	108.88	100.66	108.26
广西 Guangxi	104.51	118.93	106.08	104.11	88.54	105.29
海南 Hainan	104.26	106.36	107.04	105.70	108.34	106.26
重庆 Chongqing	103.80	125.53	105.54	120.26	100.00	0.00
四川 Sichuan	103.54	120.38	105.14	121.03	111.85	104.37
贵州 Guizhou	101.93	111.14	100.33	110.72	115.72	106.00
云南 Yunnan	100.33	112.91	98.96	110.68	110.96	115.79
陕西 Shaanxi	105.48	111.66	109.00	110.28	87.35	95.09
甘肃 Gansu	103.36	113.06	105.76	112.98	86.28	100.01
青海 Qinghai	105.75	108.75	110.05	111.51	100.00	0.00
宁夏 Ningxia	104.40	114.23	108.80	120.21	100.00	0.00
新疆 Xinjiang	126.16	100.80	137.38	96.76	89.98	98.77

2—8续表1 continued 1

地　区 Region	畜牧业产品 Livestock products		渔业产品 Fishery products	
	2003	2004	2003	2004
全　国 National Total	**101.76**	**111.08**	**100.34**	**110.19**
北　京 Beijing	102.37	107.42	109.99	106.46
天　津 Tianjin	103.29	113.65	92.66	104.41
河　北 Hebei	102.97	112.06	106.14	126.99
山　西 Shanxi	102.48	113.86	98.60	102.79
内蒙古 Inner Mongolia	105.60	112.48	109.23	112.35
辽　宁 Liaoning	102.13	124.93	99.17	117.77
吉　林 Jilin	124.51	111.81	90.52	87.34
黑龙江 Heilongjiang	100.41	119.57	119.36	104.84
上　海 Shanghai	99.70	107.81	92.95	114.74
江　苏 Jiangsu	107.06	127.44	97.74	111.85
浙　江 Zhejiang	117.64	131.17	95.75	110.30
安　徽 Anhui	105.11	120.18	103.11	110.10
福　建 Fujian	103.60	113.90	101.00	107.00
江　西 Jiangxi	108.92	125.45	97.46	110.61
山　东 Shandong	107.79	115.13	105.84	110.05
河　南 Henan	105.22	129.27	103.39	109.30
湖　北 Hubei	105.93	128.15	93.49	113.67
湖　南 Hunan	111.57	134.80	101.79	111.76
广　东 Guangdong	101.04	118.08	98.21	106.09
广　西 Guangxi	104.12	132.33	96.15	109.86
海　南 Hainan	104.43	115.20	97.39	101.46
重　庆 Chongqing	103.18	128.83	100.86	107.83
四　川 Sichuan	101.17	121.50	102.30	109.37
贵　州 Guizhou	102.55	111.69	95.88	106.20
云　南 Yunnan	100.72	116.84	98.30	111.63
陕　西 Shaanxi	100.89	115.89	115.76	110.25
甘　肃 Gansu	99.58	113.66	98.94	100.00
青　海 Qinghai	102.10	106.67	100.00	0.00
宁　夏 Ningxia	101.00	109.22	103.20	132.87
新　疆 Xinjiang	95.96	102.95	120.12	122.90

2—9 各地区种植业产品生产价格指数
Indices of the Producer Prices of Crop Products by Region

（上年=100） (the preceding year=100)

地区 Region	种植业产品 Crop products		种植业产品 Crop products 谷物(原粮) Cereal (unprocessed food grains)	
	2003	2004	2003	2004
全国 National Total	**107.42**	**115.86**	**102.34**	**128.06**
北京 Beijing	101.92	103.21	100.12	118.18
天津 Tianjin	110.75	103.11	106.40	123.60
河北 Hebei	111.76	107.10	106.09	123.91
山西 Shanxi	105.49	109.14	104.49	116.71
内蒙古 Inner Mongolia	107.23	112.26	105.07	114.92
辽宁 Liaoning	105.61	117.73	102.97	122.18
吉林 Jilin	148.11	119.78	116.25	120.41
黑龙江 Heilongjiang	116.36	117.14	98.61	122.62
上海 Shanghai	113.75	108.12	106.25	184.25
江苏 Jiangsu	110.79	124.96	115.33	130.11
浙江 Zhejiang	97.66	116.98	90.02	136.95
安徽 Anhui	108.40	117.73	105.11	132.18
福建 Fujian	101.30	104.70	103.81	138.09
江西 Jiangxi	106.23	122.60	103.42	129.64
山东 Shandong	110.23	111.40	107.03	126.51
河南 Henan	116.30	118.43	107.32	131.12
湖北 Hubei	109.71	119.58	107.63	141.53
湖南 Hunan	113.16	118.13	107.84	140.58
广东 Guangdong	103.15	108.88	104.08	134.62
广西 Guangxi	106.08	104.11	98.39	125.70
海南 Hainan	107.04	105.70	102.23	125.63
重庆 Chongqing	105.54	120.26	105.42	139.59
四川 Sichuan	105.14	121.03	105.93	132.87
贵州 Guizhou	100.33	110.72	102.14	117.47
云南 Yunnan	98.96	110.68	104.86	123.54
陕西 Shaanxi	109.00	110.28	107.35	126.98
甘肃 Gansu	105.76	112.98	99.16	118.05
青海 Qinghai	110.05	111.51	101.21	115.63
宁夏 Ningxia	108.80	120.21	101.10	125.85
新疆 Xinjiang	137.38	96.76	93.44	119.81

2—9 续表 1 continued 1

地　区 Region	种植业产品 Crop products			
	蔬菜与园艺作物 Vegetable and Holticulture crops		水果、饮料和香料作物 Fruits, beverages and perfume	
	2003	2004	2003	2004
全　国 National Total	**110.44**	**105.17**	**101.52**	**100.55**
北　京 Beijing	103.11	101.92	100.03	101.33
天　津 Tianjin	112.50	97.44	93.45	107.23
河　北 Hebei	103.99	105.64	97.11	92.88
山　西 Shanxi	101.44	107.43	103.83	100.90
内蒙古 Inner Mongolia	118.11	97.44	102.61	99.03
辽　宁 Liaoning	111.98	107.45	88.25	116.23
吉　林 Jilin	137.09	117.03	100.00	128.22
黑龙江 Heilongjiang	116.00	97.46	100.00	0.00
上　海 Shanghai	115.05	97.90	109.24	111.17
江　苏 Jiangsu	108.23	104.30	97.63	124.65
浙　江 Zhejiang	92.38	115.33	89.99	103.81
安　徽 Anhui	118.44	101.73	100.00	100.93
福　建 Fujian	96.93	100.64	108.05	103.49
江　西 Jiangxi	111.56	105.58	97.81	124.29
山　东 Shandong	112.22	105.63	87.66	113.50
河　南 Henan	101.89	109.90	106.36	112.15
湖　北 Hubei	109.83	106.20	80.45	116.28
湖　南 Hunan	113.88	101.36	113.50	86.53
广　东 Guangdong	103.65	105.55	113.06	85.13
广　西 Guangxi	116.91	137.60	113.74	94.68
海　南 Hainan	118.54	91.31	97.55	113.32
重　庆 Chongqing	108.06	106.01	94.34	103.40
四　川 Sichuan	99.91	109.77	119.22	102.93
贵　州 Guizhou	101.66	102.80	93.05	102.35
云　南 Yunnan	96.78	109.06	93.36	95.11
陕　西 Shaanxi	109.72	125.91	96.04	98.99
甘　肃 Gansu	101.25	115.44	101.43	106.07
青　海 Qinghai	99.01	100.30	100.00	0.00
宁　夏 Ningxia	100.00	112.08	100.00	119.24
新　疆 Xinjiang	144.00	112.40	100.00	119.19

2—9 续表 2 continued 2

地 区 Region	种植业产品 Crop products					
	薯类 Potato		豆类 Beans		油料 Oil-bearing crops	
	2003	2004	2003	2004	2003	2004
全 国 National Total	**92.87**	**105.75**	**119.33**	**120.29**	**119.40**	**116.58**
北 京 Beijing	101.32	101.61	102.37	113.43	92.87	109.17
天 津 Tianjin	100.00	0.00	109.12	111.83	95.69	104.28
河 北 Hebei	99.85	117.51	120.28	127.48	127.33	117.76
山 西 Shanxi	101.83	108.44	111.83	111.00	113.42	110.55
内蒙古 Inner Mongolia	100.27	107.33	116.14	119.30	107.50	117.43
辽 宁 Liaoning	102.32	105.68	127.86	114.52	137.41	108.24
吉 林 Jilin	138.18	123.49	133.09	120.09	296.92	110.57
黑龙江 Heilongjiang	114.95	113.90	133.69	112.20	100.00	113.30
上 海 Shanghai		100.28	127.97	121.56	134.13	111.10
江 苏 Jiangsu	126.65	107.74	137.18	118.93	140.46	113.84
浙 江 Zhejiang	105.65	107.47	101.33	112.30	97.88	107.43
安 徽 Anhui	91.73	103.54	128.66	112.55	120.06	111.34
福 建 Fujian	100.48	110.72	101.65	109.07	101.50	106.58
江 西 Jiangxi	85.63	115.89	104.65	117.62	119.33	118.01
山 东 Shandong	91.16	109.05	125.30	119.76	131.42	113.20
河 南 Henan	109.55	108.10	118.91	119.89	130.14	118.88
湖 北 Hubei	92.89	109.69	127.65	119.37	124.04	117.99
湖 南 Hunan	106.52	110.19	126.27	125.70	119.21	117.09
广 东 Guangdong	94.36	113.99	101.18	106.42	104.10	113.57
广 西 Guangxi	133.30	100.67	119.69	121.87	117.51	119.33
海 南 Hainan	100.39	101.26	118.09	102.62	104.54	118.78
重 庆 Chongqing	78.05	102.21	113.11	118.63	117.26	123.22
四 川 Sichuan	84.88	104.51	107.21	124.03	122.02	122.65
贵 州 Guizhou	93.35	100.30	104.97	108.15	114.96	112.05
云 南 Yunnan	108.19	102.84	100.77	119.86	117.48	108.65
陕 西 Shaanxi	88.24	105.22	113.91	118.18	125.57	121.89
甘 肃 Gansu	106.62	101.23	111.45	110.63	109.58	118.63
青 海 Qinghai	117.22	91.07	103.72	115.82	123.58	111.28
宁 夏 Ningxia	103.80	97.65	100.00	110.01	105.90	116.54
新 疆 Xinjiang	100.00	90.80	100.00	106.90	130.75	110.92

2—9 续表 3 continued 3

地区 Region	种植业产品 Crop products			
	棉花(籽棉) Cotton (unginned cotton)		麻类 Fiber crops	
	2003	2004	2003	2004
全国 National Total	**135.33**	**79.54**	**111.11**	**124.99**
北京 Beijing	100.00	100.00		
天津 Tianjin	128.75	106.42		
河北 Hebei	139.88	85.73		
山西 Shanxi	140.02	94.28		
内蒙古 Inner Mongolia	100.00	0.00		
辽宁 Liaoning	100.00	107.84		
吉林 Jilin	100.00	0.00		
黑龙江 Heilongjiang	100.00	0.00		
上海 Shanghai				
江苏 Jiangsu	164.51	73.07	100.00	100.00
浙江 Zhejiang	110.00	85.81	97.86	100.00
安徽 Anhui	135.84	78.11	100.00	100.00
福建 Fujian	100.00	0.00	98.70	102.49
江西 Jiangxi	127.85	96.80	100.00	110.18
山东 Shandong	141.35	88.60	100.00	100.00
河南 Henan	139.61	97.38	100.00	
湖北 Hubei	141.65	84.23	132.39	128.71
湖南 Hunan	158.29	101.31	126.93	127.51
广东 Guangdong	100.00	0.00	103.17	100.00
广西 Guangxi	100.00	0.00	101.20	110.84
海南 Hainan	100.00	0.00	100.00	
重庆 Chongqing	100.00	0.00	100.00	122.11
四川 Sichuan	103.03	104.80	99.63	126.07
贵州 Guizhou	100.00	0.00	100.00	100.00
云南 Yunnan	100.00	0.00	104.85	98.71
陕西 Shaanxi	156.71	99.45		
甘肃 Gansu	152.78	86.80		
青海 Qinghai	100.00	0.00		
宁夏 Ningxia	100.00	0.00		
新疆 Xinjiang	162.73	87.78		

2－9 续表 4 continued 4

地区 Region	种植业产品 Crop products			
	糖料 Sugar crops		烟叶 Tobacco	
	2003	2004	2003	2004
全 国 National Total	**90.50**	**104.86**	**97.21**	**108.42**
北 京 Beijing				
天 津 Tianjin				
河 北 Hebei	100.00	100.00	100.00	100.00
山 西 Shanxi	103.75	100.00	100.00	100.00
内蒙古 Inner Mongolia	106.99	108.55	100.00	105.37
辽 宁 Liaoning	100.00	100.00	89.10	117.20
吉 林 Jilin	138.56	100.00	100.00	108.52
黑龙江 Heilongjiang	87.94	157.89	80.35	140.15
上 海 Shanghai				
江 苏 Jiangsu	100.00	100.00	100.00	100.00
浙 江 Zhejiang	71.35	128.67	100.00	100.00
安 徽 Anhui	100.00	99.14	100.00	100.00
福 建 Fujian	98.48	105.82	97.15	111.32
江 西 Jiangxi	93.10	120.91	102.04	123.47
山 东 Shandong			160.41	82.66
河 南 Henan	100.00	100.00	115.70	95.06
湖 北 Hubei	61.81	144.90	104.30	128.46
湖 南 Hunan	95.37	102.48	90.26	130.68
广 东 Guangdong	82.49	95.74	86.03	120.90
广 西 Guangxi	91.06	103.27	104.99	129.97
海 南 Hainan	93.11	99.41		
重 庆 Chongqing	100.00	101.85	109.38	116.98
四 川 Sichuan	93.52	108.91	104.65	106.41
贵 州 Guizhou	91.59	98.98	83.01	109.51
云 南 Yunnan	94.27	102.02	97.26	113.19
陕 西 Shaanxi	80.63	100.00	134.84	118.10
甘 肃 Gansu	100.00	100.00	107.74	111.11
青 海 Qinghai				
宁 夏 Ningxia				
新 疆 Xinjiang		113.83		

2—9 续表 5 continued 5

地 区 Region	种植业产品 Crop products			
	小麦 Wheat		稻谷 Paddy	
	2003	2004	2003	2004
全 国 National Total	**102.99**	**131.16**	**99.89**	**136.30**
北 京 Beijing	101.53	123.54	100.00	141.67
天 津 Tianjin	101.94	142.11	106.15	100.00
河 北 Hebei	102.85	135.25	111.18	119.90
山 西 Shanxi	101.94	129.49		
内 蒙 古 Inner Mongolia	107.38	122.05	107.91	112.29
辽 宁 Liaoning	89.89	100.00	97.47	138.76
吉 林 Jilin	100.00	100.00	119.74	134.69
黑 龙 江 Heilongjiang	106.60	131.61	94.43	134.18
上 海 Shanghai	131.82	127.68	100.75	189.86
江 苏 Jiangsu	109.61	147.39	122.87	119.38
浙 江 Zhejiang	92.56	100.00	89.64	137.10
安 徽 Anhui	105.02	137.56	105.04	136.42
福 建 Fujian			104.95	139.57
江 西 Jiangxi			103.42	129.64
山 东 Shandong	105.38	136.58	110.05	123.86
河 南 Henan	105.79	138.21	108.18	135.23
湖 北 Hubei	103.10	150.07	108.65	138.85
湖 南 Hunan	100.00	96.81	107.64	141.10
广 东 Guangdong			104.51	135.24
广 西 Guangxi			100.61	136.15
海 南 Hainan			102.18	126.28
重 庆 Chongqing	102.34	131.58	106.02	141.46
四 川 Sichuan	106.29	136.92	106.02	133.70
贵 州 Guizhou	101.13	113.15	102.10	119.90
云 南 Yunnan	103.65	126.46	104.80	126.79
陕 西 Shaanxi	102.56	140.11	107.23	119.60
甘 肃 Gansu	97.28	117.42	118.42	0.00
青 海 Qinghai	98.41	118.27		
宁 夏 Ningxia	100.00	129.63	100.00	129.29
新 疆 Xinjiang	85.56	126.22	100.00	107.43

2—9 续表 6 continued 6

地 区 Region	种植业产品 Crop products			
	玉米 Maize (corn)		杂粮 Coarse cereals	
	2003	2004	2003	2004
全 国 National Total	**104.58**	**116.92**	**118.67**	**0.00**
北 京 Beijing	99.25	114.03		
天 津 Tianjin	107.15	119.53		
河 北 Hebei	108.13	115.97		
山 西 Shanxi	105.24	113.40	100.00	108.44
内 蒙 古 Inner Mongolia	104.85	114.59	100.00	119.26
辽 宁 Liaoning	106.05	115.25	104.21	127.75
吉 林 Jilin	115.37	114.89	104.80	137.82
黑 龙 江 Heilongjiang	105.01	114.78		
上 海 Shanghai	143.37	145.99		
江 苏 Jiangsu	122.73	115.85		
浙 江 Zhejiang	105.33	122.84		
安 徽 Anhui	105.60	110.24	100.00	116.49
福 建 Fujian	62.50	106.00	100.00	116.61
江 西 Jiangxi				
山 东 Shandong	107.76	118.29		
河 南 Henan	110.06	115.57		
湖 北 Hubei	112.49	123.63		
湖 南 Hunan	114.02	125.07		
广 东 Guangdong	91.03	115.93	108.27	100.00
广 西 Guangxi	97.89	122.90		
海 南 Hainan	103.07	112.63		
重 庆 Chongqing	102.33	130.43	109.52	100.00
四 川 Sichuan	106.68	126.92	94.87	129.82
贵 州 Guizhou	102.26	113.42		
云 南 Yunnan	105.31	116.01		
陕 西 Shaanxi	112.66	115.39	105.07	104.71
甘 肃 Gansu	103.41	116.93	97.95	123.30
青 海 Qinghai			103.71	113.27
宁 夏 Ningxia	100.00	119.32	100.00	110.47
新 疆 Xinjiang	108.82	118.74	100.00	117.29

2—9 续表 7 continued 7

地区 Region	种植业产品 Crop products			
	红薯 Sweet potato		马铃薯 White potato	
	2003	2004	2003	2004
全国 National Total	**94.54**	**108.97**	**92.21**	**104.89**
北京 Beijing	101.32	101.01	101.35	110.22
天津 Tianjin				
河北 Hebei	91.26	131.83	103.93	110.72
山西 Shanxi	104.00	98.89	101.44	110.53
内蒙古 Inner Mongolia			100.27	107.33
辽宁 Liaoning	104.16	102.42	101.39	111.74
吉林 Jilin	100.00	143.49	138.18	113.38
黑龙江 Heilongjiang	100.00	125.00	91.28	112.60
上海 Shanghai				100.28
江苏 Jiangsu				
浙江 Zhejiang	111.02	114.22	97.98	100.30
安徽 Anhui	100.00	98.98	100.00	110.14
福建 Fujian	99.50	111.05	103.81	108.73
江西 Jiangxi	77.39	115.89	160.85	145.06
山东 Shandong	91.61	107.37	87.84	121.53
河南 Henan	109.55	108.10	100.43	76.15
湖北 Hubei	89.49	106.77	94.61	111.18
湖南 Hunan	104.72	108.79	111.33	113.93
广东 Guangdong	91.59	120.80	102.41	92.69
广西 Guangxi	109.02	109.99	136.03	77.37
海南 Hainan	100.27	101.34		
重庆 Chongqing	92.02	103.60	72.47	101.66
四川 Sichuan	91.05	104.41	67.64	104.78
贵州 Guizhou	100.07	100.15	92.41	100.31
云南 Yunnan	100.87	105.80	108.77	102.61
陕西 Shaanxi	76.49	115.66	90.37	102.16
甘肃 Gansu			106.62	101.23
青海 Qinghai			117.22	91.07
宁夏 Ningxia			103.80	97.65
新疆 Xinjiang			104.38	90.80

2—9 续表 8　　continued 8

地　区 Region	种植业产品 Crop products			
	大豆 Soybeans		绿豆 Mung beans	
	2003	2004	2003	2004
全　国 National Total	**120.62**	**120.17**	**100.45**	**116.73**
北　京 Beijing	102.61	114.89	100.00	100.00
天　津 Tianjin	109.12	111.83		
河　北 Hebei	120.73	128.05	104.10	102.05
山　西 Shanxi	115.76	112.77	98.53	108.32
内蒙古 Inner Mongolia	119.34	116.07	110.37	127.33
辽　宁 Liaoning	129.15	112.35	106.81	99.28
吉　林 Jilin	133.75	109.57	123.61	147.23
黑龙江 Heilongjiang	133.69	112.20	100.00	100.00
上　海 Shanghai	127.97	120.99		
江　苏 Jiangsu	144.97	108.09	110.29	100.00
浙　江 Zhejiang	106.00	104.93	100.00	0.00
安　徽 Anhui	133.81	112.91	100.00	110.04
福　建 Fujian	103.45	109.43	100.00	100.00
江　西 Jiangxi	104.65	121.45	110.02	110.66
山　东 Shandong	125.30	119.76	83.18	116.76
河　南 Henan	118.91	119.89	120.22	102.39
湖　北 Hubei	128.62	120.35	108.78	104.17
湖　南 Hunan	126.76	125.78	105.12	122.39
广　东 Guangdong	107.72	119.41	100.00	103.45
广　西 Guangxi	120.36	121.93	105.54	107.11
海　南 Hainan	108.22	103.51	100.00	105.26
重　庆 Chongqing	116.91	122.07	217.12	107.34
四　川 Sichuan	108.91	122.40	100.87	105.84
贵　州 Guizhou	104.97	108.15	99.91	104.44
云　南 Yunnan	102.85	116.75	99.98	100.00
陕　西 Shaanxi	122.91	122.81	91.83	107.65
甘　肃 Gansu	112.53	109.68		
青　海 Qinghai	100.00	116.63		
宁　夏 Ningxia	100.00	100.00		
新　疆 Xinjiang	135.58	99.00		

2—9 续表 9 continued 9

地区 Region	种植业产品 Crop products			
	红小豆 Red beans		蚕豆 Broad beans	
	2003	2004	2003	2004
全国 National Total	**103.60**	**128.26**	**106.18**	**127.61**
北京 Beijing	100.02	100.00		
天津 Tianjin	100.00	0.00		
河北 Hebei	103.71	110.70		
山西 Shanxi	112.39	100.68	80.51	120.59
内蒙古 Inner Mongolia	104.63	107.43	103.91	118.84
辽宁 Liaoning	95.90	127.32		
吉林 Jilin	199.16	183.54		
黑龙江 Heilongjiang	138.56	102.99		
上海 Shanghai	100.00	100.00		
江苏 Jiangsu	216.11	100.00		
浙江 Zhejiang	100.00	100.00		
安徽 Anhui	100.00	103.58	100.00	120.41
福建 Fujian			83.33	127.60
江西 Jiangxi			106.57	109.95
山东 Shandong	100.00	99.56	100.00	100.00
河南 Henan	137.50	100.00	107.98	100.00
湖北 Hubei	100.00	125.00	114.09	114.84
湖南 Hunan	100.00	126.44	100.00	104.45
广东 Guangdong	60.00	114.29		
广西 Guangxi	100.00	200.00		
海南 Hainan	100.42	75.64		
重庆 Chongqing	100.00	100.00	108.47	116.14
四川 Sichuan	100.00	102.98	102.32	144.50
贵州 Guizhou	100.00	112.87	100.00	107.96
云南 Yunnan	102.00	104.91	91.78	135.60
陕西 Shaanxi	106.60	100.00	116.45	126.48
甘肃 Gansu	104.88	105.03	104.02	125.96
青海 Qinghai			119.44	124.16
宁夏 Ningxia				
新疆 Xinjiang				

2—9 续表 10 continued 10

地　区 Region	种植业产品 Crop products			
	豌豆 Peas		芸豆 Kidney beans	
	2003	2004	2003	2004
全　国 National Total	**105.27**	**114.36**	**110.33**	**107.60**
北　京 Beijing				
天　津 Tianjin				
河　北 Hebei				
山　西 Shanxi	107.80	100.00	101.12	110.34
内蒙古 Inner Mongolia	94.82	115.06	105.71	105.15
辽　宁 Liaoning				
吉　林 Jilin			100.00	104.65
黑龙江 Heilongjiang			103.60	108.11
上　海 Shanghai				
江　苏 Jiangsu				
浙　江 Zhejiang				
安　徽 Anhui	100.00	116.61	100.00	120.00
福　建 Fujian	98.08	107.77		
江　西 Jiangxi	116.49	101.56	102.79	100.00
山　东 Shandong	101.42	129.89	144.38	100.00
河　南 Henan	119.39	131.18		
湖　北 Hubei	96.26	114.97		
湖　南 Hunan	100.00	106.84	100.00	100.00
广　东 Guangdong	99.30	126.12		
广　西 Guangxi	99.77	104.72		
海　南 Hainan				
重　庆 Chongqing	102.56	100.00	100.00	100.00
四　川 Sichuan	109.63	116.76	100.31	100.00
贵　州 Guizhou	111.29	99.73	106.61	123.57
云　南 Yunnan	91.45	121.35	99.40	100.01
陕　西 Shaanxi	80.25	123.02		
甘　肃 Gansu	83.61	105.59	99.20	96.43
青　海 Qinghai	84.91	108.88		
宁　夏 Ningxia	100.00	110.90		
新　疆 Xinjiang				

2—9 续表 11 continued 11

地区 Region	种植业产品 Crop products					
	花生 Peanut		油菜籽 Rapeseeds		芝麻 Sesame	
	2003	2004	2003	2004	2003	2004
全国 National Total	**124.19**	**117.07**	**119.15**	**116.33**	**128.92**	**122.34**
北京 Beijing	92.87	109.17			99.20	100.00
天津 Tianjin	100.00	100.39			100.00	100.00
河北 Hebei	127.37	117.76	106.45	120.76	105.49	116.59
山西 Shanxi	112.51	112.83	113.78	105.28	137.83	109.17
内蒙古 Inner Mongolia	101.03	83.61	120.68	112.73	132.32	111.15
辽宁 Liaoning	138.25	108.24	107.11	100.00	103.40	100.00
吉林 Jilin	100.00	121.17			296.92	89.03
黑龙江 Heilongjiang	75.33	87.26			100.00	100.00
上海 Shanghai			134.13	111.10		
江苏 Jiangsu	145.37	97.91	134.38	114.22		
浙江 Zhejiang	95.45	107.43	90.56	118.21	109.32	117.70
安徽 Anhui	121.06	111.23	100.00	112.52	124.83	103.83
福建 Fujian	101.51	106.61			100.00	104.08
江西 Jiangxi	124.04	118.01	115.73	117.34	112.02	109.83
山东 Shandong	131.42	113.21	100.00	104.50	144.99	100.63
河南 Henan	132.86	120.93	119.86	114.45	125.35	112.25
湖北 Hubei	121.77	116.23	124.68	119.57	161.21	96.95
湖南 Hunan	124.14	121.26	121.83	118.16	118.41	116.76
广东 Guangdong	104.09	113.57	92.73	100.00	107.72	100.00
广西 Guangxi	117.51	119.30	100.00	136.94	100.99	100.00
海南 Hainan	104.60	119.23			101.90	106.23
重庆 Chongqing	112.37	127.84	118.70	117.90	186.33	133.36
四川 Sichuan	119.10	125.13	123.65	121.27	103.08	92.68
贵州 Guizhou	103.19	107.41	116.90	112.70		
云南 Yunnan	105.77	114.32	119.36	107.74		
陕西 Shaanxi	135.26	112.74	123.99	123.38	175.16	97.06
甘肃 Gansu	100.00	100.00	108.51	117.12	100.00	100.00
青海 Qinghai			123.58	111.28		
宁夏 Ningxia						
新疆 Xinjiang	113.29	94.16	130.75	104.55		

2—9 续表 12 continued 12

地　区 Region	种植业产品 Crop products					
	黄红麻 Jute and blueish dogbane		亚麻 Flax		苎麻 Ramie	
	2003	2004	2003	2004	2003	2004
全　国 National Total	**107.67**	**116.59**	**99.90**	**119.34**	**113.83**	**131.10**
北　京 Beijing						
天　津 Tianjin						
河　北 Hebei						
山　西 Shanxi						
内蒙古 Inner Mongolia						
辽　宁 Liaoning						
吉　林 Jilin						
黑龙江 Heilongjiang	100.00	100.00	103.27	100.00	100.00	100.00
上　海 Shanghai						
江　苏 Jiangsu	100.00	100.00			100.00	107.14
浙　江 Zhejiang	100.00	100.00			97.86	0.00
安　徽 Anhui	100.00	113.12			100.00	128.12
福　建 Fujian	98.70	102.49			100.00	100.00
江　西 Jiangxi	100.00	100.00	100.00	105.88	111.33	110.18
山　东 Shandong	100.00	145.84	100.00	100.00		
河　南 Henan	90.78	117.30			100.00	0.00
湖　北 Hubei	121.86	100.00			135.47	137.05
湖　南 Hunan	100.00	100.00			126.93	127.51
广　东 Guangdong	100.00	100.00	103.17	100.00	100.00	100.00
广　西 Guangxi	101.20	117.78	100.00	100.00	101.55	100.00
海　南 Hainan	95.24	100.00	100.00	100.00	100.00	100.00
重　庆 Chongqing	100.00	100.00	100.00		137.30	122.11
四　川 Sichuan	95.81	100.00	100.00		100.14	126.07
贵　州 Guizhou	100.00	100.00				
云　南 Yunnan	100.00	100.00	104.85	98.71		
陕　西 Shaanxi						
甘　肃 Gansu						
青　海 Qinghai						
宁　夏 Ningxia						
新　疆 Xinjiang	100.00	100.00	85.89	170.19	100.00	100.00

2—9 续表 13 continued 13

地区 Region	种植业产品 Crop products			
	甘蔗 Sugarcane		甜菜 Beet	
	2003	2004	2003	2004
全国 National Total	**90.49**	**104.86**	**106.56**	**106.10**
北京 Beijing				
天津 Tianjin				
河北 Hebei			102.50	100.00
山西 Shanxi			103.75	100.00
内蒙古 Inner Mongolia			106.99	108.55
辽宁 Liaoning			98.63	100.00
吉林 Jilin			138.56	100.00
黑龙江 Heilongjiang			87.94	157.89
上海 Shanghai				
江苏 Jiangsu	100.00	100.00	100.00	100.00
浙江 Zhejiang	71.35	128.67	100.00	101.48
安徽 Anhui	100.00	99.14		
福建 Fujian	98.48	105.82		
江西 Jiangxi	76.74	120.91		
山东 Shandong	100.00	100.00		
河南 Henan	100.00	100.00		
湖北 Hubei	61.81	144.90		
湖南 Hunan	95.37	102.48		
广东 Guangdong	82.49	95.74		
广西 Guangxi	91.06	103.27		
海南 Hainan	93.11	99.41		
重庆 Chongqing	110.00	101.85		
四川 Sichuan	93.52	108.91		
贵州 Guizhou	91.59	98.98	100.00	98.40
云南 Yunnan	94.27	102.02	100.00	100.00
陕西 Shaanxi	98.69	100.00	80.63	100.00
甘肃 Gansu				
青海 Qinghai				
宁夏 Ningxia				
新疆 Xinjiang			108.10	113.83

2—9 续表 14　　continued 14

地　　区 Region	种植业产品 Crop products			
	烤烟叶 Flue-cured tobacco		晒烟叶 Sun-cured tobacco	
	2003	2004	2003	2004
全　　国 National Total	**94.94**	**106.42**	**112.40**	**113.45**
北　　京 Beijing				
天　　津 Tianjin				
河　　北 Hebei	100.00	100.00		
山　　西 Shanxi	100.00	100.00		
内 蒙 古 Inner Mongolia	100.00	105.37		
辽　　宁 Liaoning	89.10	117.20	95.67	101.09
吉　　林 Jilin	112.06	120.25	100.00	100.00
黑 龙 江 Heilongjiang	80.35	140.15	143.23	99.36
上　　海 Shanghai				
江　　苏 Jiangsu			100.00	100.00
浙　　江 Zhejiang			100.00	102.29
安　　徽 Anhui				
福　　建 Fujian	97.15	111.32		
江　　西 Jiangxi	102.04	123.47		
山　　东 Shandong	160.41	82.66	105.76	103.85
河　　南 Henan	115.70	95.06		
湖　　北 Hubei	100.00	125.26	102.74	143.17
湖　　南 Hunan	90.26	130.68	96.35	104.17
广　　东 Guangdong	86.03	120.90		
广　　西 Guangxi	104.99	139.30	100.00	100.63
海　　南 Hainan				
重　　庆 Chongqing	104.86	123.37	115.26	108.68
四　　川 Sichuan	105.55	111.23	104.22	104.12
贵　　州 Guizhou	82.64	109.55	104.01	108.43
云　　南 Yunnan	97.23	113.23	100.75	108.47
陕　　西 Shaanxi	134.84	118.10	100.00	100.00
甘　　肃 Gansu	107.81	100.00	109.09	111.11
青　　海 Qinghai	100.00	100.00	100.00	100.00
宁　　夏 Ningxia	100.00	100.00	100.00	100.00
新　　疆 Xinjiang	100.00	100.00	100.00	123.03

2—9 续表 15 continued 15

地区 Region	蔬菜 Vegetable		蔬菜 Vegetable			
			叶菜类 Leaf vegetable		瓜菜类 Gourd vegetable	
	2003	2004	2003	2004	2003	2004
全国 National Total	**110.44**	**105.17**	**113.21**	**101.85**	**110.71**	**101.10**
北京 Beijing	99.92	102.84	105.14	92.10	103.79	113.29
天津 Tianjin	113.34	97.62	141.14	85.04	81.04	105.66
河北 Hebei	103.99	105.64	108.41	95.41	91.06	106.00
山西 Shanxi	101.44	107.43	95.83	93.98	100.97	101.87
内蒙古 Inner Mongolia	118.11	97.44	132.96	86.21	111.97	112.91
辽宁 Liaoning	111.98	107.45	108.10	98.48	117.99	126.06
吉林 Jilin	137.09	117.03	140.63	100.12	124.08	112.16
黑龙江 Heilongjiang	116.00	97.46	127.74	87.07	120.57	120.61
上海 Shanghai	114.29	98.81	131.29	88.63	83.72	108.70
江苏 Jiangsu	108.18	104.31	109.77	105.77	103.07	104.22
浙江 Zhejiang	109.52	115.33	119.99	108.22	78.95	127.34
安徽 Anhui	114.38	101.99	120.91	95.57	100.00	100.00
福建 Fujian	96.72	102.98	100.61	102.72	102.99	108.35
江西 Jiangxi	111.56	105.58	106.87	104.74	115.00	110.57
山东 Shandong	110.67	106.13	126.30	90.36	117.75	98.07
河南 Henan	101.89	109.90	124.46	94.92	118.67	107.32
湖北 Hubei	109.79	106.20	107.23	105.36	104.29	102.81
湖南 Hunan	114.53	102.07	122.11	101.99	112.11	96.22
广东 Guangdong	105.97	105.48	110.70	99.26	99.15	112.15
广西 Guangxi	116.91	137.60	100.37	107.67	150.27	99.72
海南 Hainan	120.02	91.14	103.44	103.08	120.64	85.40
重庆 Chongqing	104.31	106.01	107.82	105.89	103.23	110.12
四川 Sichuan	101.23	109.92	102.91	106.19	94.91	111.93
贵州 Guizhou	101.66	102.88	99.25	98.42	102.56	96.90
云南 Yunnan	97.76	111.56	95.71	105.07	90.61	105.81
陕西 Shaanxi	109.72	125.91	120.27	108.26	111.10	112.99
甘肃 Gansu	101.77	115.64	104.60	111.59	109.52	112.73
青海 Qinghai	99.01	100.30	91.08	97.58	113.59	100.95
宁夏 Ningxia	122.60	112.08	97.80	106.76	119.00	101.08
新疆 Xinjiang	144.00	112.40	144.95	108.73	233.00	131.40

2－9 续表 16

continued 16

地区 Region	蔬菜 Vegetable			
	块根、块茎菜类 Root and tuber vegetable		茄果菜类 Eggplant，tomato and chili，etc.	
	2003	2004	2003	2004
全　国 National Total	**111.62**	**103.59**	**108.55**	**103.18**
北　京 Beijing	102.48	108.15	83.65	110.21
天　津 Tianjin	107.16	90.99	98.34	98.69
河　北 Hebei	125.99	81.16	102.82	110.89
山　西 Shanxi	115.71	93.06	103.36	119.33
内蒙古 Inner Mongolia	125.81	89.59	101.81	107.86
辽　宁 Liaoning	115.16	97.44	112.27	109.64
吉　林 Jilin	133.88	110.82	138.83	127.60
黑龙江 Heilongjiang	107.34	107.97	112.67	125.97
上　海 Shanghai	138.90	105.87	85.67	109.41
江　苏 Jiangsu	124.87	96.61	110.10	103.33
浙　江 Zhejiang	66.66	109.05	102.31	123.57
安　徽 Anhui	123.42	103.47	110.61	82.90
福　建 Fujian	108.00	107.24	102.74	102.65
江　西 Jiangxi	96.10	106.67	103.40	108.60
山　东 Shandong	99.42	135.97	103.29	96.99
河　南 Henan	173.02	87.52	96.23	109.64
湖　北 Hubei	126.61	98.49	94.29	113.02
湖　南 Hunan	105.42	110.04	115.90	87.43
广　东 Guangdong	104.39	116.50	111.54	99.04
广　西 Guangxi	119.43	215.54	107.89	102.30
海　南 Hainan	98.45	102.27	134.32	90.09
重　庆 Chongqing	104.73	105.61	99.40	101.92
四　川 Sichuan	103.99	109.31	96.70	117.97
贵　州 Guizhou	109.18	99.33	99.33	107.03
云　南 Yunnan	100.60	117.29	100.67	108.61
陕　西 Shaanxi	119.43	135.58	105.41	133.46
甘　肃 Gansu	102.34	99.60	105.72	126.55
青　海 Qinghai	105.60	100.00	119.02	97.82
宁　夏 Ningxia	101.40	123.40	144.50	104.35
新　疆 Xinjiang	93.67	113.62	105.42	112.41

2—9 续表 17 continued 17

地 区 Region	蔬菜 Vegetable			
	葱蒜类 Onion and Garlic		菜用豆类 Garden beans	
	2003	2004	2003	2004
全 国 National Total	**105.98**	**115.91**	**109.98**	**104.96**
北 京 Beijing	100.55	112.77	99.35	115.14
天 津 Tianjin	97.47	108.93	112.78	136.74
河 北 Hebei	115.52	112.12	88.88	127.72
山 西 Shanxi	100.59	117.97	98.85	123.68
内蒙古 Inner Mongolia	101.82	112.18		
辽 宁 Liaoning	122.47	100.09	94.83	123.61
吉 林 Jilin	135.53	119.54	100.00	133.76
黑龙江 Heilongjiang	135.01	128.76	100.00	100.00
上 海 Shanghai	128.63	118.28	79.13	100.83
江 苏 Jiangsu	97.32	98.19	99.97	116.51
浙 江 Zhejiang	112.21	149.42	100.55	117.13
安 徽 Anhui	109.92	106.23	100.00	100.00
福 建 Fujian	104.84	105.42	103.88	107.72
江 西 Jiangxi	100.00	94.72	113.54	105.07
山 东 Shandong	109.90	117.55	99.81	110.43
河 南 Henan	81.65	143.38	100.00	100.00
湖 北 Hubei	110.91	113.63	102.75	105.34
湖 南 Hunan	117.70	99.20	111.09	103.54
广 东 Guangdong	104.55	96.62	105.60	101.97
广 西 Guangxi	173.91	111.66	147.85	108.91
海 南 Hainan	113.97	110.97	115.16	94.64
重 庆 Chongqing	105.85	105.93	96.51	114.48
四 川 Sichuan	102.90	109.88	97.93	119.46
贵 州 Guizhou	98.15	109.24	108.60	105.03
云 南 Yunnan	100.52	120.32	95.62	122.27
陕 西 Shaanxi	91.40	116.56	117.97	109.73
甘 肃 Gansu	102.57	116.53	100.00	116.10
青 海 Qinghai	104.58	114.69	100.00	100.00
宁 夏 Ningxia	100.00	108.38	85.90	148.00
新 疆 Xinjiang	100.00	103.22	155.99	100.00

2—9 续表 18 continued 18

地　　区 Region	蔬菜 Vegetable			
	水生菜类 Water vegetable		食用菌(干鲜混合) Mushroom	
	2003	2004	2003	2004
全　　国 National Total	**112.41**	**113.37**	**99.22**	**101.41**
北　　京 Beijing	100.00	103.03	111.04	101.65
天　　津 Tianjin			99.36	91.77
河　　北 Hebei			106.81	93.17
山　　西 Shanxi			95.92	110.12
内 蒙 古 Inner Mongolia			100.00	100.00
辽　　宁 Liaoning			101.76	100.00
吉　　林 Jilin			100.00	141.78
黑 龙 江 Heilongjiang			71.11	119.73
上　　海 Shanghai	105.37	147.29	100.00	100.00
江　　苏 Jiangsu	122.83	108.61	100.00	102.86
浙　　江 Zhejiang	99.88	100.00	100.00	100.00
安　　徽 Anhui	100.00	131.13	100.00	100.00
福　　建 Fujian	100.21	102.37	86.06	99.43
江　　西 Jiangxi	130.75	108.58	96.33	104.45
山　　东 Shandong	153.73	111.06	138.18	106.09
河　　南 Henan	132.52	113.86	66.39	116.57
湖　　北 Hubei	135.61	114.06	98.77	109.41
湖　　南 Hunan	143.19	109.17	108.86	107.69
广　　东 Guangdong	105.72	91.91	103.05	103.55
广　　西 Guangxi	101.68	132.20	97.79	91.81
海　　南 Hainan	100.00	100.00	100.00	100.00
重　　庆 Chongqing	110.40	106.90	100.00	100.00
四　　川 Sichuan	102.63	101.89	111.22	98.40
贵　　州 Guizhou	97.53	102.65	100.01	95.89
云　　南 Yunnan	109.07	91.24	95.80	101.77
陕　　西 Shaanxi	90.37	172.71	122.24	115.29
甘　　肃 Gansu			98.69	92.65
青　　海 Qinghai				
宁　　夏 Ningxia				
新　　疆 Xinjiang				

2—9 续表 19 continued 19

地　区 Region	蔬菜 Vegetable			
	菠菜 Spinach		芹菜 Celery	
	2003	2004	2003	2004
全　国 National Total	**113.94**	**101.57**	**127.10**	**99.28**
北　京 Beijing	115.00	96.87	109.99	105.56
天　津 Tianjin	100.00	0.00	139.74	82.92
河　北 Hebei	134.37	81.96	97.19	125.73
山　西 Shanxi	79.38	111.77	91.91	104.27
内蒙古 Inner Mongolia	116.13	103.15	211.93	100.35
辽　宁 Liaoning	103.45	111.45	115.34	91.16
吉　林 Jilin	74.04	147.24	175.42	101.32
黑龙江 Heilongjiang	120.87	131.32	106.82	108.98
上　海 Shanghai		95.69		106.11
江　苏 Jiangsu	112.25	120.10	132.10	110.25
浙　江 Zhejiang	97.42	74.72	65.66	70.94
安　徽 Anhui	100.00	105.14	122.59	90.61
福　建 Fujian	101.28	101.74	104.86	99.12
江　西 Jiangxi	136.23	115.89	150.20	104.11
山　东 Shandong	111.24	86.90	152.77	93.10
河　南 Henan	120.84	98.65	112.72	70.27
湖　北 Hubei	111.55	110.38	142.99	96.33
湖　南 Hunan	134.88	94.99	134.09	94.84
广　东 Guangdong	104.66	99.90	109.83	77.45
广　西 Guangxi	99.91	86.98	68.86	112.20
海　南 Hainan	100.00	105.62	139.87	109.69
重　庆 Chongqing	111.11	108.65	100.00	125.72
四　川 Sichuan	97.18	104.45	101.22	96.33
贵　州 Guizhou	91.68	108.45	96.90	98.33
云　南 Yunnan	102.71	102.69	96.44	100.00
陕　西 Shaanxi	131.89	113.20	97.10	118.04
甘　肃 Gansu	129.17	134.27	99.47	91.79
青　海 Qinghai	60.02	100.00	100.00	
宁　夏 Ningxia	100.00	100.00	100.00	118.58
新　疆 Xinjiang	154.54	76.47	80.66	96.84

2—9 续表 20 continued 20

地 区 Region	蔬菜 Vegetable			
	大白菜 Chinese cabbage		元白菜 Cabbage	
	2003	2004	2003	2004
全 国 National Total	**115.76**	**102.10**	**99.55**	**106.45**
北 京 Beijing	105.10	69.15	103.37	110.41
天 津 Tianjin	144.07	74.10	98.63	92.30
河 北 Hebei	126.28	77.45	75.54	108.43
山 西 Shanxi	127.15	78.16	105.45	74.73
内蒙古 Inner Mongolia	112.61	83.04	111.22	75.60
辽 宁 Liaoning	108.76	103.33	100.00	110.12
吉 林 Jilin	142.68	90.22	98.19	211.19
黑龙江 Heilongjiang	125.68	86.15	199.33	63.90
上 海 Shanghai	137.55	94.85	123.67	101.09
江 苏 Jiangsu	108.50	97.58	104.54	99.77
浙 江 Zhejiang	108.57	148.85	121.33	100.87
安 徽 Anhui	100.00	98.01	100.00	85.59
福 建 Fujian	104.18	104.49	96.12	101.00
江 西 Jiangxi	115.50	106.13	107.45	98.54
山 东 Shandong	118.58	84.10	107.72	101.17
河 南 Henan	129.23	92.88	125.18	114.38
湖 北 Hubei	106.38	116.85	106.13	107.70
湖 南 Hunan	121.47	103.39	127.19	97.62
广 东 Guangdong	115.01	112.43	100.19	96.17
广 西 Guangxi	99.42	112.96	109.71	156.81
海 南 Hainan	111.30	102.53	100.00	101.45
重 庆 Chongqing	117.83	110.85	103.40	107.01
四 川 Sichuan	96.35	112.50	102.48	111.65
贵 州 Guizhou	99.84	97.07	96.09	96.58
云 南 Yunnan	96.88	104.63	88.93	100.91
陕 西 Shaanxi	118.93	108.76	114.08	105.83
甘 肃 Gansu	86.96	97.32	112.62	103.96
青 海 Qinghai	83.82	99.47	91.29	
宁 夏 Ningxia	123.00	85.24	96.90	95.79
新 疆 Xinjiang	156.08	105.41	85.71	165.68

2—9 续表 21 continued 21

地区 Region	蔬菜 Vegetable			
	甘蓝 Wild cabbage		花椰菜 Cauliflower	
	2003	2004	2003	2004
全 国 National Total	**97.81**	**100.78**	**112.08**	**101.29**
北 京 Beijing	90.01	107.97	101.23	114.53
天 津 Tianjin	100.00	100.00	131.87	80.43
河 北 Hebei	100.00	100.00	123.41	64.06
山 西 Shanxi	31.11	112.46		
内蒙古 Inner Mongolia	100.00	117.49		
辽 宁 Liaoning	108.43	95.08	100.00	80.00
吉 林 Jilin			100.00	
黑龙江 Heilongjiang	100.00	116.50	100.00	129.04
上 海 Shanghai	100.00	0.00	128.43	98.27
江 苏 Jiangsu	100.00	100.00	107.52	100.22
浙 江 Zhejiang	100.00	116.36	101.36	
安 徽 Anhui	100.00	98.20	100.00	91.91
福 建 Fujian	99.24	96.74	103.33	101.60
江 西 Jiangxi	93.03	94.58	139.69	95.86
山 东 Shandong	101.13	92.05	183.85	97.13
河 南 Henan	100.00		117.78	110.30
湖 北 Hubei	100.00		113.80	85.78
湖 南 Hunan	106.21	105.76	106.48	100.84
广 东 Guangdong	103.19	89.61	119.17	84.53
广 西 Guangxi	100.00	0.00	120.29	
海 南 Hainan	103.03	0.00	126.57	87.48
重 庆 Chongqing	100.00	98.63	106.36	94.98
四 川 Sichuan	112.75	105.83	118.09	85.67
贵 州 Guizhou	99.61	100.00	115.07	96.71
云 南 Yunnan	100.00	104.85	88.71	112.21
陕 西 Shaanxi	136.08	103.72	100.00	51.85
甘 肃 Gansu	119.35	103.80	96.50	126.00
青 海 Qinghai	117.51	100.01		
宁 夏 Ningxia				
新 疆 Xinjiang			170.45	170.68

2—9 续表 22 continued 22

地　区 Region	蔬菜 Vegetable			
	莴笋 Asparagus lettuce		油菜 Rape	
	2003	2004	2003	2004
全　国 National Total	**102.77**	**107.36**	**109.50**	**101.61**
北　京 Beijing	104.60	98.46	101.26	111.07
天　津 Tianjin			100.00	13.00
河　北 Hebei	101.42	105.71	95.54	103.33
山　西 Shanxi	50.86	104.00	116.14	102.03
内蒙古 Inner Mongolia			109.09	100.00
辽　宁 Liaoning			110.66	92.41
吉　林 Jilin				83.88
黑龙江 Heilongjiang			102.56	
上　海 Shanghai	97.88	76.47	137.84	81.44
江　苏 Jiangsu	125.23	102.58	100.00	100.00
浙　江 Zhejiang	110.21	135.57	135.68	98.19
安　徽 Anhui	100.00	98.53	100.00	90.01
福　建 Fujian	94.25	105.28	105.19	115.60
江　西 Jiangxi	104.67	90.01	182.07	95.13
山　东 Shandong	140.20	113.95	171.08	89.87
河　南 Henan	100.00	66.18	100.00	0.00
湖　北 Hubei	111.28	104.13	100.00	0.00
湖　南 Hunan	131.25	100.18	117.25	90.93
广　东 Guangdong	101.39		109.92	98.95
广　西 Guangxi	112.48	82.81	105.45	
海　南 Hainan	100.00	101.95	100.00	105.17
重　庆 Chongqing	103.37	99.59	100.00	
四　川 Sichuan	103.67	106.69	115.11	116.47
贵　州 Guizhou	99.72	98.72	121.82	117.48
云　南 Yunnan	94.27	109.38	104.24	126.77
陕　西 Shaanxi	113.59	87.16	147.12	99.52
甘　肃 Gansu	116.12	176.17	104.88	115.26
青　海 Qinghai	100.00	105.27	99.52	90.35
宁　夏 Ningxia			100.00	108.07
新　疆 Xinjiang			100.00	121.21

2—9 续表 23 continued 23

地 区 Region	蔬菜 Vegetable			
	黄瓜 Cucumber		冬瓜 White gourd	
	2003	2004	2003	2004
全 国 National Total	**113.37**	**103.66**	**122.81**	**92.92**
北 京 Beijing	104.86	110.41	101.40	118.38
天 津 Tianjin	81.04	105.66	100.00	100.00
河 北 Hebei	91.07	106.01	107.14	139.28
山 西 Shanxi	105.99	119.29	100.00	100.00
内蒙古 Inner Mongolia	111.97	112.91	98.79	
辽 宁 Liaoning	117.99	126.06		
吉 林 Jilin	124.08	112.16		
黑龙江 Heilongjiang	121.30	122.40		
上 海 Shanghai	77.49	106.95	91.44	127.89
江 苏 Jiangsu	95.26	103.95	103.67	101.25
浙 江 Zhejiang	112.35	126.85	71.25	123.12
安 徽 Anhui		112.79		97.07
福 建 Fujian	104.91	100.88	106.77	119.07
江 西 Jiangxi	85.95	105.98	166.15	93.03
山 东 Shandong	115.76	98.70	119.66	101.09
河 南 Henan	118.67	107.32	101.98	117.08
湖 北 Hubei	102.24	113.30	111.88	105.02
湖 南 Hunan	111.10	102.63	109.47	96.00
广 东 Guangdong	109.15	101.66	89.77	120.92
广 西 Guangxi	133.73	114.73	112.27	95.29
海 南 Hainan	106.83	81.93	124.54	64.94
重 庆 Chongqing	104.45	113.32	98.57	111.73
四 川 Sichuan	90.56	111.79	98.00	109.02
贵 州 Guizhou	99.53	95.73	91.67	95.98
云 南 Yunnan	91.69	102.67	88.35	100.66
陕 西 Shaanxi	111.28	112.84		
甘 肃 Gansu	109.16	114.45		
青 海 Qinghai	137.88	102.62		
宁 夏 Ningxia	119.00	101.08		
新 疆 Xinjiang	233.00	101.91	99.07	120.93

2—9 续表 24 continued 24

地区 Region	蔬菜 Vegetable			
	西葫芦 Summer squash		苦瓜 Balsam pear	
	2003	2004	2003	2004
全国 National Total	**107.46**	**99.41**	**110.73**	**113.19**
北京 Beijing	107.32	120.87	100.00	104.59
天津 Tianjin	100.00	100.00		
河北 Hebei	91.62	92.20		
山西 Shanxi	93.35	71.69		
内蒙古 Inner Mongolia	125.00	100.00		
辽宁 Liaoning	100.00	100.00		
吉林 Jilin	100.00	100.00		
黑龙江 Heilongjiang	115.58	112.65		
上海 Shanghai			100.00	
江苏 Jiangsu	100.00	98.34	100.00	100.00
浙江 Zhejiang			87.21	110.98
安徽 Anhui				
福建 Fujian	96.91	100.32	108.52	99.04
江西 Jiangxi	95.80	107.66	116.60	88.66
山东 Shandong	107.55	95.68	91.83	100.40
河南 Henan	104.31		100.00	
湖北 Hubei	100.00	119.02	96.13	81.32
湖南 Hunan	132.18	83.72	125.51	87.52
广东 Guangdong	88.67	121.27	101.85	121.52
广西 Guangxi	202.38	115.33	94.38	98.05
海南 Hainan	97.70	92.45	138.18	118.62
重庆 Chongqing	100.00		111.07	105.71
四川 Sichuan	100.00	95.57	101.46	116.86
贵州 Guizhou	73.82	107.23	100.00	111.84
云南 Yunnan	100.00	127.69	88.56	117.53
陕西 Shaanxi	75.92	143.23	123.45	111.91
甘肃 Gansu	116.42	109.44		
青海 Qinghai				
宁夏 Ningxia				
新疆 Xinjiang				

2—9 续表 25 continued 25

地 区 Region	蔬菜 Vegetable			
	萝卜 Radish		胡萝卜 Carrot	
	2003	2004	2003	2004
全 国 National Total	**110.46**	**103.08**	**115.09**	**102.90**
北 京 Beijing	104.20	107.94	100.02	108.78
天 津 Tianjin	107.16	90.99	100.00	
河 北 Hebei	119.96	97.80	147.95	77.95
山 西 Shanxi	108.02	107.60	122.47	79.87
内蒙古 Inner Mongolia	78.45	122.38	135.20	83.08
辽 宁 Liaoning	128.56	97.44	100.00	0.00
吉 林 Jilin	128.69	125.11	144.27	115.13
黑龙江 Heilongjiang	107.20	107.97	105.83	
上 海 Shanghai	126.80	99.86	100.00	
江 苏 Jiangsu	107.83	92.41	167.92	103.07
浙 江 Zhejiang	51.25	115.91	100.00	106.67
安 徽 Anhui	100.00	95.60	100.00	110.57
福 建 Fujian	107.71	95.65	100.00	105.33
江 西 Jiangxi	101.66	104.84	99.43	120.00
山 东 Shandong	104.86	91.76	106.76	100.31
河 南 Henan	173.02	87.52	209.34	114.67
湖 北 Hubei	126.34	93.41	93.20	113.24
湖 南 Hunan	106.63	95.51	95.96	111.09
广 东 Guangdong	106.36	99.98	91.65	103.63
广 西 Guangxi	111.18	114.35	80.13	146.46
海 南 Hainan	98.50	97.37	100.00	
重 庆 Chongqing	102.61	103.49	106.82	110.35
四 川 Sichuan	108.17	103.18	100.41	106.93
贵 州 Guizhou	104.46	96.29	100.61	97.38
云 南 Yunnan	93.73	97.22	85.28	90.50
陕 西 Shaanxi	139.38	128.32	108.99	147.92
甘 肃 Gansu	89.77	114.25	107.65	109.23
青 海 Qinghai	105.60	100.00	100.20	119.47
宁 夏 Ningxia	101.40	120.88	100.00	129.27
新 疆 Xinjiang	86.60	100.00	96.84	83.45

2—9 续表 26 continued 26

地 区 Region	蔬菜 Vegetable			
	生姜 Ginger		芋头 Taro	
	2003	2004	2003	2004
全 国 National Total	**95.91**	**145.13**	**111.54**	**107.38**
北 京 Beijing	100.00		100.00	
天 津 Tianjin	100.00		100.00	
河 北 Hebei	100.00		100.00	
山 西 Shanxi	100.00		100.00	
内蒙古 Inner Mongolia	100.00		100.00	
辽 宁 Liaoning	100.00		100.00	
吉 林 Jilin	100.00		100.00	
黑龙江 Heilongjiang	100.00		100.00	
上 海 Shanghai	100.00		100.00	
江 苏 Jiangsu	100.00	100.00	100.00	
浙 江 Zhejiang	100.00		100.00	122.31
安 徽 Anhui	111.40	106.84	100.00	102.04
福 建 Fujian	108.77	116.74	109.75	116.52
江 西 Jiangxi	75.73	102.90	101.11	120.56
山 东 Shandong	96.33	158.82	109.81	101.80
河 南 Henan	100.00		100.00	
湖 北 Hubei	100.00	114.77	100.00	98.04
湖 南 Hunan	130.91	147.89	96.18	106.40
广 东 Guangdong	105.64	194.40	95.09	101.11
广 西 Guangxi	103.27	237.63	93.77	103.85
海 南 Hainan	89.04	101.18	125.00	
重 庆 Chongqing	115.91	114.67	103.34	92.13
四 川 Sichuan	99.42	132.20	95.30	110.03
贵 州 Guizhou	121.40	108.00	80.25	102.32
云 南 Yunnan	106.29	132.43	101.12	106.62
陕 西 Shaanxi	100.00		104.49	97.22
甘 肃 Gansu	100.00		100.00	
青 海 Qinghai	100.00		100.00	
宁 夏 Ningxia	100.00		100.00	
新 疆 Xinjiang	100.00		100.00	120.00

2—9 续表 27 continued 27

地 区 Region	蔬菜 Vegetable			
	茄子 Eggplant		西红柿 Tomato	
	2003	2004	2003	2004
全 国 National Total	**117.82**	**108.01**	**103.82**	**104.06**
北 京 Beijing	65.89	114.10	87.16	108.89
天 津 Tianjin	86.50	94.02	91.34	104.20
河 北 Hebei	111.34	125.11	102.37	110.21
山 西 Shanxi	108.59	133.06	95.40	123.94
内蒙古 Inner Mongolia	88.31	137.66	90.76	108.03
辽 宁 Liaoning	118.88	110.53	107.45	111.08
吉 林 Jilin	162.50	115.61	181.19	119.96
黑龙江 Heilongjiang	113.47	157.02	90.89	78.21
上 海 Shanghai	78.78	106.94	84.26	116.05
江 苏 Jiangsu	114.60	107.61	104.49	104.09
浙 江 Zhejiang	71.35	114.11	89.79	103.80
安 徽 Anhui	100.00	103.15	100.00	108.14
福 建 Fujian	101.36	105.58	104.80	104.12
江 西 Jiangxi	107.17	109.46	101.11	107.18
山 东 Shandong	104.55	101.41	99.27	92.04
河 南 Henan	95.55	170.70	86.80	96.74
湖 北 Hubei	103.06	117.16	87.89	110.87
湖 南 Hunan	120.04	97.00	106.00	98.46
广 东 Guangdong	114.92	110.31	111.69	102.02
广 西 Guangxi	122.26	118.32	102.21	103.67
海 南 Hainan	115.17	120.05	108.58	86.22
重 庆 Chongqing	118.58	99.93	91.94	99.75
四 川 Sichuan	97.04	122.59	100.25	105.37
贵 州 Guizhou	94.52	105.01	91.37	106.35
云 南 Yunnan	108.28	116.13	87.09	100.19
陕 西 Shaanxi	124.72	124.22	113.50	112.80
甘 肃 Gansu	86.53	136.54	118.48	117.49
青 海 Qinghai	121.01		100.00	96.23
宁 夏 Ningxia	145.20	82.29	145.10	112.33
新 疆 Xinjiang	126.75	84.34	104.64	125.04

2—9 续表 28 continued 28

地 区 Region	蔬菜 Vegetable			
	辣椒 Chili		青椒 Sweetbell	
	2003	2004	2003	2004
全 国 National Total	**111.06**	**103.62**	**109.38**	**96.48**
北 京 Beijing	97.93	109.90	93.18	109.03
天 津 Tianjin	110.46	110.24	100.00	0.00
河 北 Hebei	98.86	68.56	103.28	109.29
山 西 Shanxi	115.64	97.41	118.41	96.60
内 蒙 古 Inner Mongolia	143.94	88.86	85.05	98.78
辽 宁 Liaoning	101.04	103.57	109.98	105.20
吉 林 Jilin	95.88	130.49	130.91	118.82
黑 龙 江 Heilongjiang	107.37	115.74	103.33	107.44
上 海 Shanghai	100.00	100.00	114.47	86.18
江 苏 Jiangsu	109.42	97.59	106.47	103.11
浙 江 Zhejiang	91.25	139.55	139.89	146.28
安 徽 Anhui	110.61	82.90	100.00	102.40
福 建 Fujian	101.91	112.61	101.98	94.86
江 西 Jiangxi	103.21	108.37	104.40	98.01
山 东 Shandong	107.13	100.61	115.14	99.29
河 南 Henan	117.93	99.61	91.91	122.74
湖 北 Hubei	91.54	111.46	100.00	112.57
湖 南 Hunan	115.00	81.66	95.64	95.97
广 东 Guangdong	128.50	88.61	95.97	95.42
广 西 Guangxi	119.00	103.22	106.05	85.63
海 南 Hainan	141.87	92.46	127.64	73.73
重 庆 Chongqing	109.39	106.77	103.44	109.35
四 川 Sichuan	90.61	125.99	104.25	110.63
贵 州 Guizhou	100.70	107.38	103.13	105.28
云 南 Yunnan	101.62	108.04	105.66	107.90
陕 西 Shaanxi	102.46	138.51	143.19	107.49
甘 肃 Gansu	122.71	127.22	71.26	115.31
青 海 Qinghai	118.44	100.00	251.69	140.16
宁 夏 Ningxia	110.90	107.68	100.00	
新 疆 Xinjiang	101.71	108.41	98.98	

2—9 续表 29 continued 29

地区 Region	蔬菜 Vegetable			
	大葱 Scallion		蒜苔 Garlic stalk	
	2003	2004	2003	2004
全国 National Total	**110.21**	**111.81**	**115.60**	**115.10**
北京 Beijing	100.55	106.28	100.00	157.14
天津 Tianjin	101.75	141.16	100.00	
河北 Hebei	115.63	108.82	84.39	138.94
山西 Shanxi	105.84	123.25	109.10	
内蒙古 Inner Mongolia	100.86	117.02	105.57	
辽宁 Liaoning	128.70	105.10	100.00	
吉林 Jilin	102.60	101.62	100.00	89.50
黑龙江 Heilongjiang	124.70	128.76	108.07	134.93
上海 Shanghai	100.00		100.00	
江苏 Jiangsu	106.37	121.04	107.21	103.08
浙江 Zhejiang	182.35	98.15	100.00	
安徽 Anhui	97.37	108.27	100.00	89.93
福建 Fujian	66.19	105.40	100.00	
江西 Jiangxi	145.88	113.54	183.92	100.82
山东 Shandong	135.80	113.75	129.55	110.10
河南 Henan	116.88	120.34	117.52	128.31
湖北 Hubei	124.56	110.51	116.01	115.39
湖南 Hunan	118.92	105.90	105.68	113.17
广东 Guangdong	119.38	109.04	100.00	58.40
广西 Guangxi	101.71	94.43	100.00	
海南 Hainan	103.83	98.20	100.00	93.99
重庆 Chongqing	109.88	108.79	100.00	109.36
四川 Sichuan	105.60	103.03	100.00	95.94
贵州 Guizhou	86.05	110.71	119.67	108.52
云南 Yunnan	96.58	119.33	97.51	113.70
陕西 Shaanxi	91.60	119.88	145.81	90.72
甘肃 Gansu	94.08	91.26	180.58	102.82
青海 Qinghai	100.00	99.97	88.69	168.02
宁夏 Ningxia	100.00	87.42	100.00	
新疆 Xinjiang	110.01	130.86		

2—9 续表 30 continued 30

地 区 Region	蔬菜 Vegetable			
	蒜头 Garlic head		洋葱 Onion	
	2003	2004	2003	2004
全 国 National Total	**94.67**	**117.72**	**99.13**	**101.15**
北 京 Beijing	100.00	146.67	100.00	123.75
天 津 Tianjin	101.13	81.28	100.00	
河 北 Hebei	91.84	109.38	100.00	101.01
山 西 Shanxi	88.32	111.06	100.00	
内蒙古 Inner Mongolia	100.37	83.33	108.09	83.30
辽 宁 Liaoning	100.00	102.46	100.00	
吉 林 Jilin	184.92	139.28	100.00	
黑龙江 Heilongjiang	104.35	110.17	105.67	
上 海 Shanghai	128.63	116.15	100.00	121.75
江 苏 Jiangsu	92.73	91.55	100.00	
浙 江 Zhejiang	105.28	119.38	100.00	
安 徽 Anhui	100.00	116.40	100.00	103.68
福 建 Fujian	106.32	100.52	94.91	114.37
江 西 Jiangxi	110.53	105.47	130.26	107.77
山 东 Shandong	98.97	127.41	119.73	115.01
河 南 Henan	61.61	188.27	96.45	
湖 北 Hubei	94.28	123.03	100.00	113.36
湖 南 Hunan	106.70	99.76	81.27	104.82
广 东 Guangdong	104.31	95.94	100.00	
广 西 Guangxi	173.91	102.06	100.00	
海 南 Hainan	100.00	125.00	100.00	
重 庆 Chongqing	100.08	104.33	100.00	
四 川 Sichuan	80.16	113.60	102.27	105.68
贵 州 Guizhou	108.33	105.12	100.00	111.11
云 南 Yunnan	101.61	121.23	100.00	54.09
陕 西 Shaanxi	73.66	105.41	100.00	
甘 肃 Gansu	100.00	116.12	100.00	137.36
青 海 Qinghai	95.00	114.90	100.00	111.11
宁 夏 Ningxia	100.00	117.17		
新 疆 Xinjiang	100.00		100.00	

2—9 续表 31 continued 31

地 区 Region	食用菌 Mushroom		食用菌 Mushroom 香菇(干品) Mushroom (dried)	
	2003	2004	2003	2004
全 国 National Total	**99.22**	**101.41**	**96.93**	**100.33**
北 京 Beijing	111.04	101.65	100.00	100.00
天 津 Tianjin	99.36	91.77	100.00	
河 北 Hebei	106.81	93.17	100.00	89.45
山 西 Shanxi	95.92	110.12	86.60	101.28
内蒙古 Inner Mongolia	100.00		100.00	
辽 宁 Liaoning	101.76	0.00		
吉 林 Jilin	74.85	141.78		
黑龙江 Heilongjiang	71.11	119.73		
上 海 Shanghai	100.00			
江 苏 Jiangsu	100.00	102.86		
浙 江 Zhejiang	100.00			
安 徽 Anhui	100.00		100.00	86.81
福 建 Fujian	86.06	99.43	104.72	94.96
江 西 Jiangxi	96.33	104.45	57.80	106.37
山 东 Shandong	138.18	106.09	100.00	101.59
河 南 Henan	66.39	116.57	66.39	116.57
湖 北 Hubei	98.77	109.41	73.79	105.50
湖 南 Hunan	108.86	107.69	100.00	
广 东 Guangdong	103.05	103.55	105.48	
广 西 Guangxi	97.79	91.81	103.05	
海 南 Hainan	100.00	0.00	100.00	
重 庆 Chongqing	100.00			
四 川 Sichuan	111.22	98.40	100.00	77.78
贵 州 Guizhou	100.01	95.89	100.00	100.00
云 南 Yunnan	95.80	101.77	100.00	
陕 西 Shaanxi	122.24	115.29	117.00	94.70
甘 肃 Gansu	98.69	92.65		
青 海 Qinghai	100.00	0.00		
宁 夏 Ningxia	100.00	0.00		
新 疆 Xinjiang	100.00	0.00		

2—9 续表 32 continued 32

地　区　Region	食用菌　Mushroom			
	蘑菇(鲜品) Mushroom (fresh)		黑木耳(干品) Black edible fungus (dried)	
	2003	2004	2003	2004
全　国　National Total	**98.10**	**100.50**	**112.90**	**115.47**
北　京　Beijing	111.04	102.58		
天　津　Tianjin	99.36	91.77		
河　北　Hebei	106.81	93.17		
山　西　Shanxi	98.96	113.84		
内蒙古　Inner Mongolia	92.31	106.38		
辽　宁　Liaoning	101.76	100.00	100.00	0.00
吉　林　Jilin	74.85	141.78	100.00	0.00
黑龙江　Heilongjiang	100.00	100.00	71.11	119.73
上　海　Shanghai				
江　苏　Jiangsu	124.87	100.00	100.00	100.00
浙　江　Zhejiang	100.00	0.00	100.00	
安　徽　Anhui	100.00	97.71	100.00	108.45
福　建　Fujian	97.44	100.20	100.00	111.80
江　西　Jiangxi	107.77	104.37		
山　东　Shandong	138.18	107.15		
河　南　Henan	120.54	141.19	100.00	
湖　北　Hubei	100.41	106.13	105.79	127.97
湖　南　Hunan	131.38	106.33	100.00	162.86
广　东　Guangdong	100.00	0.00	100.00	
广　西　Guangxi	115.77	97.85	97.79	
海　南　Hainan	100.00	0.00	100.00	
重　庆　Chongqing	100.00	111.11		
四　川　Sichuan	111.39	97.46	100.23	111.43
贵　州　Guizhou	100.05	95.89		
云　南　Yunnan	95.80	101.77	100.00	108.01
陕　西　Shaanxi	100.00	0.00	123.17	118.98
甘　肃　Gansu	91.20	86.12		
青　海　Qinghai	100.00	18.54		
宁　夏　Ningxia	100.00	90.11		
新　疆　Xinjiang		0.00		

2—9 续表 33 continued 33

地 区 Region	花卉 Flowers		花卉 Flowers 康乃馨 Carnation	
	2003	2004	2003	2004
全 国 National Total	**96.41**	**0.00**	**175.57**	**112.47**
北 京 Beijing	100.00	98.68	100.00	0.00
天 津 Tianjin	128.33	99.30	100.00	0.00
河 北 Hebei				
山 西 Shanxi				
内蒙古 Inner Mongolia				
辽 宁 Liaoning				
吉 林 Jilin				
黑龙江 Heilongjiang				
上 海 Shanghai	100.00	96.56	100.00	0.00
江 苏 Jiangsu	100.00	100.00	99.99	99.99
浙 江 Zhejiang	100.00	0.00	100.00	0.00
安 徽 Anhui	100.00	0.00	100.00	0.00
福 建 Fujian	100.00	68.76	100.00	0.00
江 西 Jiangxi	100.00	0.00	100.00	0.00
山 东 Shandong	100.00	79.22	100.00	98.00
河 南 Henan	100.00	0.00	100.00	0.00
湖 北 Hubei	100.00	0.00	100.00	0.00
湖 南 Hunan	100.00	0.00	100.00	0.00
广 东 Guangdong	102.47	119.31	100.00	0.00
广 西 Guangxi	100.00	0.00	100.00	0.00
海 南 Hainan	96.92	93.70	100.00	0.00
重 庆 Chongqing	194.81	0.00	194.81	0.00
四 川 Sichuan	100.00	0.00		0.00
贵 州 Guizhou	100.00	0.00	100.00	0.00
云 南 Yunnan	95.45	105.92	124.90	110.62
陕 西 Shaanxi	100.00	0.00		
甘 肃 Gansu	98.47	85.03		
青 海 Qinghai	100.00	0.00		
宁 夏 Ningxia	100.00	0.00		
新 疆 Xinjiang	100.00	0.00		

2—9 续表 34　　continued 34

地　区　Region	水果 Fruits		水果 Fruits 苹果 Apple	
	2003	2004	2003	2004
全　国　National Total	**102.04**	**98.63**	**103.51**	**102.50**
北　京　Beijing	100.03	101.33	108.98	89.14
天　津　Tianjin	93.45	107.23	94.22	104.76
河　北　Hebei	97.11	92.88	107.55	92.77
山　西　Shanxi	103.83	100.90	104.42	100.38
内蒙古　Inner Mongolia	102.61	99.03	100.00	97.24
辽　宁　Liaoning	88.25	116.23	82.52	106.28
吉　林　Jilin	100.00	128.22	100.00	0.00
黑龙江　Heilongjiang	100.00		100.00	0.00
上　海　Shanghai	109.24	111.17	100.00	0.00
江　苏　Jiangsu	93.85	113.83	100.00	0.00
浙　江　Zhejiang	79.77	101.23	100.00	0.00
安　徽　Anhui		100.81		0.00
福　建　Fujian	109.28	102.15	100.00	0.00
江　西　Jiangxi	96.48			
山　东　Shandong	87.66	113.50	93.62	104.46
河　南　Henan	106.36	112.15	105.21	101.93
湖　北　Hubei	92.98	111.04	100.00	0.00
湖　南　Hunan	109.86	85.50	100.00	0.00
广　东　Guangdong	113.98	83.19	100.00	0.00
广　西　Guangxi	120.87	90.96	100.00	0.00
海　南　Hainan	97.55	113.32	100.00	0.00
重　庆　Chongqing	94.34	103.04	100.00	0.00
四　川　Sichuan	119.22	100.96	123.24	92.59
贵　州　Guizhou	91.71	103.75	100.00	0.00
云　南　Yunnan	94.84	87.75	92.40	88.35
陕　西　Shaanxi	96.04	99.00	98.61	98.82
甘　肃　Gansu	101.43	106.07	101.10	97.07
青　海　Qinghai	100.00	0.00	100.00	0.00
宁　夏　Ningxia	107.60	119.24	55.40	81.81
新　疆　Xinjiang	100.00	119.09		123.64

2—9 续表 35 continued 35

地 区 Region	水果 Fruits			
	梨 Pear		柑桔 Citrus	
	2003	2004	2003	2004
全 国 National Total	**102.91**	**95.31**	**100.50**	**94.73**
北 京 Beijing	95.99	104.37		
天 津 Tianjin	97.01	82.80		
河 北 Hebei	109.44	87.70		
山 西 Shanxi	106.88	89.44		
内蒙古 Inner Mongolia	110.64	91.66		
辽 宁 Liaoning	102.77	103.29		
吉 林 Jilin	100.00	113.74		
黑龙江 Heilongjiang				
上 海 Shanghai			107.84	127.40
江 苏 Jiangsu	100.00	110.78	100.00	100.00
浙 江 Zhejiang	100.00	0.00	88.79	100.59
安 徽 Anhui		104.60		102.04
福 建 Fujian	61.56	0.00	103.75	103.77
江 西 Jiangxi	100.00	0.00	105.67	113.59
山 东 Shandong	106.20	112.03	100.00	0.00
河 南 Henan	105.00	84.00	100.00	0.00
湖 北 Hubei			102.08	106.32
湖 南 Hunan			109.69	84.39
广 东 Guangdong	100.00	94.64	99.23	106.94
广 西 Guangxi	100.00	95.92	100.79	102.93
海 南 Hainan	100.00	0.00	100.00	0.00
重 庆 Chongqing	94.61	107.58	94.29	100.02
四 川 Sichuan	169.17	102.23	109.43	97.40
贵 州 Guizhou	81.47	96.36	95.81	103.51
云 南 Yunnan	78.79	60.00	96.43	84.20
陕 西 Shaanxi	107.42	95.71	86.10	100.00
甘 肃 Gansu	101.68	116.00		
青 海 Qinghai	100.00			
宁 夏 Ningxia	100.00	132.94		
新 疆 Xinjiang	100.00	100.01		

2—9 续表 36 continued 36

地区 Region	水果 Fruits			
	红富士苹果 Hongfushi apple		国光苹果 Guoguang apple	
	2003	2004	2003	2004
全国 National Total	**103.84**	**102.48**	**91.60**	**98.21**
北京 Beijing	114.43	85.77	85.52	100.31
天津 Tianjin	94.22	113.33	101.11	
河北 Hebei	106.33	97.60	110.38	81.55
山西 Shanxi	103.26	101.52	106.67	94.51
内蒙古 Inner Mongolia			100.00	93.75
辽宁 Liaoning	84.22	120.26	79.47	92.31
吉林 Jilin			100.00	100.00
黑龙江 Heilongjiang			100.00	100.00
上海 Shanghai				
江苏 Jiangsu	100.00	100.00	100.00	100.00
浙江 Zhejiang				
安徽 Anhui				
福建 Fujian				
江西 Jiangxi				
山东 Shandong	93.62	104.32	100.00	106.04
河南 Henan	105.21	101.93	100.00	0.00
湖北 Hubei	100.00	0.00	100.00	0.00
湖南 Hunan	100.00	0.00	100.00	0.00
广东 Guangdong		0.00	100.00	0.00
广西 Guangxi	100.00	0.00	100.00	0.00
海南 Hainan		0.00	100.00	0.00
重庆 Chongqing	100.00	0.00	100.00	0.00
四川 Sichuan	131.58	0.00	100.00	92.59
贵州 Guizhou	100.00	0.00	100.00	0.00
云南 Yunnan	92.40	87.07	100.00	0.00
陕西 Shaanxi	97.08	98.15	100.00	0.00
甘肃 Gansu	104.10	93.65	100.00	100.02
青海 Qinghai	100.00	97.61	100.00	42.44
宁夏 Ningxia	100.00	81.81	100.00	0.00
新疆 Xinjiang	93.65	123.64		0.00

2—9 续表 37 continued 37

地区 Region	水果 Fruits			
	秦冠苹果 Qinguan apple		香蕉苹果 Banana apple	
	2003	2004	2003	2004
全国 National Total	**107.81**	**108.62**	**110.85**	**105.10**
北京 Beijing	100.00	0.00	100.00	160.00
天津 Tianjin	100.00	0.00		87.06
河北 Hebei	100.00	0.00	100.00	
山西 Shanxi	106.93	102.32	106.67	100.00
内蒙古 Inner Mongolia	100.00	112.50	100.00	
辽宁 Liaoning	90.91			
吉林 Jilin	100.00			
黑龙江 Heilongjiang				
上海 Shanghai	100.00			0.00
江苏 Jiangsu	100.00		100.00	0.00
浙江 Zhejiang	100.00		100.00	0.00
安徽 Anhui	100.00			0.00
福建 Fujian	100.00		100.00	0.00
江西 Jiangxi	100.00		100.00	0.00
山东 Shandong	100.00	97.41	119.64	94.04
河南 Henan	153.04	109.40	128.58	110.56
湖北 Hubei		0.00	100.00	0.00
湖南 Hunan	100.00	0.00		0.00
广东 Guangdong	100.00	0.00	100.00	0.00
广西 Guangxi		0.00	100.00	0.00
海南 Hainan	100.00	0.00	100.00	0.00
重庆 Chongqing	100.00	0.00	100.00	0.00
四川 Sichuan	100.00	0.00	100.00	0.00
贵州 Guizhou	100.00	0.00	100.00	0.00
云南 Yunnan	100.00	91.86	100.00	0.00
陕西 Shaanxi	125.07	109.48		
甘肃 Gansu	153.21	79.06	97.05	114.75
青海 Qinghai		0.00	100.00	0.00
宁夏 Ningxia	100.00	0.00	100.00	0.00
新疆 Xinjiang	100.00	0.00	100.00	0.00

2—9 续表 38　　continued 38

地区 Region	水果 Fruits					
	雪花梨 Snowflake pear		鸭梨 Ya-pear		酥梨 Soft-pear	
	2003	2004	2003	2004	2003	2004
全国 National Total	**109.54**	**93.96**	**103.56**	**98.29**	**106.64**	**95.31**
北京 Beijing	100.00	0.00	89.46	104.37	114.24	0.00
天津 Tianjin	100.00	86.18	95.00	80.33	100.00	0.00
河北 Hebei	107.46	88.64	111.77	86.60	100.00	0.00
山西 Shanxi	100.00	0.00	100.00	0.00	106.88	89.44
内蒙古 Inner Mongolia	100.00	0.00	100.00	0.00	100.18	0.00
辽宁 Liaoning	100.00	0.00	100.00	0.00	111.80	119.77
吉林 Jilin		0.00	100.00	0.00	100.00	0.00
黑龙江 Heilongjiang	100.00	0.00	100.00	0.00	100.00	0.00
上海 Shanghai						
江苏 Jiangsu	100.00	100.00	100.00	0.00	100.00	0.00
浙江 Zhejiang	100.00	81.02		105.41	100.00	0.00
安徽 Anhui	100.00	0.00	100.00	0.00	100.00	104.60
福建 Fujian	103.77	0.00	99.96	0.00	100.00	0.00
江西 Jiangxi	100.00	111.11	100.00	0.00		0.00
山东 Shandong	100.00	100.00	106.20	112.03	100.00	105.41
河南 Henan	100.00	0.00	105.00	85.71	73.87	84.00
湖北 Hubei	100.00	103.92	100.00	109.39	100.00	0.00
湖南 Hunan	88.01	94.23	108.43	85.94	105.56	0.00
广东 Guangdong						
广西 Guangxi	100.00	69.44	100.00	0.00	100.00	0.00
海南 Hainan						
重庆 Chongqing	94.61	107.58	100.00	0.00	100.00	0.00
四川 Sichuan	101.51	99.58	118.06	95.74	100.00	106.25
贵州 Guizhou	100.02	104.73	81.47	96.23	100.00	100.00
云南 Yunnan	71.89	60.00	89.45	0.00	100.00	0.00
陕西 Shaanxi	95.05	97.40	100.00	0.00	107.67	95.66
甘肃 Gansu	100.00	108.08		0.00	101.70	121.65
青海 Qinghai	100.00	0.00	100.00	0.00		0.00
宁夏 Ningxia	100.00	0.00	100.00	0.00	100.00	132.94
新疆 Xinjiang	100.00	100.01		0.00	100.00	0.00

2—9 续表 39　　　　continued 39

地　区 Region	水果 Fruits			
	西瓜 Watermelon		甜瓜 Muskmelon	
	2003	2004	2003	2004
全　国 National Total	**88.54**	**110.00**	**91.83**	**107.34**
北　京 Beijing	99.60	106.41	100.00	103.14
天　津 Tianjin	83.65	95.39	100.00	0.00
河　北 Hebei	82.26	131.40	84.75	115.96
山　西 Shanxi	101.68	123.57	126.18	94.69
内蒙古 Inner Mongolia	101.22	101.17	107.94	90.19
辽　宁 Liaoning	76.10	204.65	89.57	122.24
吉　林 Jilin	163.40	131.10	161.42	0.00
黑龙江 Heilongjiang	129.81	104.41	100.00	0.00
上　海 Shanghai	109.50	124.54	100.00	116.05
江　苏 Jiangsu	88.91	0.00	94.57	0.00
浙　江 Zhejiang	115.32	94.29	100.00	110.51
安　徽 Anhui	100.00	109.91	100.00	112.85
福　建 Fujian	103.35	99.73	73.33	99.61
江　西 Jiangxi	87.29	95.07	114.85	102.44
山　东 Shandong	81.66	119.75	93.85	118.78
河　南 Henan	109.38	136.44	105.30	150.45
湖　北 Hubei	79.05	128.02	100.00	97.78
湖　南 Hunan	118.44	87.43	100.00	93.38
广　东 Guangdong	103.23	82.63	100.00	78.83
广　西 Guangxi	103.04	88.23	93.87	119.92
海　南 Hainan	98.02	116.12	87.51	110.31
重　庆 Chongqing	100.00	120.51	100.00	
四　川 Sichuan	128.86	91.69	100.00	
贵　州 Guizhou	81.12	104.88	100.00	100.00
云　南 Yunnan	128.81	94.14	100.00	
陕　西 Shaanxi	112.27	114.81	111.77	79.50
甘　肃 Gansu	97.43	140.45	103.84	101.46
青　海 Qinghai				
宁　夏 Ningxia	125.60	126.04	100.00	
新　疆 Xinjiang	127.87	95.98	88.18	86.37

2—9 续表 40 continued 40

地区 Region	水果 Fruits			
	香瓜 Musk melon		草莓 Strawberry	
	2003	2004	2003	2004
全国 National Total	**108.59**	**110.86**	**110.38**	**105.37**
北京 Beijing				
天津 Tianjin				
河北 Hebei			100.23	101.81
山西 Shanxi	72.62	178.10	100.00	105.26
内蒙古 Inner Mongolia	103.72	149.99		
辽宁 Liaoning	100.00	0.00	93.76	84.92
吉林 Jilin	100.58	98.60	100.00	82.08
黑龙江 Heilongjiang		108.18		
上海 Shanghai	100.00	0.00	96.78	100.00
江苏 Jiangsu	100.00	0.00	100.00	0.00
浙江 Zhejiang	100.00	0.00	100.00	117.81
安徽 Anhui		0.00	100.00	0.00
福建 Fujian	100.00	0.00	100.00	0.00
江西 Jiangxi	100.00	109.05	100.00	0.00
山东 Shandong	100.00	102.06	98.66	120.65
河南 Henan	100.00	0.00	138.82	0.00
湖北 Hubei	100.00	0.00	100.00	0.00
湖南 Hunan	126.40	94.79	100.00	102.23
广东 Guangdong	105.06	106.30	100.00	0.00
广西 Guangxi	88.09	126.20	100.00	0.00
海南 Hainan	100.00	100.00	100.00	0.00
重庆 Chongqing	100.00	0.00	100.00	0.00
四川 Sichuan	106.17	0.00	176.73	138.74
贵州 Guizhou	100.00	0.00	111.91	97.30
云南 Yunnan	100.00	0.00	100.00	0.00
陕西 Shaanxi			102.18	158.67
甘肃 Gansu				
青海 Qinghai				
宁夏 Ningxia				
新疆 Xinjiang				

2—9 续表 41 continued 41

地区 Region	水果 Fruits			
	桃 Peach		杏 Apricot	
	2003	2004	2003	2004
全国 National Total	**89.42**	**96.66**	**98.72**	**99.61**
北京 Beijing	90.01	96.64	103.30	95.83
天津 Tianjin	100.00	92.21	100.00	0.00
河北 Hebei	90.65	75.61	99.80	142.85
山西 Shanxi	85.32	96.39	97.09	95.14
内蒙古 Inner Mongolia	100.00	0.00	100.00	0.00
辽宁 Liaoning	137.73	93.93	100.00	117.85
吉林 Jilin				
黑龙江 Heilongjiang				
上海 Shanghai	70.15	100.25	100.00	0.00
江苏 Jiangsu	94.13	93.56	100.00	0.00
浙江 Zhejiang	71.25	105.06	100.00	0.00
安徽 Anhui	100.00	85.72	100.00	100.00
福建 Fujian	98.48	85.06	119.70	0.00
江西 Jiangxi	73.12	104.66	100.00	0.00
山东 Shandong	81.84	106.90	86.67	101.44
河南 Henan	97.10	108.32	100.00	0.00
湖北 Hubei	99.30	95.34	100.00	0.00
湖南 Hunan	98.04	86.55	106.72	109.25
广东 Guangdong	105.42	83.04		
广西 Guangxi	95.49	59.13		
海南 Hainan				
重庆 Chongqing	100.00	105.81	109.55	111.11
四川 Sichuan	105.91	109.34	100.00	111.11
贵州 Guizhou	119.95	93.47	99.85	120.00
云南 Yunnan	104.03	102.74	100.00	114.58
陕西 Shaanxi	99.18	90.43	100.74	88.87
甘肃 Gansu	84.15	95.81	104.29	94.20
青海 Qinghai	112.62	83.58	105.35	91.29
宁夏 Ningxia	100.00	143.59	100.00	
新疆 Xinjiang	100.00	100.00	93.41	85.78

2—9 续表 42 continued 42

地　区 Region	水果 Fruits					
	葡萄 Grape		红枣 Chinese date		柿子 Persimmon	
	2003	2004	2003	2004	2003	2004
全　国 National Total	**99.14**	**95.36**	**91.62**	**108.02**	**97.86**	**92.29**
北　京 Beijing	128.06	91.39	53.39	124.85	101.87	96.63
天　津 Tianjin	96.95	122.58	93.39	0.00	100.00	0.00
河　北 Hebei	92.86	85.65	90.27	114.67	108.87	105.06
山　西 Shanxi	98.33	100.19	106.82	89.87	95.58	97.79
内蒙古 Inner Mongolia	120.00	0.00	100.00	0.00	100.00	0.00
辽　宁 Liaoning	92.48	111.02	90.61	54.48	100.00	0.00
吉　林 Jilin	93.81	113.19	100.00	0.00	100.00	0.00
黑龙江 Heilongjiang					100.00	100.00
上　海 Shanghai	129.46	0.00	100.00	0.00	100.00	0.00
江　苏 Jiangsu	98.11	97.87	100.00	100.00	100.00	0.00
浙　江 Zhejiang	100.00	84.91	100.00	162.96	100.00	96.32
安　徽 Anhui	100.00	0.00	100.00	100.00	100.00	84.50
福　建 Fujian	91.58	96.26	100.00	0.00	132.32	87.25
江　西 Jiangxi	100.00	0.00	100.00	113.64	100.00	0.00
山　东 Shandong	84.98	116.58	79.77	105.04	110.35	87.41
河　南 Henan	109.70	0.00	100.00	0.00	92.75	269.22
湖　北 Hubei	100.00	0.00	100.00	0.00	100.00	99.51
湖　南 Hunan	97.50	81.59	103.88	90.88	105.20	100.28
广　东 Guangdong	100.00	0.00	100.00	0.00	88.62	103.85
广　西 Guangxi	93.25	92.00	100.00	0.00	93.38	115.01
海　南 Hainan						
重　庆 Chongqing	53.23	124.37	100.00	0.00	100.00	106.67
四　川 Sichuan	108.14	104.85	104.35	127.85	83.27	105.46
贵　州 Guizhou	92.57	119.64	100.00	0.00	100.00	0.00
云　南 Yunnan	73.79	86.78	78.74	0.00	105.85	103.96
陕　西 Shaanxi	66.29	114.17	84.61	90.88	98.95	97.13
甘　肃 Gansu	100.96	65.21	167.35	101.01	100.00	86.18
青　海 Qinghai	100.00	0.00	100.00	0.00		
宁　夏 Ningxia	100.00	118.13	100.00	75.00		
新　疆 Xinjiang	104.20	106.14	170.42	133.77		

2—9 续表 43 continued 43

地 区 Region	其他水果 Other fruits		其他水果 Other fruits			
			香蕉 Banana		菠萝 Pineapple	
	2003	2004	2003	2004	2003	2004
全 国 National Total	**114.98**	**101.61**	**111.31**	**114.25**	**87.93**	**100.36**
北 京 Beijing	100.00	97.44				
天 津 Tianjin	100.00	123.33				
河 北 Hebei	100.00	93.08				
山 西 Shanxi	100.00	94.87				
内蒙古 Inner Mongolia						
辽 宁 Liaoning	100.00	101.66				
吉 林 Jilin	100.00	113.19				
黑龙江 Heilongjiang						
上 海 Shanghai	100.00	100.25				
江 苏 Jiangsu						
浙 江 Zhejiang						
安 徽 Anhui	100.00	85.72				
福 建 Fujian	135.49	92.25	154.20	115.87	73.97	125.63
江 西 Jiangxi	100.00	108.18				
山 东 Shandong	100.00	109.64				
河 南 Henan	100.00	108.32				
湖 北 Hubei	100.00	95.34				
湖 南 Hunan	100.00	85.87				
广 东 Guangdong	136.83	73.01	112.73	102.22	100.00	108.65
广 西 Guangxi	128.48	82.94	107.93	107.00	100.00	116.67
海 南 Hainan	98.72	115.98	104.42	120.15	89.45	91.66
重 庆 Chongqing	100.00	115.09	100.00	101.02	100.00	0.00
四 川 Sichuan	96.58	106.64	102.56	110.06	100.00	0.00
贵 州 Guizhou	100.10	104.10	100.00	0.00	100.00	0.00
云 南 Yunnan	100.90	98.18	101.74	113.96	100.00	100.30
陕 西 Shaanxi		103.80				
甘 肃 Gansu	100.00	87.47				
青 海 Qinghai						
宁 夏 Ningxia	100.00	116.07				
新 疆 Xinjiang	100.00	105.39				

2—9 续表 44 continued 44

地 区 Region	茶叶 Tea					
	红毛茶 Black tea		绿毛茶 Green tea		乌龙茶 Oolong tea	
	2003	2004	2003	2004	2003	2004
全 国 National Total	**83.22**	**109.41**	**100.56**	**110.48**	**94.56**	**107.50**
北 京 Beijing						
天 津 Tianjin						
河 北 Hebei						
山 西 Shanxi						
内蒙古 Inner Mongolia						
辽 宁 Liaoning						
吉 林 Jilin						
黑龙江 Heilongjiang						
上 海 Shanghai	100.00	100.00	100.00	100.00		
江 苏 Jiangsu	101.36	100.00	109.61	102.05		
浙 江 Zhejiang			188.58	112.51		
安 徽 Anhui	100.00	97.70	114.55	102.11		
福 建 Fujian	103.91	108.64	100.51	99.34	106.39	113.48
江 西 Jiangxi	80.00	100.00	93.69	124.29		
山 东 Shandong	100.00	100.00	100.00	104.85		
河 南 Henan			79.06	141.26		
湖 北 Hubei			71.80	119.75		
湖 南 Hunan	100.00	39.53	86.11	138.85		
广 东 Guangdong			100.75	103.58	88.35	105.75
广 西 Guangxi			100.79	105.50		
海 南 Hainan			100.00	0.00		
重 庆 Chongqing			100.00	107.69		
四 川 Sichuan			90.53	121.46		
贵 州 Guizhou			99.84	97.08		
云 南 Yunnan	84.00	117.51	98.54	108.17		
陕 西 Shaanxi	100.00	100.00	121.48	93.23		
甘 肃 Gansu						
青 海 Qinghai						
宁 夏 Ningxia						
新 疆 Xinjiang						

2—10 各地区林业产品生产价格指数
Indices of the Producer Prices of Forest Products by Region

(上年=100) (the preceding year=100)

地 区 Region	林业产品 Forest products		林业产品 Forest products: 竹木采运 Felling and transport of bamboo and wood		林业产品 Forest products: 林产品的采集 Gathering of forest products	
	2003	2004	2003	2004	2003	2004
全 国 National Total	**107.01**	**104.62**		**104.81**		**104.05**
北 京 Beijing	100.85	111.40				111.40
天 津 Tianjin	98.75	98.80				98.80
河 北 Hebei	95.00	112.34				112.34
山 西 Shanxi	98.63	106.33		105.56		107.49
内蒙古 Inner Mongolia	97.21	98.97		103.69		
辽 宁 Liaoning	104.90	95.05		90.10		95.35
吉 林 Jilin	100.00	250.55				250.55
黑龙江 Heilongjiang	100.00	83.75		83.75		
上 海 Shanghai	100.00	0.00				
江 苏 Jiangsu	101.40	99.36		101.95		94.38
浙 江 Zhejiang	116.57	98.75		98.75		0.00
安 徽 Anhui	97.65	102.78		106.26		75.52
福 建 Fujian	101.50	102.30		102.88		102.78
江 西 Jiangxi	103.35	109.06		109.14		107.82
山 东 Shandong	90.09	110.24		106.35		111.70
河 南 Henan	103.52	103.81		103.81		0.00
湖 北 Hubei	141.73	100.09		100.09		0.00
湖 南 Hunan	107.55	111.10		111.23		110.86
广 东 Guangdong	100.66	108.26		107.59		111.23
广 西 Guangxi	88.54	105.29		105.28		107.63
海 南 Hainan	108.34	106.26		103.33		106.72
重 庆 Chongqing	100.00	0.00				
四 川 Sichuan	111.85	104.37		102.52		97.60
贵 州 Guizhou	115.72	106.00		103.41		109.84
云 南 Yunnan	110.96	115.79		104.33		119.70
陕 西 Shaanxi	87.35	95.09		105.53		94.90
甘 肃 Gansu	86.28	100.01		0.00		100.01
青 海 Qinghai	100.00	0.00				
宁 夏 Ningxia	100.00	0.00				
新 疆 Xinjiang	89.98	98.77		95.40		104.71

2—10续表1 continued 1

地　区 Region	木材采运 Felling and transport of wood				竹材采运 Felling and transport of bamboo	
	原木 Log		薪材 Firewood			
	2003	2004	2003	2004	2003	2004
全　国 National Total		**104.19**		**104.31**		**108.89**
北　京 Beijing						
天　津 Tianjin						
河　北 Hebei						
山　西 Shanxi		105.56				
内蒙古 Inner Mongolia		104.79		100.13		
辽　宁 Liaoning		96.28		83.91		
吉　林 Jilin						
黑龙江 Heilongjiang		83.75				
上　海 Shanghai						
江　苏 Jiangsu		102.09				99.93
浙　江 Zhejiang		96.91				113.77
安　徽 Anhui		103.92		106.17		114.24
福　建 Fujian		98.28		107.18		106.81
江　西 Jiangxi		109.47		110.07		102.70
山　东 Shandong		106.35		103.17		
河　南 Henan		103.81		101.74		
湖　北 Hubei		105.34		96.18		85.16
湖　南 Hunan		104.91		90.45		124.40
广　东 Guangdong		106.52		93.66		110.94
广　西 Guangxi		105.28		101.13		110.42
海　南 Hainan		100.51		107.69		101.79
重　庆 Chongqing						
四　川 Sichuan		103.67				100.68
贵　州 Guizhou		103.15		108.68		104.75
云　南 Yunnan		99.87		103.30		134.98
陕　西 Shaanxi				111.06		100.40
甘　肃 Gansu						
青　海 Qinghai				94.95		
宁　夏 Ningxia						
新　疆 Xinjiang		95.94		88.76		

2—10 续表 2 continued 2

地 区 Region	林产品采集 Gathering of forest products					
	橡胶 Rubber		油桐籽 Seeds of tung oil tree		油茶籽 Seeds of tea-oil tree	
	2003	2004	2003	2004	2003	2004
全 国 National Total	**121.49**	**117.47**	**180.53**	**114.47**	**113.54**	**115.56**
北 京 Beijing						
天 津 Tianjin						
河 北 Hebei						
山 西 Shanxi						
内 蒙 古 Inner Mongolia						
辽 宁 Liaoning						
吉 林 Jilin						
黑 龙 江 Heilongjiang						
上 海 Shanghai						
江 苏 Jiangsu						
浙 江 Zhejiang						
安 徽 Anhui						
福 建 Fujian	100.00	0.00	100.00	102.22	100.00	100.00
江 西 Jiangxi	100.00	0.00	108.56	102.15	106.60	111.73
山 东 Shandong	100.00	0.00	100.00	0.00	100.00	0.00
河 南 Henan						
湖 北 Hubei			100.00	114.10	100.00	0.00
湖 南 Hunan			125.94	129.02	105.23	111.92
广 东 Guangdong			100.00	0.00	100.00	116.67
广 西 Guangxi			163.71	167.18	124.10	133.98
海 南 Hainan	118.85	112.28	100.00	0.00	100.00	0.00
重 庆 Chongqing			100.00	0.00	100.00	106.67
四 川 Sichuan			100.00	103.91	100.00	100.00
贵 州 Guizhou			184.65	109.52	100.00	0.00
云 南 Yunnan	125.64	126.65	112.69	124.22	100.00	0.00
陕 西 Shaanxi			163.60	93.40		
甘 肃 Gansu						
青 海 Qinghai						
宁 夏 Ningxia						
新 疆 Xinjiang						

2—10 续表 3 continued 3

地　区 Region	林产品采集 Gathering of forest products			
	棕片 Palm fibre		松脂 Rosin	
	2003	2004	2003	2004
全　国 National Total	**94.10**	**102.30**	**102.85**	**107.74**
北　京 Beijing				
天　津 Tianjin				
河　北 Hebei				
山　西 Shanxi				
内蒙古 Inner Mongolia				
辽　宁 Liaoning				
吉　林 Jilin				
黑龙江 Heilongjiang				
上　海 Shanghai				
江　苏 Jiangsu				
浙　江 Zhejiang				
安　徽 Anhui				
福　建 Fujian	100.60	0.00	99.66	0.00
江　西 Jiangxi	98.75	96.00	75.15	106.77
山　东 Shandong				
河　南 Henan				
湖　北 Hubei				
湖　南 Hunan	85.87	112.00	100.00	0.00
广　东 Guangdong	100.00	113.33	114.84	116.85
广　西 Guangxi	100.00	0.00	104.11	112.78
海　南 Hainan	100.00	0.00	103.09	94.40
重　庆 Chongqing				
四　川 Sichuan	100.00	101.23	100.00	0.00
贵　州 Guizhou	89.00	112.50	100.00	0.00
云　南 Yunnan	114.47	80.00	103.34	121.94
陕　西 Shaanxi				
甘　肃 Gansu				
青　海 Qinghai				
宁　夏 Ningxia				
新　疆 Xinjiang				

2—10 续表 4 continued 4

地区 Region	林产品采集 Gathering of forest products			
	核桃 Walnut		板栗 Chinese chestnut	
	2003	2004	2003	2004
全国 National Total	**96.39**	**102.66**	**96.85**	**96.37**
北京 Beijing	114.28	106.82	96.80	115.25
天津 Tianjin	100.79	98.80	89.13	0.00
河北 Hebei	99.13	104.05	91.50	134.85
山西 Shanxi	105.10	116.71	81.23	
内蒙古 Inner Mongolia				
辽宁 Liaoning	106.67	90.28	105.56	96.44
吉林 Jilin	100.00	61.47	100.00	0.00
黑龙江 Heilongjiang				
上海 Shanghai				
江苏 Jiangsu	0.00	0.00	94.63	0.00
浙江 Zhejiang	100.00	0.00	100.00	89.65
安徽 Anhui	100.00	129.65	100.00	64.70
福建 Fujian	100.00	0.00	106.59	75.47
江西 Jiangxi	100.00	0.00	101.94	91.51
山东 Shandong	95.98	104.38	77.15	114.14
河南 Henan	84.21	122.70	134.27	110.95
湖北 Hubei	100.00	100.00	100.00	86.65
湖南 Hunan	100.00		101.41	85.16
广东 Guangdong	100.00		110.93	85.71
广西 Guangxi	100.00		95.67	99.03
海南 Hainan			100.00	0.00
重庆 Chongqing				
四川 Sichuan	108.50	98.08	98.95	111.83
贵州 Guizhou	103.61	102.69	89.86	108.08
云南 Yunnan	94.87	113.83	82.17	124.98
陕西 Shaanxi	95.23	111.20	108.17	105.98
甘肃 Gansu	99.49	126.55		
青海 Qinghai	100.00	114.29		
宁夏 Ningxia				
新疆 Xinjiang	89.98	104.71		

2—11 各地区畜牧业产品生产价格指数
Indices of the Producer Prices of Livestock Products by Region

（上年=100） (the preceding year=100)

地 区 Region	畜牧业产品 Livestock products		畜产品 Livestock products			
			大牲畜 Livestock		猪 Hog	
	2003	2004	2003	2004	2003	2004
全 国 National Total	**101.76**	**111.08**	**99.84**	**104.16**	**102.86**	**112.84**
北 京 Beijing	102.37	107.42	103.49	102.20	104.10	117.57
天 津 Tianjin	103.29	113.65	99.96	100.16	107.65	125.29
河 北 Hebei	102.97	112.06	101.43	102.25	107.68	125.25
山 西 Shanxi	102.48	113.86	104.46	102.35	103.16	126.72
内蒙古 Inner Mongolia	105.60	112.48	100.81	107.76	103.96	119.96
辽 宁 Liaoning	102.13	124.93	100.00	105.87	101.95	133.99
吉 林 Jilin	124.51	111.81	114.39	104.60	134.09	116.11
黑龙江 Heilongjiang	100.41	119.57	92.95	96.85	101.91	124.47
上 海 Shanghai	99.70	107.81	100.00	102.75	90.51	127.27
江 苏 Jiangsu	107.06	127.44	101.14	91.00	109.88	138.92
浙 江 Zhejiang	117.64	131.17	106.23	0.00	121.31	137.46
安 徽 Anhui	105.11	120.18	101.19	105.25	108.42	132.86
福 建 Fujian	103.60	113.90	97.47	105.40	108.07	121.77
江 西 Jiangxi	108.92	125.45	102.93	108.00	110.52	126.84
山 东 Shandong	107.79	115.13	104.51	103.29	112.00	128.07
河 南 Henan	105.22	129.27	99.98	103.84	106.80	147.50
湖 北 Hubei	105.93	128.15	98.17	103.70	106.96	132.95
湖 南 Hunan	111.57	134.80	92.52	106.62	110.97	137.66
广 东 Guangdong	101.04	118.08	102.13	99.36	103.16	124.86
广 西 Guangxi	104.12	132.33	102.63	125.63	104.23	133.76
海 南 Hainan	104.43	115.20	107.31	109.71	106.75	123.64
重 庆 Chongqing	103.18	128.83	104.00	103.62	103.62	130.79
四 川 Sichuan	101.17	121.50	101.99	101.99	102.58	129.71
贵 州 Guizhou	102.55	111.69	102.80	104.60	103.08	112.95
云 南 Yunnan	100.72	116.84	103.20	104.26	100.07	119.65
陕 西 Shaanxi	100.89	115.89	103.74	109.07	99.99	132.84
甘 肃 Gansu	99.58	113.66	101.25	110.50	99.26	115.89
青 海 Qinghai	102.10	106.67	101.99	105.10	103.61	122.32
宁 夏 Ningxia	101.00	109.22	100.90	105.48	90.50	122.59
新 疆 Xinjiang	95.96	102.95	95.96	100.07	100.00	118.51

2—11 续表 1 continued 1

地　区 Region	畜牧业产品 Livestock products			
	家禽(毛重) Poultry		禽蛋 Eggs	
	2003	2004	2003	2004
全　国 National Total	**101.00**	**111.25**	**101.06**	**112.58**
北　京 Beijing	100.77	103.68	103.28	109.66
天　津 Tianjin	96.40	104.08	101.62	118.54
河　北 Hebei	101.97	111.27	97.97	113.91
山　西 Shanxi	106.46	103.33	96.51	111.97
内蒙古 Inner Mongolia	105.52	112.76	105.68	119.98
辽　宁 Liaoning	101.88	111.64	102.92	115.94
吉　林 Jilin	117.60	119.65	124.80	116.24
黑龙江 Heilongjiang	98.95	119.76	90.67	125.63
上　海 Shanghai	89.95	95.12	227.59	116.19
江　苏 Jiangsu	106.58	112.00	106.48	114.05
浙　江 Zhejiang	113.55	114.72	103.45	115.02
安　徽 Anhui	102.17	112.78	95.16	112.01
福　建 Fujian	102.81	113.23	101.14	116.71
江　西 Jiangxi	107.05	106.27	93.05	113.57
山　东 Shandong	107.34	104.28	105.78	114.61
河　南 Henan	108.03	114.35	101.20	117.20
湖　北 Hubei	105.43	111.52	102.85	114.08
湖　南 Hunan	105.38	116.55	100.34	116.62
广　东 Guangdong	96.20	106.23	102.96	114.83
广　西 Guangxi	102.36	111.10	102.32	103.19
海　南 Hainan	100.82	105.94	100.33	103.12
重　庆 Chongqing	98.55	117.21	103.01	111.95
四　川 Sichuan	98.84	114.40	99.59	109.33
贵　州 Guizhou	97.44	108.46	99.29	107.61
云　南 Yunnan	99.55	109.51	96.43	105.29
陕　西 Shaanxi	106.45	113.83	96.80	111.23
甘　肃 Gansu	109.88	110.84	95.76	113.16
青　海 Qinghai	98.54	101.88	101.21	108.21
宁　夏 Ningxia	97.10	109.39	97.70	111.02
新　疆 Xinjiang	100.00	106.29	100.00	94.67

2—11 续表 2 continued 2

地 区 Region	畜产品 Livestock products					
	牛 Live cattle		羊 Sheep raising		马 Horse	
	2003	2004	2003	2004	2003	2004
全 国 National Total	**101.68**	**103.93**	**96.34**	**103.72**	**102.52**	**108.63**
北 京 Beijing	100.00	103.63	100.00	102.44		
天 津 Tianjin	100.10	99.47	99.70	97.38		
河 北 Hebei	101.69	103.07	101.06	100.72		
山 西 Shanxi	107.37	107.44	103.09	101.18		
内 蒙 古 Inner Mongolia	99.83	103.34	101.22	106.99	104.11	112.37
辽 宁 Liaoning	101.63	105.33	99.26	109.27		
吉 林 Jilin	114.39	100.40	121.10	98.36		
黑 龙 江 Heilongjiang	92.94	96.58	98.67	97.48		
上 海 Shanghai	100.00	0.00	100.00	0.00		
江 苏 Jiangsu	101.08	100.00	100.64	0.00		
浙 江 Zhejiang	100.00	0.00	100.00	139.31		
安 徽 Anhui	101.37	102.45	100.00	108.34		
福 建 Fujian	98.45	102.04	96.64	114.77		
江 西 Jiangxi	106.94	108.00	100.00	100.88		
山 东 Shandong	105.29	103.96	102.73	102.05		
河 南 Henan	97.16	104.17	104.17	102.82	100.00	0.00
湖 北 Hubei	97.88	105.99	100.81	97.70	100.00	0.00
湖 南 Hunan	83.09	108.44	120.68	105.62	100.00	125.00
广 东 Guangdong	105.28	102.73	93.86	113.42	100.00	0.00
广 西 Guangxi	103.08	129.37	92.31	105.30	111.11	0.00
海 南 Hainan	108.60	109.22	104.71	110.69		
重 庆 Chongqing	104.56	101.75	102.31	111.09		
四 川 Sichuan	91.39	100.04	112.18	102.75		
贵 州 Guizhou	103.76	104.41	100.00	106.12	100.09	108.74
云 南 Yunnan	101.99	107.18	103.57	103.77	100.00	103.21
陕 西 Shaanxi	102.60	101.14	105.50	105.33	100.00	0.00
甘 肃 Gansu	101.76	104.58	101.20	114.58	100.00	0.00
青 海 Qinghai	105.11	101.80	101.15	103.27	100.05	100.40
宁 夏 Ningxia	106.60	102.61	98.40	101.76	100.00	0.00
新 疆 Xinjiang	101.80	101.05	93.94	102.00	100.00	100.00

2—11 续表 3 continued 3

地 区 Region	畜产品 Livestock products					
	牛肉 Beef		羊肉 Mutton		猪肉 Pork	
	2003	2004	2003	2004	2003	2004
全 国 National Total	**105.20**	**102.28**	**104.93**	**103.13**	**103.42**	**121.99**
北 京 Beijing	104.98	102.93	100.00	100.00	103.30	109.77
天 津 Tianjin			100.00	0.00	100.00	0.00
河 北 Hebei	102.53		102.13	100.00	99.19	124.78
山 西 Shanxi	105.54	100.55	106.98	107.03	103.28	110.56
内蒙古 Inner Mongolia	100.89	110.39	100.48	113.56	107.73	119.18
辽 宁 Liaoning	103.14		100.00	118.68	98.80	127.71
吉 林 Jilin	100.00		100.00	130.43	100.00	112.39
黑龙江 Heilongjiang	100.00	88.23	100.00	114.29	100.72	113.92
上 海 Shanghai	100.00	0.00	100.00		100.00	102.27
江 苏 Jiangsu	100.00	100.00	100.00		100.00	0.00
浙 江 Zhejiang	100.00	0.00	100.00		100.00	123.18
安 徽 Anhui	100.00	115.74	100.00		100.00	129.00
福 建 Fujian	100.00	111.80	90.96		106.09	121.77
江 西 Jiangxi	100.00	112.88	100.00		108.26	127.61
山 东 Shandong	100.00	105.73	100.00	95.97	102.84	122.22
河 南 Henan	100.00		100.00		99.99	117.97
湖 北 Hubei	100.00	100.00	100.00	107.58	90.91	119.25
湖 南 Hunan	103.97		144.93	100.00	107.59	128.68
广 东 Guangdong	100.00	109.09	100.00		103.62	130.65
广 西 Guangxi	100.00		100.00		102.96	115.18
海 南 Hainan	104.85	109.16	100.71	112.51	104.08	113.85
重 庆 Chongqing	100.00	0.00	100.00	106.30	102.37	115.89
四 川 Sichuan	100.00	103.35	100.00	98.17	102.58	108.36
贵 州 Guizhou	100.00	93.75	100.00		99.95	114.65
云 南 Yunnan	93.75	100.00	120.00		101.95	110.98
陕 西 Shaanxi	100.00	112.22	99.62	104.01	107.61	117.71
甘 肃 Gansu	105.69	105.49	105.09	114.45	101.02	116.69
青 海 Qinghai	100.00		100.00	102.94	100.00	107.21
宁 夏 Ningxia	100.00	107.39	100.00	95.44	100.00	114.16
新 疆 Xinjiang	101.80	90.05	93.94	85.72	102.60	105.63

2—11 续表 4 continued 4

地　区 Region	畜产品 Livestock products					
	鸡 Chicken		鸭 Duck		鹅 Goose	
	2003	2004	2003	2004	2003	2004
全　国 National Total	**101.02**	**111.22**	**95.81**	**116.32**	**101.83**	**113.47**
北　京 Beijing	102.98	105.08	95.66	100.74	100.00	
天　津 Tianjin	98.05	102.46	92.96	113.65	100.00	
河　北 Hebei	101.97	111.28	107.30	114.12	100.94	110.55
山　西 Shanxi	106.46	103.33	100.00	0.00	100.00	
内蒙古 Inner Mongolia	106.07	112.27	97.89	113.22	101.03	116.86
辽　宁 Liaoning	114.81	111.62	92.59	117.40	98.25	110.28
吉　林 Jilin	114.24	117.88	121.82	125.78	128.45	122.44
黑龙江 Heilongjiang	97.80	118.69	99.67	132.75	109.20	112.10
上　海 Shanghai	89.95	95.12	100.00	0.00	100.00	0.00
江　苏 Jiangsu	107.48	112.24	104.22	111.34	102.69	112.42
浙　江 Zhejiang	118.95	116.80	109.33	112.58	100.00	134.80
安　徽 Anhui	102.91	113.77	99.98	107.94	100.63	122.12
福　建 Fujian	104.94	113.23	100.93	114.10	103.28	100.29
江　西 Jiangxi	108.19	101.08	107.22	109.06	101.40	115.60
山　东 Shandong	106.88	103.94	112.95	108.92	104.98	102.07
河　南 Henan	108.03	114.35	120.10	116.87	103.34	109.99
湖　北 Hubei	105.45	112.52	105.49	105.83	100.00	
湖　南 Hunan	106.09	111.31	102.55	121.51	111.57	123.59
广　东 Guangdong	94.89	104.96	96.60	106.60	103.55	106.58
广　西 Guangxi	102.23	109.76	101.42	114.89	102.70	122.95
海　南 Hainan	100.44	106.06	101.81	105.65	110.13	103.10
重　庆 Chongqing	101.69	114.54	96.32	119.46	95.97	116.41
四　川 Sichuan	99.53	111.89	99.30	121.35	95.35	112.16
贵　州 Guizhou	96.59	108.91	101.60	107.32	97.16	105.65
云　南 Yunnan	99.55	109.50	97.69	110.66	104.22	107.96
陕　西 Shaanxi	107.05	113.86	100.00	95.24	94.28	
甘　肃 Gansu	109.88	110.84	100.00	0.00		
青　海 Qinghai	98.54	101.88	100.00	0.00	100.00	
宁　夏 Ningxia	97.10	109.39		0.00	100.00	
新　疆 Xinjiang	103.12	106.29	86.30	150.94	91.34	

2—11 续表 5 continued 5

地 区 Region	畜产品 Livestock products					
	鸡蛋 Chicken's eggs		鸭 蛋 Duck's eggs		鹅蛋 Goose's eggs	
	2003	2004	2003	2004	2003	2004
全 国 National Total	**101.06**	**112.54**	**101.61**	**113.95**	**100.35**	**105.95**
北 京 Beijing	103.28	109.66	100.00	0.00	100.00	
天 津 Tianjin	101.62	118.54	100.00	0.00	100.00	
河 北 Hebei	97.97	113.98	102.91	100.00	96.34	112.24
山 西 Shanxi	96.51	111.97	100.00	0.00	100.00	
内蒙古 Inner Mongolia	105.70	119.99	104.52	110.24	100.07	118.50
辽 宁 Liaoning	102.84	115.45	94.54	125.42	114.50	115.44
吉 林 Jilin	121.84	116.90	135.59	116.58	130.12	106.87
黑龙江 Heilongjiang	90.59	125.78	99.26	118.16	98.29	115.88
上 海 Shanghai	156.03	116.19	392.67	0.00	100.00	
江 苏 Jiangsu	106.50	113.99	101.17	124.75	100.00	100.14
浙 江 Zhejiang	108.64	100.39	101.25	128.61	100.00	
安 徽 Anhui	94.65	112.43	99.38	109.90	100.00	
福 建 Fujian	101.20	111.36	101.10	120.00	100.00	
江 西 Jiangxi	102.28	111.32	90.92	114.39	100.00	
山 东 Shandong	107.10	115.10	96.47	113.06	91.69	104.50
河 南 Henan	101.20	117.20	109.86	106.03	103.45	
湖 北 Hubei	103.70	112.26	99.84	120.69	100.00	
湖 南 Hunan	104.04	113.93	98.05	118.29	100.00	
广 东 Guangdong	99.93	106.76	103.02	118.07	100.00	
广 西 Guangxi	102.03	108.31	102.34	103.12	100.00	
海 南 Hainan	98.99	99.23	102.20	108.58	100.00	
重 庆 Chongqing	102.03	112.27	104.58	115.20	96.86	99.25
四 川 Sichuan	98.75	110.44	99.55	108.09	105.83	104.80
贵 州 Guizhou	99.87	108.15	96.97	105.35	96.87	108.33
云 南 Yunnan	96.45	104.74	96.84	110.00	84.45	101.51
陕 西 Shaanxi	96.80	111.23	90.88		100.00	
甘 肃 Gansu	95.76	113.16	106.67		100.00	
青 海 Qinghai	101.21	108.21	100.00		100.00	
宁 夏 Ningxia	97.70	111.02	100.00		100.00	
新 疆 Xinjiang	107.46	94.67	109.52	103.64	100.00	96.70

2—11 续表 6 continued 6

地 区 Region	畜产品 Livestock products			
	牛奶 Cow milk		羊奶 Sheep milk	
	2003	2004	2003	2004
全 国 National Total	**103.67**	**103.73**	**105.90**	**105.30**
北 京 Beijing	98.96	100.75	100.00	
天 津 Tianjin	100.56	103.31	100.00	
河 北 Hebei	101.02	102.66	99.58	95.37
山 西 Shanxi	108.33	95.23	100.00	0.00
内蒙古 Inner Mongolia	104.37	100.19	100.00	100.00
辽 宁 Liaoning	100.00	0.00	100.00	
吉 林 Jilin	191.79	102.85	100.00	
黑龙江 Heilongjiang	111.50	102.62	100.00	
上 海 Shanghai	97.06	102.75	100.00	
江 苏 Jiangsu	100.00	100.00	100.00	100.00
浙 江 Zhejiang		124.41		
安 徽 Anhui	104.87	105.35	100.00	
福 建 Fujian	100.69	101.81	98.99	100.00
江 西 Jiangxi	100.00		100.00	
山 东 Shandong	112.44	100.48	124.41	77.79
河 南 Henan	100.00	0.00	100.00	
湖 北 Hubei	100.00	0.00	100.00	
湖 南 Hunan	130.65	87.84	100.00	
广 东 Guangdong	103.70	88.43	100.00	
广 西 Guangxi	100.00	0.00	100.00	
海 南 Hainan	100.00	0.00	100.00	
重 庆 Chongqing	106.67	0.00	100.00	
四 川 Sichuan	128.64	105.68	100.00	101.40
贵 州 Guizhou	91.74	99.84	100.00	
云 南 Yunnan	118.87	104.84	84.04	87.08
陕 西 Shaanxi	106.74	111.04	111.84	104.62
甘 肃 Gansu	100.88	108.06	100.00	103.40
青 海 Qinghai	98.85	100.48	100.00	
宁 夏 Ningxia	109.50	111.85	100.00	
新 疆 Xinjiang	97.72	101.21	100.00	100.00

2—11 续表 7 continued 7

地　　区　Region	畜产品　Livestock products			
	山羊毛 Goat's wool		绵羊毛 Sheep's wool	
	2003	2004	2003	2004
全　　国　National Total	**85.72**	**98.98**	**100.87**	**105.47**
北　　京　Beijing	100.00	0.00	100.00	100.00
天　　津　Tianjin		0.00	100.00	0.00
河　　北　Hebei	95.76	95.88	105.70	122.57
山　　西　Shanxi	97.75	99.47	99.18	109.30
内 蒙 古　Inner Mongolia	106.41	87.56	106.64	100.35
辽　　宁　Liaoning	100.00	123.44	100.00	0.00
吉　　林　Jilin	100.00	0.00	119.37	86.50
黑 龙 江　Heilongjiang	100.00	0.00	135.06	95.94
上　　海　Shanghai	100.00	0.00	100.00	0.00
江　　苏　Jiangsu	100.00	0.00		100.00
浙　　江　Zhejiang	100.00	0.00		0.00
安　　徽　Anhui	100.00	0.00	100.00	0.00
福　　建　Fujian	100.00	0.00		0.00
江　　西　Jiangxi	100.00	0.00	100.00	0.00
山　　东　Shandong	100.00	104.81	35.54	116.13
河　　南　Henan	157.81	100.00	90.56	0.00
湖　　北　Hubei	100.00	0.00	100.00	0.00
湖　　南　Hunan	100.00	0.00	100.00	0.00
广　　东　Guangdong	100.00	0.00	100.00	0.00
广　　西　Guangxi	100.00	0.00	100.00	0.00
海　　南　Hainan	100.00	0.00	100.00	0.00
重　　庆　Chongqing	100.00	0.00		0.00
四　　川　Sichuan	100.00	0.00	100.00	101.62
贵　　州　Guizhou	100.00	0.00	100.00	0.00
云　　南　Yunnan	100.00	0.00	100.00	0.00
陕　　西　Shaanxi	100.00	0.00	107.50	0.00
甘　　肃　Gansu	88.25	100.00	102.82	108.41
青　　海　Qinghai	100.00	85.71	102.48	114.43
宁　　夏　Ningxia	100.00	107.35	118.40	112.38
新　　疆　Xinjiang	100.00	0.00	124.81	97.79

2—11 续表 8　　continued 8

地　区　Region	畜产品　Livestock products			
	山羊绒 Cashmere		绵羊绒 Sheep's down	
	2003	2004	2003	2004
全　国　National Total	**104.92**	**104.71**	**123.64**	**104.55**
北　京　Beijing	100.00	101.15	100.00	
天　津　Tianjin		0.00	100.00	
河　北　Hebei	100.77	0.00	100.00	
山　西　Shanxi	87.06	107.53	100.00	
内蒙古　Inner Mongolia	111.85	110.56	104.88	
辽　宁　Liaoning	96.55	95.73	100.00	
吉　林　Jilin	100.00	527.71	100.00	
黑龙江　Heilongjiang	100.00	120.00	100.00	
上　海　Shanghai	100.00		100.00	0.00
江　苏　Jiangsu	100.00			0.00
浙　江　Zhejiang	100.00			0.00
安　徽　Anhui			100.00	0.00
福　建　Fujian	100.00			0.00
江　西　Jiangxi	100.00			0.00
山　东　Shandong	100.00	114.56	100.00	0.00
河　南　Henan	100.00		100.00	
湖　北　Hubei	100.00		100.00	
湖　南　Hunan	100.00		100.00	
广　东　Guangdong	100.00		100.00	
广　西　Guangxi	100.00		100.00	
海　南　Hainan	100.00		100.00	
重　庆　Chongqing	100.00	0.00	100.00	0.00
四　川　Sichuan	100.00	104.81		102.17
贵　州　Guizhou		0.00	100.00	0.00
云　南　Yunnan	100.00	0.00		0.00
陕　西　Shaanxi	121.36	84.63	100.00	0.00
甘　肃　Gansu	90.19	99.06	93.72	106.93
青　海　Qinghai	101.68	108.50	146.25	
宁　夏　Ningxia	100.00	111.11	100.00	
新　疆　Xinjiang	133.33	126.68	100.00	100.00

2—12 各地区渔业产品生产价格指数
Indices of the Producers Prices of Fishery Products by Region

（上年=100） (the preceding year=100)

地 区 Region	渔业产品 Fishery products		渔业产品 Fishery products			
			海水产品 Seawater aquatic products		内陆水域水产品 Aquatic products in inland water areas	
	2003	2004	2003	2004	2003	2004
全 国 National Total	**100.34**	**110.19**	**101.13**	**109.00**	**98.83**	**112.30**
北 京 Beijing	109.99	106.46			109.99	106.46
天 津 Tianjin	92.66	104.41	101.05	104.10	93.62	105.99
河 北 Hebei	106.14	126.99	108.89	136.98	100.76	107.47
山 西 Shanxi	98.60	102.79			98.60	102.79
内蒙古 Inner Mongolia	109.23	112.35			109.23	112.35
辽 宁 Liaoning	99.17	117.77	104.21	119.03	88.06	103.97
吉 林 Jilin	90.52	87.34			90.52	87.34
黑龙江 Heilongjiang	119.36	104.84			119.36	104.84
上 海 Shanghai	92.95	114.74	100.00	105.91	92.95	124.46
江 苏 Jiangsu	97.74	111.85	106.59	105.11	94.97	112.02
浙 江 Zhejiang	95.75	110.30	97.69		81.93	110.30
安 徽 Anhui	103.11	110.10			103.11	110.10
福 建 Fujian	101.00	107.00	101.14	106.10	101.09	107.40
江 西 Jiangxi	97.46	110.61		0.00	97.46	110.61
山 东 Shandong	105.84	110.05	104.81	109.10	110.90	114.26
河 南 Henan	103.39	109.30			103.39	109.30
湖 北 Hubei	93.49	113.67			93.49	113.67
湖 南 Hunan	101.79	111.76			101.79	111.76
广 东 Guangdong	98.21	106.09	99.89	108.68	97.93	105.67
广 西 Guangxi	96.15	109.86	83.18	90.39	98.53	115.75
海 南 Hainan	97.39	101.46	97.78	100.55	94.32	108.67
重 庆 Chongqing	100.86	107.83			100.86	107.83
四 川 Sichuan	102.30	109.37			102.30	109.37
贵 州 Guizhou	95.88	106.20			95.88	106.20
云 南 Yunnan	98.30	111.63			98.30	111.63
陕 西 Shaanxi	115.76	110.25			115.76	110.25
甘 肃 Gansu	98.94	100.00			98.94	100.00
青 海 Qinghai	100.00				100.00	
宁 夏 Ningxia	103.20	132.87			103.20	132.87
新 疆 Xinjiang	120.12	122.90			120.12	122.90

2—12 续表 1 continued 1

地 区 Region	海水产品 Seawater aquatic products		海水产品 Seawater aquatic products 鱼类 Seawater Fish	
	2003	2004	2003	2004
全 国 National Total	**101.13**	**109.00**	**103.98**	**109.16**
天 津 Tianjin	101.05	104.10	100.00	103.64
河 北 Hebei	108.89	136.98	100.00	0.00
辽 宁 Liaoning	104.21	119.03	113.06	127.51
上 海 Shanghai	100.00	105.91	100.00	93.92
江 苏 Jiangsu	106.59	105.11	104.36	105.50
浙 江 Zhejiang	97.69		100.00	0.00
福 建 Fujian	101.14	106.10	101.28	109.27
山 东 Shandong	104.81	109.10	103.58	115.46
广 东 Guangdong	99.89	108.68	94.67	97.65
广 西 Guangxi	83.18	90.39	91.17	88.79
海 南 Hainan	97.78	100.55	96.85	100.13

2—12 续表 2 continued 2

地 区 Region	海水产品 Seawater aquatic products			
	贝类 Seawater shellfish		藻类 Seaweeds	
	2003	2004	2003	2004
全 国 National Total	**97.80**	**109.17**	**102.66**	**120.68**
天 津 Tianjin			100.00	
河 北 Hebei	114.15	163.16	100.00	
辽 宁 Liaoning	92.94	101.91	100.00	87.84
上 海 Shanghai	100.00	0.00		0.00
江 苏 Jiangsu	102.96	100.00	100.00	100.00
浙 江 Zhejiang	100.00	0.00	100.00	0.00
福 建 Fujian	101.36	105.18	102.07	107.59
山 东 Shandong	102.27	103.97	117.61	135.00
广 东 Guangdong	123.92	113.86	100.00	0.00
广 西 Guangxi	73.99	92.36	100.00	0.00
海 南 Hainan	95.10	111.11	105.23	131.62

2—12 续表 3 continued 3

地 区 Region	海水产品 Seawater aquatic products					
	大黄鱼 Large yellow croaker		小黄鱼 Small yellow croaker		带鱼 Hairtail	
	2003	2004	2003	2004	2003	2004
全 国 National Total	**94.01**	**108.66**	**97.68**	**110.53**	**102.75**	**107.29**
天 津 Tianjin	100.00		100.00		100.00	
河 北 Hebei	100.00				100.00	
辽 宁 Liaoning	88.56	115.44	113.08	130.60	119.03	138.13
上 海 Shanghai	100.00	0.00	100.00	0.00	100.00	0.00
江 苏 Jiangsu	100.00	100.00	100.28	100.36	114.65	118.38
浙 江 Zhejiang	100.00	0.00	100.00	0.00		0.00
福 建 Fujian	116.76	105.54	106.97	95.85	104.14	112.01
山 东 Shandong	100.00	120.00	92.28	108.05	113.16	134.27
广 东 Guangdong	100.00	0.00	100.00	0.00	94.78	100.34
广 西 Guangxi	100.00	0.00	106.02	97.33	100.00	0.00
海 南 Hainan	100.00	0.00	101.49	104.28	101.49	96.05

2—12 续表 4 continued 4

地 区 Region	海水产品 Seawater aquatic products					
	鳕鱼 Cod		鲳鱼 Silvery pomfret		鲅鱼 Spanish mackerel	
	2003	2004	2003	2004	2003	2004
全 国 National Total	**96.64**	**93.92**	**96.95**	**113.63**	**107.18**	**109.76**
天 津 Tianjin	100.00			103.64	100.00	0.00
河 北 Hebei	100.00		100.00		100.00	0.00
辽 宁 Liaoning	100.00		100.00		116.64	125.33
上 海 Shanghai		93.92	100.00		100.00	0.00
江 苏 Jiangsu	100.00	0.00	96.79	117.93	100.00	100.00
浙 江 Zhejiang	100.00	0.00	100.00	0.00	100.00	0.00
福 建 Fujian	100.00	0.00	100.62	109.65	100.00	0.00
山 东 Shandong	96.64	0.00	99.99	94.91	105.00	113.11
广 东 Guangdong	100.00	0.00	100.00	0.00	100.00	0.00
广 西 Guangxi	100.00	0.00		0.00	100.00	0.00
海 南 Hainan	100.00	0.00	103.39	111.92	103.28	0.00

2—12 续表 5 continued 5

地 区 Region	海水产品 Seawater aquatic products					
	对虾 Prawn		毛虾 Shrimp		梭子蟹 Swimming crab	
	2003	2004	2003	2004	2003	2004
全 国 National Total	**101.93**	**103.32**	**110.09**	**105.65**	**109.68**	**108.61**
天 津 Tianjin	84.39	0.00	100.00	0.00	117.70	135.53
河 北 Hebei	99.92	90.14	146.41	82.14	84.85	99.45
辽 宁 Liaoning	95.61	103.35	93.45		95.68	81.19
上 海 Shanghai	100.00	109.88	100.00		100.00	101.23
江 苏 Jiangsu	100.00	100.00		100.00	100.00	100.00
浙 江 Zhejiang	100.00		100.00		100.00	
福 建 Fujian	99.71	100.13	98.04	105.47	106.98	133.33
山 东 Shandong	108.63	100.12	103.22		109.45	106.94
广 东 Guangdong	90.17	122.91	109.32	95.86	100.00	
广 西 Guangxi	83.74	92.71	100.00		132.58	98.58
海 南 Hainan	101.37	102.00	106.67	109.27	97.64	119.75

2－12续表6 continued 6

地　区 Region	内陆水域水产品 Aquatic products in inland water areas		淡水产品 Aquatic products in inland water areas 淡水鱼类 Freshwater fish		淡水虾蟹类 Freshwater shrimps and crabs	
	2003	2004	2003	2004	2003	2004
全　国 National Total	**98.83**	**112.30**	**98.65**	**111.52**	**104.13**	**122.97**
北　京 Beijing	109.99	106.46	109.99	111.09	100.00	0.00
天　津 Tianjin	93.62	105.99	92.49	107.56	109.98	101.24
河　北 Hebei	100.76	107.47	100.76	107.47	100.00	0.00
山　西 Shanxi	98.60	102.79	98.60	102.79	100.00	0.00
内蒙古 Inner Mongolia	109.23	112.35	109.23	112.35	100.00	0.00
辽　宁 Liaoning	88.06	103.97	88.06	103.97	100.00	0.00
吉　林 Jilin	90.52	87.34	90.52	87.34	100.00	0.00
黑龙江 Heilongjiang	119.36	104.84	119.36	104.84	100.00	0.00
上　海 Shanghai	92.95	124.46	94.60	130.59	89.31	100.17
江　苏 Jiangsu	94.97	112.02	98.92	119.36	90.23	102.74
浙　江 Zhejiang	81.93	110.30	90.05	120.42	64.33	92.37
安　徽 Anhui	103.11	110.10	105.76	109.33	86.66	113.35
福　建 Fujian	101.09	107.40	101.37	114.97	98.64	118.05
江　西 Jiangxi	97.46	110.61	97.60	110.61	91.48	0.00
山　东 Shandong	110.90	114.26	110.90	113.64	100.00	120.00
河　南 Henan	103.39	109.30	103.39	109.30	100.00	0.00
湖　北 Hubei	93.49	113.67	92.03	113.41	131.59	120.36
湖　南 Hunan	101.79	111.76	99.71	112.15	129.12	162.90
广　东 Guangdong	97.93	105.67	100.28	106.82	96.93	90.38
广　西 Guangxi	98.53	115.75	98.53	115.75	100.00	0.00
海　南 Hainan	94.32	108.67	94.05	110.12	98.45	101.46
重　庆 Chongqing	100.86	107.83	100.86	107.83	100.00	0.00
四　川 Sichuan	102.30	109.37	102.30	109.37	100.00	0.00
贵　州 Guizhou	95.88	106.20	95.88	106.20	100.00	0.00
云　南 Yunnan	98.30	111.63	98.30	111.63	100.00	0.00
陕　西 Shaanxi	115.76	110.25	115.76	110.25	100.00	0.00
甘　肃 Gansu	98.94	100.00	98.94	100.00	100.00	0.00
青　海 Qinghai	100.00	0.00	100.00	0.00	100.00	0.00
宁　夏 Ningxia	103.20	132.87	103.20	132.87	100.00	0.00
新　疆 Xinjiang	120.12	122.90	120.12	122.90	100.00	0.00

2—12 续表 7 continued 7

地　区 Region	内陆水域水产品 Aquatic products in inland water areas			
	青鱼 Black carp		草鱼 Grass carp	
	2003	2004	2003	2004
全　国 National Total	**99.28**	**106.65**	**97.33**	**115.47**
北　京 Beijing			101.57	114.35
天　津 Tianjin	100.00		98.08	101.74
河　北 Hebei	100.00		103.71	109.00
山　西 Shanxi	100.00		100.00	0.00
内蒙古 Inner Mongolia			132.47	111.19
辽　宁 Liaoning	100.00		97.46	0.00
吉　林 Jilin	100.00		100.00	0.00
黑龙江 Heilongjiang			100.00	0.00
上　海 Shanghai	100.00		94.02	128.04
江　苏 Jiangsu	97.42	101.53	103.40	120.08
浙　江 Zhejiang	100.00	0.00	98.79	123.78
安　徽 Anhui	77.54	111.99	96.88	111.42
福　建 Fujian	72.90	133.98	94.27	112.86
江　西 Jiangxi	102.58	105.26	108.12	115.26
山　东 Shandong	100.00	134.12	100.00	111.25
河　南 Henan	100.83	103.06	100.00	123.60
湖　北 Hubei	106.32	102.91	88.19	113.55
湖　南 Hunan	104.70	98.99	95.22	117.07
广　东 Guangdong	101.22	114.89	101.56	110.68
广　西 Guangxi	100.00	0.00	99.99	108.61
海　南 Hainan	100.00	0.00	100.00	114.61
重　庆 Chongqing	100.00	107.69	120.96	108.50
四　川 Sichuan	115.70	104.12	97.56	110.78
贵　州 Guizhou	100.09		92.37	98.28
云　南 Yunnan	100.00		98.10	112.62
陕　西 Shaanxi			117.35	115.42
甘　肃 Gansu	100.00			0.00
青　海 Qinghai			100.00	0.00
宁　夏 Ningxia	100.00			157.58
新　疆 Xinjiang	100.00		103.86	114.36

2—12 续表 8 continued 8

地区 Region	内陆水域水产品 Aquatic products in inland water areas			
	鲤鱼 Carp		鲢鱼 Silver carp	
	2003	2004	2003	2004
全国 National Total	**101.06**	**112.06**	**97.28**	**113.29**
北京 Beijing	106.08	116.79	138.64	106.17
天津 Tianjin	103.60	107.78	92.28	115.87
河北 Hebei	97.46	118.22	108.18	101.91
山西 Shanxi	100.00	113.79	100.00	107.21
内蒙古 Inner Mongolia	102.78	110.25	112.14	118.31
辽宁 Liaoning	97.21		69.53	0.00
吉林 Jilin	100.00			0.00
黑龙江 Heilongjiang	119.98	103.27	103.08	110.75
上海 Shanghai	100.00		99.71	128.89
江苏 Jiangsu	100.21	109.41	98.33	122.89
浙江 Zhejiang	74.44	100.00	84.65	0.00
安徽 Anhui	115.78	111.91	109.15	104.69
福建 Fujian	104.43	107.76	103.88	103.02
江西 Jiangxi	91.88	108.08	81.43	110.14
山东 Shandong	106.23	118.64	119.91	111.86
河南 Henan	105.20	117.90	101.40	99.82
湖北 Hubei	93.23	110.97	90.60	118.80
湖南 Hunan	106.55	101.90	99.25	114.48
广东 Guangdong	105.35	103.85	103.03	103.79
广西 Guangxi	103.90	107.59	97.30	122.53
海南 Hainan		108.92	100.00	105.17
重庆 Chongqing	95.57	123.29	102.17	104.71
四川 Sichuan	104.95	108.79	100.52	106.55
贵州 Guizhou	97.42	110.20	100.00	104.86
云南 Yunnan	102.84	102.59	99.01	101.55
陕西 Shaanxi	121.05	112.61	97.72	101.41
甘肃 Gansu	98.94	100.00	100.00	0.00
青海 Qinghai	136.36	0.00		0.00
宁夏 Ningxia	103.20	129.77	100.00	95.38
新疆 Xinjiang	138.31	126.66	110.32	108.97

2—12 续表 9 continued 9

地 区 Region	内陆水域水产品 Aquatic products in inland water areas					
	鲫鱼 Crucian carp		罗非鱼 Tilapia		鲶鱼 Oriental sheatfish	
	2003	2004	2003	2004	2003	2004
全 国 National Total	**98.06**	**109.33**	**96.57**	**104.88**	**98.02**	**108.62**
北 京 Beijing	100.00	0.00	99.01	109.30	100.00	0.00
天 津 Tianjin	87.36	110.68	100.00	0.00	100.00	0.00
河 北 Hebei	97.70	104.43	100.00	0.00	100.00	0.00
山 西 Shanxi	100.00	0.00	98.52	101.59		0.00
内 蒙 古 Inner Mongolia	114.31	110.37	100.00	100.00	100.00	0.00
辽 宁 Liaoning	100.00	103.97	100.00	0.00	111.18	0.00
吉 林 Jilin	90.52	87.34	100.00	0.00	95.57	0.00
黑 龙 江 Heilongjiang	114.69	107.73	100.00	0.00	100.00	0.00
上 海 Shanghai	92.46	136.40	100.00	0.00	100.00	0.00
江 苏 Jiangsu	93.30	115.38	100.00	100.00	100.00	100.00
浙 江 Zhejiang	114.39	127.53	100.00	0.00	100.00	0.00
安 徽 Anhui	98.14	109.44		0.00	100.00	106.16
福 建 Fujian	101.99	106.99	100.31	106.80	100.00	0.00
江 西 Jiangxi	119.04	102.56	100.00	0.00		90.97
山 东 Shandong	100.00	110.06	100.00	102.86	103.45	104.59
河 南 Henan	92.31	118.22	100.00	0.00	100.00	0.00
湖 北 Hubei	95.10	111.13	100.00	0.00		111.80
湖 南 Hunan	101.49	99.65	100.00	0.00	116.67	108.68
广 东 Guangdong	98.90	99.76	90.38	101.94	99.40	111.23
广 西 Guangxi	100.00	0.00	98.97	80.44	68.95	93.82
海 南 Hainan	100.00	105.90	97.29	112.94	100.00	0.00
重 庆 Chongqing	100.00	102.54		0.00	100.00	0.00
四 川 Sichuan	109.01	113.55	100.00	0.00	91.67	102.89
贵 州 Guizhou	138.61	103.77	100.00	0.00	100.00	0.00
云 南 Yunnan	98.53	107.41	98.93	99.97	100.00	0.00
陕 西 Shaanxi	100.00	100.00	100.00	0.00		0.00
甘 肃 Gansu		0.00	100.00	0.00	100.00	0.00
青 海 Qinghai	100.00	0.00		0.00	100.00	0.00
宁 夏 Ningxia	100.00	127.95	100.00	0.00		0.00
新 疆 Xinjiang	83.36	121.04	94.86	107.14	100.00	0.00

3

农产品集贸市场价格

Prices of the Agricultural Products at the Rural Market Fairs

3—1 全国农产品集贸市场年度价格及走势
Annual RMF Prices of the Agricultural Products

		2000	2001	2002	2003	2004
一、价 格	Price					
(元/公斤)	(yuan/ kg)					
籼 稻	Long-grained nonglutinous rice	1.01	1.05	1.04	1.08	1.51
优质籼稻	High quality long-grained nonglutinous rice	1.18	1.24	1.16	1.25	1.72
粳 稻	Round-grained rice	1.27	1.31	1.15	1.20	1.72
小 麦	Wheat	1.02	1.09	1.06	1.14	1.52
玉 米	Corn	0.88	1.08	1.03	1.14	1.40
大 豆	Soybeans	2.53	2.43	2.38	2.96	3.88
籼 米	Polished long-grained nonglutinous rice			1.62	1.79	2.48
优质籼米	High quality polished long-grained nonglutinous rice			1.90	2.10	2.87
粳 米	Polished round-grained rice			1.92	2.02	2.84
面 粉	Wheat flour			1.71	1.82	2.35
二、价格变动	Index					
(上年=100)	(preceding year=100)					
籼 稻	Long-grained nonglutinous rice	82.44	104.70	98.63	103.63	140.41
优质籼稻	High quality long-grained nonglutinous rice		105.10	93.62	107.46	137.92
粳 稻	Round-grained rice	91.39	102.89	87.99	104.06	143.26
小 麦	Wheat	82.02	107.09	96.46	107.64	133.30
玉 米	Corn	81.99	122.78	95.18	111.31	122.57
大 豆	Soybeans	93.23	96.36	97.75	124.51	130.98
籼 米	Polished long-grained nonglutinous rice				110.56	138.91
优质籼米	High quality polished long-grained nonglutinous rice				110.41	136.75
粳 米	Polished round-grained rice				105.03	140.48
面 粉	Wheat flour				106.20	129.65

Note: RMF refer to the selected Rural Market Faires.

3－1 续表 1 continued 1

		2000	2001	2002	2003	2004
一、价　格	Price					
(元/公斤)	(yuan/ kg)					
棉花(籽棉)	Cotton (unginned cotton)	3.33	3.55	3.35	4.80	5.60
花生仁	Peanut kernel			4.32	5.60	6.75
油菜籽	Rapeseeds			1.92	2.40	2.85
花生油	Peanut oil	8.49	8.04	7.88	9.43	11.15
菜籽油	Rape oil	6.73	5.98	5.79	6.85	7.99
豆　油	Soybean oil	6.37	5.50	5.50	6.74	7.71
烤　烟	Flue-cured tobacco			7.70	8.54	10.08
大白菜	Chinese cabbage			0.75	1.01	1.00
黄　瓜	Cucumber			1.81	2.07	2.03
西红柿	Tomato			1.88	2.21	2.18
菜　椒	Green bell			2.21	2.62	2.60
四季豆	Kidney Beans			2.48	2.69	2.80
红富士苹果	Hongfushi Apple			2.93	3.35	3.47
香　蕉	Banana			2.91	3.11	3.49
橙　子	Orange			2.88	3.41	3.55
二、价格变动	Index					
(上年=100)	(preceding year=100)					
棉花(籽棉)	Cotton (unginned cotton)		106.65	94.41	143.16	116.59
花生仁	Peanut kernel				129.60	120.66
油菜籽	Rapeseeds				125.07	118.98
花生油	Peanut oil		94.69	97.99	119.78	118.18
菜籽油	Rape oil		88.95	96.73	118.43	116.64
豆　油	Soybean oil		86.43	99.92	122.53	114.47
烤　烟	Flue-cured tobacco				110.97	117.98
大白菜	Chinese cabbage				134.02	98.68
黄　瓜	Cucumber				114.14	98.06
西红柿	Tomato				117.08	98.93
菜　椒	Green bell				118.89	99.21
四季豆	Kidney Beans				108.47	104.08
红富士苹果	Hongfushi Apple				114.22	103.81
香　蕉	Banana				107.03	112.22
橙　子	Orange				118.58	104.07

3—1 续表 2 continued 2

		2000	2001	2002	2003	2004
一、价 格	Price					
(元/公斤)	(yuan/ kg)					
草 鱼	Grass carp	7.25	7.24	7.10	7.24	9.10
鲤 鱼	Carp	7.73	7.52	6.84	7.01	8.90
鲢 鱼	Silver carp			5.71	5.70	7.03
带 鱼	Hairtail			8.95	9.33	10.13
活 猪	Hog	5.51	5.80	5.56	6.12	8.44
仔 猪	Piglet	7.16	7.64	7.37	7.91	12.14
猪 肉	Pork	9.68	10.18	9.85	10.70	13.97
牛 肉	Beef	12.53	12.86	13.66	14.99	16.21
羊 肉	Mutton	14.55	14.58	15.16	16.16	16.98
活 鸡	Live chicken			8.39	8.80	10.09
鸡 蛋	Eggs	4.98	5.20	5.43	5.37	6.40
二、价格变动	Index					
(上年=100)	(preceding year=100)					
草 鱼	Grass carp		99.83	98.04	102.06	125.70
鲤 鱼	Carp		97.31	90.94	102.48	126.98
鲢 鱼	Silver carp				99.85	123.28
带 鱼	Hairtail				104.26	108.49
活 猪	Hog		105.31	95.92	109.90	137.97
仔 猪	Piglet		106.81	96.46	107.23	153.60
猪 肉	Pork		105.27	96.74	108.54	130.60
牛 肉	Beef		102.62	106.25	109.74	108.10
羊 肉	Mutton		100.14	103.99	106.61	105.05
活 鸡	Live chicken				104.90	114.68
鸡 蛋	Eggs		104.27	104.51	98.89	119.14

3－2 全国农产品集贸市场季度价格及走势
Quarterly RMF Prices of the Agricultural Products

（第一季度） (1st quarter)

		2000	2001	2002	2003	2004
一、价 格	Price					
（元/公斤）	(yuan/ kg)					
籼 稻	Long-grained nonglutinous rice	1.06	1.01	1.02	1.05	1.36
优质籼稻	High quality long-grained nonglutinous rice	1.22	1.21	1.15	1.22	1.56
粳 稻	Round-grained rice	1.31	1.28	1.17	1.14	1.53
小 麦	Wheat	1.09	1.06	1.08	1.12	1.39
玉 米	Corn	0.85	1.01	1.01	1.06	1.31
大 豆	Soybeans	2.43	2.47	2.31	2.74	3.61
籼 米	Polished long-grained nonglutinous rice			1.60	1.73	2.23
优质籼米	High quality polished long-grained nonglutinous rice			1.88	2.04	2.59
粳 米	Polished round-grained rice			1.92	1.96	2.50
面 粉	Wheat flour			1.72	1.78	2.22
棉 花	Cotton (unginned cotton)	2.96	3.72	2.97	4.22	6.00
花生仁	Peanut kernel			4.08	5.11	6.56
油菜籽	Rapeseeds			1.93	2.22	2.79
花生油	Peanut oil	8.70	8.19	7.78	8.85	11.00
菜籽油	Rape oil	7.31	6.17	5.62	6.41	8.01
豆 油	Soybean oil	6.80	5.61	5.25	6.31	7.84
烤 烟	Flue-cured tobacco			7.58	8.19	9.30
活 猪	Hog	5.48	5.90	5.71	5.77	7.54
仔 猪	Piglet	6.60	7.79	7.56	7.54	9.65
猪 肉	Pork	9.48	10.37	10.01	10.05	12.64
牛 肉	Beef	12.32	13.02	13.45	14.82	16.00
羊 肉	Mutton	14.72	14.80	15.22	16.32	16.98
活 鸡	Live chicken			8.53	8.79	9.44
鸡 蛋	Eggs	4.96	5.01	5.53	5.28	5.93
草 鱼	Grass carp	6.93	7.22	7.18	7.14	8.01
鲤 鱼	Carp	7.31	7.69	6.76	6.86	7.92
鲢 鱼	Silver carp			5.53	5.51	6.38
带 鱼	Hairtail			8.95	9.47	9.60
大白菜	Chinese cabbage			0.54	0.95	0.90
黄 瓜	Cucumber			2.54	3.06	3.01
西红柿	Tomato			2.47	2.89	3.03
菜 椒	Green bell			3.14	3.61	3.55
四季豆	Kidney Beans			3.40	3.81	3.80
红富士苹果	Hongfushi Apple			2.72	3.13	3.14
香 蕉	Banana			3.24	3.13	3.51
橙 子	Orange			2.87	3.17	3.49

3-2续表 continued

		2000	2001	2002	2003	2004
二、价格变动	Index					
（上季度=100）	(preceding quarter=100)					
籼　稻	Long-grained nonglutinous rice	98.32	101.77	95.63	102.49	117.09
优质籼稻	High quality long-grained nonglutinous rice		102.38	92.03	106.84	115.64
粳　稻	Round-grained rice	103.06	100.03	90.26	102.35	116.27
小　麦	Wheat	96.34	103.48	96.53	107.17	111.94
玉　米	Corn	89.59	108.82	95.21	106.54	106.61
大　豆	Soybeans	95.28	100.43	97.49	111.24	109.94
籼　米	Polished long-grained nonglutinous rice				106.45	115.60
优质籼米	High quality polished long-grained nonglutinous rice				106.38	114.21
粳　米	Polished round-grained rice				102.58	114.71
面　粉	Wheat flour				105.18	112.36
棉　花	Cotton (unginned cotton)		104.47	99.08	104.14	99.75
花生仁	Peanut kernel				113.29	107.05
油菜籽	Rapeseeds				110.84	101.19
花生油	Peanut oil		99.18	99.51	109.78	103.76
菜籽油	Rape oil		96.98	96.66	103.80	103.96
豆　油	Soybean oil		94.37	97.95	106.76	103.11
烤　烟	Flue-cured tobacco				114.16	106.95
活　猪	Hog		102.12	96.50	101.21	106.07
仔　猪	Piglet		103.68	101.92	103.01	108.28
猪　肉	Pork		101.28	97.03	100.48	102.64
牛　肉	Beef		102.50	103.13	103.60	102.53
羊　肉	Mutton		101.85	103.07	105.65	102.84
活　鸡	Live chicken				105.49	100.90
鸡　蛋	Eggs		98.33	102.61	97.51	99.35
草　鱼	Grass carp		99.16	99.86	102.94	108.80
鲤　鱼	Carp		101.56	93.71	101.78	110.49
鲢　鱼	Silver carp				97.35	108.51
带　鱼	Hairtail				106.00	102.66
大白菜	Chinese cabbage				136.19	95.21
黄　瓜	Cucumber				146.48	126.55
西红柿	Tomato				146.34	123.01
菜　椒	Green bell				167.37	137.48
四季豆	Kidney Beans				156.22	141.90
红富士苹果	Hongfushi Apple				112.00	101.77
香　蕉	Banana				115.06	107.15
橙　子	Orange				114.18	98.90

3—3 全国农产品集贸市场季度价格及走势
Quarterly RMF Prices of the Agricultural Products

（第二季度） (2nd quarter)

		2000	2001	2002	2003	2004
一、价 格	Price					
（元/公斤）	(yuan/ kg)					
籼 稻	Long-grained nonglutinous rice	1.01	1.06	1.06	1.05	1.58
优质籼稻	High quality long-grained nonglutinous rice	1.19	1.26	1.19	1.21	1.79
粳 稻	Round-grained rice	1.23	1.32	1.17	1.16	1.79
小 麦	Wheat	1.01	1.10	1.06	1.10	1.55
玉 米	Corn	0.84	1.10	1.04	1.13	1.45
大 豆	Soybeans	2.61	2.47	2.35	2.89	4.02
籼 米	Polished long-grained nonglutinous rice			1.61	1.74	2.59
优质籼米	High quality polished long-grained nonglutinous rice			1.89	2.05	2.98
粳 米	Polished round-grained rice			1.92	1.97	2.97
面 粉	Wheat flour			1.72	1.76	2.40
棉 花	Cotton (unginned cotton)	3.37	3.80	3.14	4.39	6.04
花生仁	Peanut kernel			4.22	5.52	6.79
油菜籽	Rapeseeds			1.82	2.22	2.85
花生油	Peanut oil	8.53	8.15	7.68	9.10	11.22
菜籽油	Rape oil	6.80	6.05	5.55	6.59	8.13
豆 油	Soybean oil	6.55	5.62	5.22	6.52	7.94
烤 烟	Flue-cured tobacco			8.07	8.62	9.65
活 猪	Hog	5.27	5.65	5.34	5.57	8.23
仔 猪	Piglet	7.08	7.82	7.36	7.35	11.44
猪 肉	Pork	9.22	9.92	9.57	9.84	13.63
牛 肉	Beef	12.51	12.69	13.29	14.65	15.90
羊 肉	Mutton	14.45	14.45	14.97	15.86	16.85
活 鸡	Live chicken			8.32	8.36	9.78
鸡 蛋	Eggs	4.82	5.02	5.31	5.00	6.08
草 鱼	Grass carp	7.35	7.26	7.11	7.19	9.60
鲤 鱼	Carp	8.06	7.68	6.82	6.90	9.63
鲢 鱼	Silver carp			5.78	5.64	7.25
带 鱼	Hairtail			8.82	9.29	10.14
大白菜	Chinese cabbage			0.77	1.05	1.05
黄 瓜	Cucumber			1.46	1.56	1.61
西红柿	Tomato			1.76	2.05	1.95
菜 椒	Green bell			2.14	2.69	2.71
四季豆	Kidney Beans			2.32	2.51	2.70
红富士苹果	Hongfushi Apple			3.15	3.42	3.67
香 蕉	Banana			3.08	3.05	3.84
橙 子	Orange			2.91	3.30	3.59

3－3 续表 continued

		2000	2001	2002	2003	2004
二、价格变动	Index					
(上季度＝100)	(preceding quarter＝100)					
籼　稻	Long-grained nonglutinous rice	95.27	104.51	104.12	99.46	116.49
优质籼稻	High quality long-grained nonglutinous rice	97.28	104.54	103.40	98.99	114.82
粳　稻	Round-grained rice	93.88	103.05	100.54	102.27	116.88
小　麦	Wheat	93.25	103.78	98.27	98.41	111.36
玉　米	Corn	99.61	108.73	102.77	105.97	110.61
大　豆	Soybeans	107.69	99.84	101.95	105.53	111.37
籼　米	Polished long-grained nonglutinous rice			100.70	100.49	116.51
优质籼米	High quality polished long-grained nonglutinous rice			100.30	100.64	115.33
粳　米	Polished round-grained rice			100.29	100.25	119.04
面　粉	Wheat flour			99.78	98.63	108.04
棉　花	Cotton (unginned cotton)	113.84	102.16	105.53	103.98	100.60
花生仁	Peanut kernel			103.37	108.05	103.61
油菜籽	Rapeseeds			94.27	99.79	102.14
花生油	Peanut oil	98.05	99.51	98.81	102.82	101.94
菜籽油	Rape oil	92.98	98.00	98.71	102.70	101.57
豆　油	Soybean oil	96.42	100.18	99.56	103.39	101.24
烤　烟	Flue-cured tobacco			106.41	105.25	103.77
活　猪	Hog	96.17	95.81	93.48	96.56	109.21
仔　猪	Piglet	107.33	100.30	97.35	97.40	118.52
猪　肉	Pork	97.33	95.67	95.58	97.98	107.82
牛　肉	Beef	101.54	97.43	98.79	98.84	99.42
羊　肉	Mutton	98.14	97.63	98.40	97.21	99.23
活　鸡	Live chicken			97.52	95.10	103.57
鸡　蛋	Eggs	97.11	100.20	96.13	94.69	102.63
草　鱼	Grass carp	106.06	100.60	99.00	100.72	119.97
鲤　鱼	Carp	110.21	99.93	100.89	100.63	121.61
鲢　鱼	Silver carp			104.60	102.47	113.70
带　鱼	Hairtail			98.52	98.07	105.57
大白菜	Chinese cabbage			143.86	109.85	116.46
黄　瓜	Cucumber			57.31	51.05	53.53
西红柿	Tomato			71.40	71.16	64.12
菜　椒	Green bell			68.00	74.46	76.36
四季豆	Kidney Beans			68.12	65.95	71.17
红富士苹果	Hongfushi Apple			115.72	109.17	116.85
香　蕉	Banana			95.10	97.51	109.54
橙　子	Orange			101.30	103.97	102.97

3—4 全国农产品集贸市场季度价格及走势
Quarterly RMF Prices of the Agricultural Products

（第三季度） (3rd quarter)

		2000	2001	2002	2003	2004
一、价 格	Price					
(元/公斤)	(yuan/ kg)					
籼 稻	Long-grained nonglutinous rice	0.96	1.07	1.05	1.05	1.56
优质籼稻	High quality long-grained nonglutinous rice	1.13	1.24	1.16	1.22	1.79
粳 稻	Round-grained rice	1.28	1.35	1.16	1.17	1.79
小 麦	Wheat	0.96	1.10	1.05	1.09	1.55
玉 米	Corn	0.89	1.14	1.06	1.15	1.46
大 豆	Soybeans	2.60	2.43	2.39	2.93	4.07
籼 米	Polished long-grained nonglutinous rice			1.63	1.76	2.58
优质籼米	High quality polished long-grained nonglutinous rice			1.92	2.04	2.97
粳 米	Polished round-grained rice			1.94	1.97	2.96
面 粉	Wheat flour			1.71	1.75	2.39
棉 花	Cotton (unginned cotton)	3.43	3.69	3.25	4.58	5.58
花生仁	Peanut kernel			4.46	5.63	6.87
油菜籽	Rapeseeds			1.92	2.40	2.90
花生油	Peanut oil	8.46	7.98	7.98	9.17	11.25
菜籽油	Rape oil	6.43	5.91	5.81	6.72	8.04
豆 油	Soybean oil	6.18	5.43	5.62	6.52	7.71
烤 烟	Flue-cured tobacco			7.96	8.66	10.31
活 猪	Hog	5.51	5.74	5.51	6.01	8.99
仔 猪	Piglet	7.43	7.54	7.24	7.82	13.62
猪 肉	Pork	9.76	10.12	9.83	10.58	14.91
牛 肉	Beef	12.59	12.69	13.62	14.91	16.37
羊 肉	Mutton	14.52	14.29	15.00	15.95	16.81
活 鸡	Live chicken			8.38	8.70	10.54
鸡 蛋	Eggs	5.06	5.37	5.46	5.23	6.82
草 鱼	Grass carp	7.43	7.28	7.16	7.28	9.64
鲤 鱼	Carp	7.97	7.49	7.04	7.11	9.38
鲢 鱼	Silver carp			5.88	5.78	7.44
带 鱼	Hairtail			9.10	9.22	10.47
大白菜	Chinese cabbage			1.00	1.09	1.29
黄 瓜	Cucumber			1.16	1.27	1.44
西红柿	Tomato			1.33	1.42	1.66
菜 椒	Green bell			1.39	1.62	1.75
四季豆	Kidney Beans			1.78	1.77	2.11
红富士苹果	Hongfushi Apple			3.05	3.75	3.86
香 蕉	Banana			2.59	3.00	3.44
橙 子	Orange			2.95	3.66	3.72

3—4 续表 continued

		2000	2001	2002	2003	2004
二、价格变动	Index					
(上季度=100)	(preceding quarter=100)					
籼　稻	Long-grained nonglutinous rice	95.36	100.81	98.67	100.12	98.90
优质籼稻	High quality long-grained nonglutinous rice	94.96	98.23	97.50	100.81	99.64
粳　稻	Round-grained rice	104.08	102.60	98.66	100.33	99.56
小　麦	Wheat	95.07	99.88	98.72	98.92	99.88
玉　米	Corn	105.53	103.55	102.02	101.88	100.42
大　豆	Soybeans	99.49	98.40	101.61	101.27	101.30
籼　米	Polished long-grained nonglutinous rice			101.06	101.23	99.31
优质籼米	High quality polished long-grained nonglutinous rice			101.41	99.78	99.42
粳　米	Polished round-grained rice			100.60	100.12	99.77
面　粉	Wheat flour			99.84	99.94	99.86
棉　花	Cotton (unginned cotton)	101.69	97.14	103.55	104.28	92.30
花生仁	Peanut kernel			105.60	101.94	101.18
油菜籽	Rapeseeds			105.61	107.88	102.00
花生油	Peanut oil	99.26	97.93	103.80	100.79	100.32
菜籽油	Rape oil	94.61	97.66	104.73	101.99	98.79
豆　油	Soybean oil	94.25	96.59	107.52	100.05	97.08
烤　烟	Flue-cured tobacco			98.59	100.42	106.89
活　猪	Hog	104.55	101.70	103.25	107.82	109.26
仔　猪	Piglet	104.94	96.47	98.31	106.38	119.05
猪　肉	Pork	105.82	102.00	102.73	107.45	109.44
牛　肉	Beef	100.61	100.02	102.51	101.77	102.91
羊　肉	Mutton	100.53	98.92	100.13	100.57	99.79
活　鸡	Live chicken			100.77	104.07	107.76
鸡　蛋	Eggs	104.91	107.13	102.82	104.47	112.14
草　鱼	Grass carp	101.04	100.20	100.80	101.35	100.32
鲤　鱼	Carp	98.88	97.51	103.12	103.05	97.44
鲢　鱼	Silver carp			101.68	102.44	102.65
带　鱼	Hairtail			103.12	99.23	103.29
大白菜	Chinese cabbage			129.81	104.22	122.87
黄　瓜	Cucumber			79.93	81.07	89.28
西红柿	Tomato			75.69	68.93	85.33
菜　椒	Green bell			64.96	60.27	64.52
四季豆	Kidney Beans			76.69	70.52	77.94
红富士苹果	Hongfushi Apple			96.95	109.58	105.17
香　蕉	Banana			84.01	98.19	89.52
橙　子	Orange			101.38	110.86	103.48

3—5 全国农产品集贸市场季度价格及走势
Quarterly RMF Prices of the Agricultural Products

（第四季度） (4th quarter)

		2000	2001	2002	2003	2004
一、价　格	Price					
（元/公斤）	(yuan/ kg)					
籼　稻	Long-grained nonglutinous rice	1.00	1.07	1.03	1.16	1.54
优质籼稻	High quality long-grained nonglutinous rice	1.18	1.25	1.14	1.35	1.75
粳　稻	Round-grained rice	1.28	1.29	1.11	1.32	1.75
小　麦	Wheat	1.03	1.12	1.04	1.24	1.56
玉　米	Corn	0.93	1.06	1.00	1.23	1.38
大　豆	Soybeans	2.46	2.37	2.46	3.28	3.82
籼　米	Polished long-grained nonglutinous rice			1.62	1.93	2.53
优质籼米	High quality polished long-grained nonglutinous rice			1.91	2.26	2.94
粳　米	Polished round-grained rice			1.91	2.18	2.92
面　粉	Wheat flour			1.69	1.97	2.41
棉　花	Cotton (unginned cotton)	3.56	3.00	4.05	6.02	4.77
花生仁	Peanut kernel			4.51	6.13	6.78
油菜籽	Rapeseeds			2.01	2.75	2.88
花生油	Peanut oil	8.26	7.82	8.06	10.60	11.12
菜籽油	Rape oil	6.36	5.81	6.18	7.70	7.80
豆　油	Soybean oil	5.94	5.36	5.91	7.60	7.37
烤　烟	Flue-cured tobacco			7.18	8.69	11.05
活　猪	Hog	5.77	5.92	5.70	7.10	8.99
仔　猪	Piglet	7.52	7.42	7.32	8.92	13.86
猪　肉	Pork	10.24	10.32	10.00	12.31	14.70
牛　肉	Beef	12.71	13.04	14.31	15.60	16.57
羊　肉	Mutton	14.53	14.76	15.44	16.51	17.27
活　鸡	Live chicken			8.33	9.36	10.61
鸡　蛋	Eggs	5.09	5.39	5.42	5.97	6.76
草　鱼	Grass carp	7.28	7.19	6.93	7.36	9.16
鲤　鱼	Carp	7.57	7.22	6.74	7.17	8.67
鲢　鱼	Silver carp			5.66	5.88	7.04
带　鱼	Hairtail			8.94	9.35	10.29
大白菜	Chinese cabbage			0.70	0.94	0.75
黄　瓜	Cucumber			2.09	2.38	2.04
西红柿	Tomato			1.97	2.47	2.09
菜　椒	Green bell			2.15	2.58	2.40
四季豆	Kidney Beans			2.44	2.68	2.60
红富士苹果	Hongfushi Apple			2.80	3.09	3.23
香　蕉	Banana			2.72	3.27	3.19
橙　子	Orange			2.78	3.53	3.41

3—5 续表 continued

		2000	2001	2002	2003	2004
二、价格变动	Index					
(上季度=100)	(preceding quarter=100)					
籼稻	Long-grained nonglutinous rice	103.86	99.64	98.02	110.66	98.64
优质籼稻	High quality long-grained nonglutinous rice	104.44	100.93	98.27	110.88	97.99
粳稻	Round-grained rice	99.97	95.61	96.29	112.92	98.13
小麦	Wheat	106.46	101.50	99.63	114.55	100.95
玉米	Corn	104.39	93.08	94.26	107.21	94.65
大豆	Soybeans	94.64	97.48	103.13	111.95	93.96
籼米	Polished long-grained nonglutinous rice			99.60	109.66	98.09
优质籼米	High quality polished long-grained nonglutinous rice			99.88	110.81	99.15
粳米	Polished round-grained rice			98.90	110.40	98.43
面粉	Wheat flour			98.78	112.56	100.60
棉花	Cotton (unginned cotton)	103.80	81.34	124.69	131.53	85.57
花生仁	Peanut kernel			101.17	108.86	98.62
油菜籽	Rapeseeds			104.61	114.99	99.16
花生油	Peanut oil	97.61	97.88	101.11	115.57	98.87
菜籽油	Rape oil	98.89	98.45	106.35	114.70	97.06
豆油	Soybean oil	96.25	98.69	105.17	116.54	95.70
烤烟	Flue-cured tobacco			90.18	100.40	107.15
活猪	Hog	104.77	102.98	103.54	118.20	100.03
仔猪	Piglet	101.17	98.42	101.16	114.07	101.72
猪肉	Pork	104.94	101.94	101.71	116.40	98.57
牛肉	Beef	100.93	102.73	105.04	104.65	101.25
羊肉	Mutton	100.05	103.30	103.00	103.49	102.71
活鸡	Live chicken			99.39	107.62	100.62
鸡蛋	Eggs	100.69	100.21	99.20	114.14	99.12
草鱼	Grass carp	97.99	98.78	96.76	101.01	95.09
鲤鱼	Carp	94.99	96.32	95.76	100.78	92.35
鲢鱼	Silver carp			96.23	101.69	94.60
带鱼	Hairtail			98.24	101.47	98.29
大白菜	Chinese cabbage			69.84	86.43	58.61
黄瓜	Cucumber			179.59	188.14	141.56
西红柿	Tomato			147.90	174.22	125.78
菜椒	Green bell			155.21	159.37	137.66
四季豆	Kidney Beans			137.29	151.16	123.27
红富士苹果	Hongfushi Apple			91.62	82.34	83.61
香蕉	Banana			105.08	109.10	92.93
橙子	Orange			94.12	96.49	91.77

3－6 全国农产品集贸市场月度价格及走势
Monthly RMF Prices of the Agricultural Products

（1月份） (Jan.)

		2000	2001	2002	2003	2004
一、价 格	Price					
（元/公斤）	(yuan/ kg)					
籼 稻	Long-grained nonglutinous rice	1.10	1.02	1.00	1.06	1.23
优质籼稻	High quality long-grained nonglutinous rice	1.21	1.21	1.13	1.20	1.43
粳 稻	Round-grained rice	1.32	1.25	1.15	1.12	1.39
小 麦	Wheat	1.12	1.06	1.08	1.13	1.34
玉 米	Corn	0.85	0.97	1.00	1.05	1.29
大 豆	Soybeans	2.37	2.47	2.34	2.72	3.52
籼 米	Polished long-grained nonglutinous rice			1.58	1.73	2.03
优质籼米	High quality polished long-grained nonglutinous rice			1.88	2.04	2.40
粳 米	Polished round-grained rice			1.90	1.97	2.29
面 粉	Wheat flour			1.73	1.78	2.15
棉 花	Cotton (unginned cotton)	2.89	3.73	2.89	4.11	5.95
花生仁	Peanut kernel			4.06	5.02	6.55
油菜籽	Rapeseeds			2.02	2.24	2.81
花生油	Peanut oil	8.70	8.10	7.72	8.79	10.99
菜籽油	Rape oil	7.34	6.17	5.63	6.35	8.04
豆 油	Soybean oil	6.80	5.52	5.22	6.28	7.76
烤 烟	Flue-cured tobacco			7.52	7.86	9.33
活 猪	Hog	5.51	5.92	5.80	5.91	7.46
仔 猪	Piglet	6.37	7.59	7.42	7.52	9.22
猪 肉	Pork	9.30	10.63	10.09	10.20	12.73
牛 肉	Beef	11.37	13.41	13.35	14.93	16.10
羊 肉	Mutton	14.20	15.06	15.14	16.42	17.05
活 鸡	Live chicken			8.35	9.14	10.12
鸡 蛋	Eggs	4.57	5.16	5.69	5.51	6.18
草 鱼	Grass carp	6.96	7.34	7.11	7.26	7.70
鲤 鱼	Carp	7.23	7.80	6.85	7.01	7.60
鲢 鱼	Silver carp			5.42	5.69	6.26
带 鱼	Hairtail			8.91	9.66	9.64
大白菜	Chinese cabbage			0.53	0.81	0.88
黄 瓜	Cucumber			2.56	3.35	3.53
西红柿	Tomato			2.48	2.77	3.23
菜 椒	Green bell			3.14	3.58	3.50
四季豆	Kidney Beans			3.26	3.60	3.66
红富士苹果	Hongfushi Apple			2.66	3.17	3.14
香 蕉	Banana			3.06	3.10	3.57
橙 子	Orange			2.66	3.28	3.53

3—6 续表 continued

		2000	2001	2002	2003	2004
二、价格变动	Index					
（上月＝100）	(preceding month＝100)					
籼　稻	Long-grained nonglutinous rice	103.62	101.04	92.80	102.31	101.25
优质籼稻	High quality long-grained nonglutinous rice		102.10	89.27	105.01	102.42
粳　稻	Round-grained rice	104.26	98.04	90.13	100.15	102.01
小　麦	Wheat	101.34	100.19	95.82	107.39	99.91
玉　米	Corn	91.12	100.67	97.34	102.91	100.91
大　豆	Soybeans	92.43	100.34	100.24	107.81	103.98
籼　米	Polished long-grained nonglutinous rice				105.90	101.37
优质籼米	High quality polished long-grained nonglutinous rice				105.69	101.09
粳　米	Polished round-grained rice				102.71	102.20
面　粉	Wheat flour				103.94	101.91
棉　花	Cotton (unginned cotton)		103.57	99.53	99.77	101.16
花生仁	Peanut kernel				108.17	103.44
油菜籽	Rapeseeds				108.83	98.62
花生油	Peanut oil		97.59	100.01	107.21	98.96
菜籽油	Rape oil		99.29	98.74	101.05	101.32
豆　油	Soybean oil		93.85	98.56	101.55	101.13
烤　烟	Flue-cured tobacco				102.66	105.20
活　猪	Hog		100.69	96.92	102.09	101.65
仔　猪	Piglet		100.39	99.68	102.43	102.16
猪　肉	Pork		104.12	97.66	100.76	101.43
牛　肉	Beef		105.29	101.37	102.28	102.12
羊　肉	Mutton		103.28	101.08	104.09	102.24
活　鸡	Live chicken				108.97	106.83
鸡　蛋	Eggs		101.14	105.74	101.47	101.37
草　鱼	Grass carp		100.90	98.46	105.63	104.80
鲤　鱼	Carp		103.12	95.65	105.89	106.08
鲢　鱼	Silver carp				100.87	106.98
带　鱼	Hairtail				108.06	104.51
大白菜	Chinese cabbage				113.80	99.34
黄　瓜	Cucumber				127.67	122.41
西红柿	Tomato				120.29	116.80
菜　椒	Green bell				143.48	122.07
四季豆	Kidney Beans				129.33	118.69
红富士苹果	Hongfushi Apple				109.32	103.43
香　蕉	Banana				112.15	106.42
橙　子	Orange				116.00	101.37

3—7 全国农产品集贸市场月度价格及走势
Monthly RMF Prices of the Agricultural Products

（2月份）　　　　（Feb.）

		2000	2001	2002	2003	2004
一、价　格	Price					
（元/公斤）	(yuan/ kg)					
籼　稻	Long-grained nonglutinous rice	1.08	1.02	1.00	1.05	1.28
优质籼稻	High quality long-grained nonglutinous rice	1.23	1.20	1.13	1.23	1.47
粳　稻	Round-grained rice	1.31	1.27	1.16	1.13	1.44
小　麦	Wheat	1.09	1.06	1.07	1.12	1.35
玉　米	Corn	0.85	1.03	1.01	1.06	1.29
大　豆	Soybeans	2.44	2.49	2.30	2.71	3.56
籼　米	Polished long-grained nonglutinous rice			1.59	1.73	2.09
优质籼米	High quality polished long-grained nonglutinous rice			1.90	2.03	2.45
粳　米	Polished round-grained rice			1.92	1.98	2.36
面　粉	Wheat flour			1.72	1.80	2.17
棉　花	Cotton (unginned cotton)	2.99	3.76	2.96	4.23	5.99
花生仁	Peanut kernel			4.09	5.05	6.49
油菜籽	Rapeseeds			1.90	2.29	2.77
花生油	Peanut oil	8.64	8.21	7.85	8.88	10.96
菜籽油	Rape oil	7.32	6.19	5.66	6.35	7.95
豆　油	Soybean oil	6.79	5.67	5.28	6.28	7.78
烤　烟	Flue-cured tobacco			7.51	8.15	9.25
活　猪	Hog	5.46	5.94	5.81	5.74	7.42
仔　猪	Piglet	6.43	7.88	7.59	7.52	9.37
猪　肉	Pork	9.66	10.31	10.17	10.03	12.49
牛　肉	Beef	12.84	12.95	13.65	14.86	15.96
羊　肉	Mutton	15.08	14.72	15.47	16.34	16.85
活　鸡	Live chicken			8.86	8.70	9.00
鸡　蛋	Eggs	5.32	4.93	5.61	5.29	5.82
草　鱼	Grass carp	6.92	7.15	7.30	7.06	7.89
鲤　鱼	Carp	7.29	7.63	6.79	6.83	7.85
鲢　鱼	Silver carp			5.53	5.41	6.32
带　鱼	Hairtail			9.13	9.46	9.58
大白菜	Chinese cabbage			0.55	0.88	0.87
黄　瓜	Cucumber			2.82	2.99	2.75
西红柿	Tomato			2.58	2.87	3.08
菜　椒	Green bell			3.40	3.43	3.36
四季豆	Kidney Beans			3.67	3.81	3.62
红富士苹果	Hongfushi Apple			2.74	3.13	3.11
香　蕉	Banana			3.32	3.15	3.46
橙　子	Orange			3.02	3.15	3.42

3—7 续表 continued

		2000	2001	2002	2003	2004
二、价格变动	Index					
（上月＝100）	(preceding month＝100)					
籼稻	Long-grained nonglutinous rice	98.18	100.16	100.16	99.67	104.12
优质籼稻	High quality long-grained nonglutinous rice	101.65	99.06	100.13	101.97	103.14
粳稻	Round-grained rice	99.24	101.78	100.67	101.13	103.86
小麦	Wheat	97.32	99.75	99.46	99.15	100.67
玉米	Corn	100.00	105.71	100.78	101.03	100.00
大豆	Soybeans	102.95	100.84	97.98	99.79	101.30
籼米	Polished long-grained nonglutinous rice			100.50	100.08	103.03
优质籼米	High quality polished long-grained nonglutinous rice			100.75	99.60	102.26
粳米	Polished round-grained rice			101.11	100.68	102.77
面粉	Wheat flour			99.83	101.19	100.58
棉花	Cotton (unginned cotton)	103.42	100.71	102.50	102.90	100.71
花生仁	Peanut kernel			100.84	100.57	99.09
油菜籽	Rapeseeds			94.24	102.19	98.67
花生油	Peanut oil	99.31	101.33	101.62	100.96	99.78
菜籽油	Rape oil	99.73	100.37	100.54	100.03	98.86
豆油	Soybean oil	99.85	102.65	101.30	100.05	100.23
烤烟	Flue-cured tobacco			99.90	103.75	99.17
活猪	Hog	99.09	100.38	100.25	97.15	99.43
仔猪	Piglet	100.94	103.88	102.35	99.96	101.68
猪肉	Pork	103.87	96.97	100.72	98.32	98.07
牛肉	Beef	112.93	96.59	102.22	99.51	99.09
羊肉	Mutton	106.20	97.73	102.20	99.49	98.81
活鸡	Live chicken			106.08	95.19	88.86
鸡蛋	Eggs	116.41	95.64	98.57	95.97	94.16
草鱼	Grass carp	99.43	97.39	102.59	97.31	102.57
鲤鱼	Carp	100.83	97.83	99.07	97.39	103.29
鲢鱼	Silver carp			102.15	95.14	101.00
带鱼	Hairtail			102.46	97.91	99.37
大白菜	Chinese cabbage			104.14	109.05	99.07
黄瓜	Cucumber			110.13	89.33	78.08
西红柿	Tomato			104.18	103.66	95.40
菜椒	Green bell			108.34	95.81	96.04
四季豆	Kidney Beans			112.30	105.58	98.94
红富士苹果	Hongfushi Apple			103.14	98.60	99.06
香蕉	Banana			108.67	101.33	96.88
橙子	Orange			113.67	95.95	96.92

3－8 全国农产品集贸市场月度价格及走势
Monthly RMF Prices of the Agricultural Products

（3月份） (Mar.)

		2000	2001	2002	2003	2004
一、价 格	Price					
（元/公斤）	(yuan/ kg)					
籼 稻	Long-grained nonglutinous rice	0.99	1.01	1.05	1.05	1.56
优质籼稻	High quality long-grained nonglutinous rice	1.23	1.21	1.19	1.23	1.78
粳 稻	Round-grained rice	1.29	1.31	1.19	1.17	1.78
小 麦	Wheat	1.05	1.06	1.08	1.10	1.50
玉 米	Corn	0.84	1.03	1.02	1.08	1.36
大 豆	Soybeans	2.47	2.46	2.28	2.80	3.74
籼 米	Polished long-grained nonglutinous rice			1.63	1.73	2.55
优质籼米	High quality polished long-grained nonglutinous rice			1.87	2.04	2.91
粳 米	Polished round-grained rice			1.93	1.94	2.84
面 粉	Wheat flour			1.71	1.76	2.34
棉 花	Cotton (unginned cotton)	3.00	3.66	3.07	4.32	6.07
花生仁	Peanut kernel			4.10	5.25	6.63
油菜籽	Rapeseeds			1.86	2.14	2.79
花生油	Peanut oil	8.75	8.27	7.77	8.89	11.05
菜籽油	Rape oil	7.28	6.15	5.56	6.53	8.04
豆 油	Soybean oil	6.80	5.64	5.24	6.36	7.97
烤 烟	Flue-cured tobacco			7.73	8.56	9.31
活 猪	Hog	5.47	5.83	5.51	5.67	7.73
仔 猪	Piglet	6.99	7.91	7.68	7.58	10.38
猪 肉	Pork	9.47	10.18	9.78	9.91	12.69
牛 肉	Beef	12.76	12.71	13.34	14.67	15.93
羊 肉	Mutton	14.88	14.61	15.05	16.19	17.04
活 鸡	Live chicken			8.38	8.52	9.21
鸡 蛋	Eggs	5.00	4.93	5.28	5.05	5.79
草 鱼	Grass carp	6.92	7.17	7.13	7.08	8.43
鲤 鱼	Carp	7.42	7.64	6.64	6.73	8.31
鲢 鱼	Silver carp			5.63	5.42	6.55
带 鱼	Hairtail			8.83	9.31	9.59
大白菜	Chinese cabbage			0.54	1.17	0.94
黄 瓜	Cucumber			2.25	2.84	2.77
西红柿	Tomato			2.34	3.02	2.79
菜 椒	Green bell			2.89	3.81	3.78
四季豆	Kidney Beans			3.27	4.02	4.11
红富士苹果	Hongfushi Apple			2.77	3.10	3.17
香 蕉	Banana			3.34	3.15	3.49
橙 子	Orange			2.94	3.09	3.52

3—8 续表 continued

		2000	2001	2002	2003	2004
二、价格变动	Index					
(上月=100)	(preceding month=100)					
籼　稻	Long-grained nonglutinous rice	91.67	99.26	104.57	99.38	122.46
优质籼稻	High quality long-grained nonglutinous rice	100.00	100.69	105.37	100.03	121.27
粳　稻	Round-grained rice	98.47	103.57	102.48	104.06	123.49
小　麦	Wheat	96.33	100.20	100.80	97.67	111.50
玉　米	Corn	98.82	100.77	100.60	101.86	105.44
大　豆	Soybeans	101.23	99.08	99.24	103.14	104.96
籼　米	Polished long-grained nonglutinous rice			103.01	100.12	121.98
优质籼米	High quality polished long-grained nonglutinous rice			98.47	100.49	118.59
粳　米	Polished round-grained rice			100.15	98.18	120.44
面　粉	Wheat flour			99.06	98.20	107.87
棉　花	Cotton (unginned cotton)	100.40	97.51	103.50	102.17	101.17
花生仁	Peanut kernel			100.23	104.01	102.14
油菜籽	Rapeseeds			97.92	93.49	100.64
花生油	Peanut oil	101.27	100.72	98.98	100.17	100.83
菜籽油	Rape oil	99.45	99.29	98.12	102.86	101.14
豆　油	Soybean oil	100.15	99.42	99.25	101.25	102.44
烤　烟	Flue-cured tobacco			102.94	105.06	100.57
活　猪	Hog	100.18	98.11	94.88	98.87	104.29
仔　猪	Piglet	108.71	100.37	101.12	100.83	110.75
猪　肉	Pork	98.03	98.72	96.17	98.81	101.64
牛　肉	Beef	99.38	98.08	97.72	98.72	99.83
羊　肉	Mutton	98.67	99.28	97.26	99.12	101.11
活　鸡	Live chicken			94.58	97.87	102.38
鸡　蛋	Eggs	93.98	99.94	94.08	95.58	99.55
草　鱼	Grass carp	100.00	100.26	97.69	100.27	106.76
鲤　鱼	Carp	101.78	100.07	97.83	98.66	105.93
鲢　鱼	Silver carp			101.68	100.22	103.59
带　鱼	Hairtail			96.71	98.41	100.10
大白菜	Chinese cabbage			97.78	132.44	107.39
黄　瓜	Cucumber			79.76	94.79	100.48
西红柿	Tomato			90.51	105.33	90.68
菜　椒	Green bell			85.12	111.25	112.31
四季豆	Kidney Beans			89.17	105.54	113.57
红富士苹果	Hongfushi Apple			101.04	99.01	102.08
香　蕉	Banana			100.61	99.99	101.05
橙　子	Orange			97.27	98.39	102.76

3－9 全国农产品集贸市场月度价格及走势
Monthly RMF Prices of the Agricultural Products

（4月份） （Apr.）

		2000	2001	2002	2003	2004
一、价格	Price					
（元/公斤）	(yuan/ kg)					
籼稻	Long-grained nonglutinous rice	1.02	1.04	1.05	1.04	1.58
优质籼稻	High quality long-grained nonglutinous rice	1.16	1.25	1.19	1.20	1.80
粳稻	Round-grained rice	1.22	1.28	1.17	1.18	1.81
小麦	Wheat	1.04	1.08	1.07	1.10	1.57
玉米	Corn	0.82	1.08	1.01	1.10	1.44
大豆	Soybeans	2.57	2.45	2.32	2.87	3.97
籼米	Polished long-grained nonglutinous rice			1.59	1.73	2.60
优质籼米	High quality polished long-grained nonglutinous rice			1.85	2.05	3.01
粳米	Polished round-grained rice			1.90	1.98	3.01
面粉	Wheat flour			1.71	1.76	2.41
棉花	Cotton (unginned cotton)	3.28	3.85	3.24	4.38	6.13
花生仁	Peanut kernel			4.03	5.41	6.74
油菜籽	Rapeseeds			1.78	2.12	2.88
花生油	Peanut oil	8.59	8.16	7.45	9.06	11.30
菜籽油	Rape oil	6.94	6.19	5.60	6.53	8.11
豆油	Soybean oil	6.60	5.74	5.19	6.53	8.04
烤烟	Flue-cured tobacco			8.08	8.35	9.47
活猪	Hog	5.38	5.72	5.31	5.63	8.08
仔猪	Piglet	7.00	7.96	7.53	7.45	11.19
猪肉	Pork	9.22	10.05	9.51	9.87	13.33
牛肉	Beef	12.58	12.67	12.99	14.67	15.86
羊肉	Mutton	14.55	14.53	15.01	15.97	16.99
活鸡	Live chicken			8.41	8.44	9.57
鸡蛋	Eggs	4.87	4.95	5.21	5.06	5.92
草鱼	Grass carp	7.19	7.25	7.10	7.15	9.22
鲤鱼	Carp	7.76	7.73	6.69	6.83	8.92
鲢鱼	Silver carp			5.67	5.57	6.88
带鱼	Hairtail			8.82	9.36	9.74
大白菜	Chinese cabbage			0.70	1.36	1.12
黄瓜	Cucumber			1.79	2.38	2.11
西红柿	Tomato			2.11	2.82	2.48
菜椒	Green bell			2.62	3.94	3.48
四季豆	Kidney Beans			2.94	3.59	3.48
红富士苹果	Hongfushi Apple			3.02	3.19	3.44
香蕉	Banana			3.32	3.12	3.80
橙子	Orange			2.82	3.22	3.52

3－9 续表 continued

		2000	2001	2002	2003	2004
二、价格变动	Index					
（上月＝100）	(preceding month＝100)					
籼　稻	Long-grained nonglutinous rice	103.03	102.69	99.86	99.48	100.92
优质籼稻	High quality long-grained nonglutinous rice	94.31	103.26	99.62	97.72	100.63
粳　稻	Round-grained rice	94.57	97.66	98.52	100.86	101.59
小　麦	Wheat	99.05	101.83	99.05	100.48	104.53
玉　米	Corn	97.62	104.49	99.40	102.01	106.22
大　豆	Soybeans	104.05	99.56	101.96	102.54	106.17
籼　米	Polished long-grained nonglutinous rice			97.19	100.27	101.97
优质籼米	High quality polished long-grained nonglutinous rice			99.15	100.43	103.39
粳　米	Polished round-grained rice			98.51	101.94	106.12
面　粉	Wheat flour			99.91	99.58	103.09
棉　花	Cotton (unginned cotton)	109.09	104.99	105.63	101.44	101.06
花生仁	Peanut kernel			98.35	103.08	101.64
油菜籽	Rapeseeds			95.68	98.79	103.46
花生油	Peanut oil	98.17	98.65	95.95	101.94	102.17
菜籽油	Rape oil	95.33	100.60	100.77	99.94	100.85
豆　油	Soybean oil	97.06	101.81	98.96	102.65	100.84
烤　烟	Flue-cured tobacco			104.51	97.55	101.73
活　猪	Hog	98.35	98.20	96.32	99.22	104.48
仔　猪	Piglet	100.14	100.66	98.04	98.27	107.84
猪　肉	Pork	97.36	98.73	97.26	99.62	105.00
牛　肉	Beef	98.59	99.72	97.35	100.04	99.59
羊　肉	Mutton	97.78	99.44	99.73	98.64	99.71
活　鸡	Live chicken			100.38	99.05	103.88
鸡　蛋	Eggs	97.40	100.32	98.79	100.11	102.32
草　鱼	Grass carp	103.90	101.14	99.66	100.91	109.42
鲤　鱼	Carp	104.58	101.20	100.77	101.45	107.27
鲢　鱼	Silver carp			100.81	102.70	105.04
带　鱼	Hairtail			99.95	100.56	101.58
大白菜	Chinese cabbage			130.74	116.14	119.68
黄　瓜	Cucumber			79.90	83.93	76.32
西红柿	Tomato			90.27	93.47	88.64
菜　椒	Green bell			90.48	103.30	92.19
四季豆	Kidney Beans			90.02	89.40	84.53
红富士苹果	Hongfushi Apple			109.18	102.93	108.41
香　蕉	Banana			99.29	99.31	108.91
橙　子	Orange			95.81	104.21	100.01

3－10 全国农产品集贸市场月度价格及走势
Monthly RMF Prices of the Agricultural Products

(5月份) (May.)

		2000	2001	2002	2003	2004
一、价 格	Price					
(元/公斤)	(yuan/ kg)					
籼 稻	Long-grained nonglutinous rice	1.00	1.08	1.07	1.05	1.58
优质籼稻	High quality long-grained nonglutinous rice	1.19	1.29	1.20	1.20	1.79
粳 稻	Round-grained rice	1.23	1.30	1.17	1.15	1.79
小 麦	Wheat	1.00	1.14	1.07	1.10	1.55
玉 米	Corn	0.84	1.11	1.04	1.13	1.45
大 豆	Soybeans	2.63	2.49	2.36	2.91	4.02
籼 米	Polished long-grained nonglutinous rice			1.62	1.73	2.59
优质籼米	High quality polished long-grained nonglutinous rice			1.90	2.05	2.97
粳 米	Polished round-grained rice			1.93	1.97	2.96
面 粉	Wheat flour			1.73	1.76	2.40
棉 花	Cotton (unginned cotton)	3.40	3.75	3.04	4.44	6.06
花生仁	Peanut kernel			4.23	5.54	6.79
油菜籽	Rapeseeds			1.81	2.26	2.84
花生油	Peanut oil	8.53	8.11	7.78	9.15	11.24
菜籽油	Rape oil	6.83	6.00	5.51	6.58	8.17
豆 油	Soybean oil	6.54	5.53	5.23	6.58	7.94
烤 烟	Flue-cured tobacco			7.93	8.68	9.72
活 猪	Hog	5.27	5.62	5.39	5.56	8.15
仔 猪	Piglet	7.04	7.72	7.35	7.25	11.26
猪 肉	Pork	9.20	9.92	9.60	9.82	13.53
牛 肉	Beef	12.57	12.74	13.35	14.55	15.90
羊 肉	Mutton	14.52	14.42	15.09	15.74	16.80
活 鸡	Live chicken			8.26	8.30	9.81
鸡 蛋	Eggs	4.85	5.02	5.39	4.99	5.91
草 鱼	Grass carp	7.40	7.20	7.12	7.17	9.65
鲤 鱼	Carp	8.22	7.60	6.83	6.90	9.72
鲢 鱼	Silver carp			5.74	5.63	7.24
带 鱼	Hairtail			8.84	9.33	10.14
大白菜	Chinese cabbage			0.75	0.96	1.03
黄 瓜	Cucumber			1.54	1.39	1.60
西红柿	Tomato			1.80	1.99	1.97
菜 椒	Green bell			2.33	2.47	2.84
四季豆	Kidney Beans			2.35	2.42	2.77
红富士苹果	Hongfushi Apple			3.05	3.42	3.67
香 蕉	Banana			3.12	3.05	3.94
橙 子	Orange			2.90	3.21	3.64

3－10续表 continued

		2000	2001	2002	2003	2004
二、价格变动	Index					
(上月＝100)	(preceding month＝100)					
籼　稻	Long-grained nonglutinous rice	98.04	103.89	101.93	101.14	99.76
优质籼稻	High quality long-grained nonglutinous rice	102.59	103.03	100.84	100.34	99.42
粳　稻	Round-grained rice	100.82	101.23	99.97	97.07	99.06
小　麦	Wheat	96.15	104.98	100.09	100.15	98.93
玉　米	Corn	102.44	102.99	102.80	102.97	100.90
大　豆	Soybeans	102.33	101.66	101.68	101.60	101.25
籼　米	Polished long-grained nonglutinous rice			101.78	99.87	99.28
优质籼米	High quality polished long-grained nonglutinous rice			102.60	100.15	98.87
粳　米	Polished round-grained rice			101.88	99.58	98.20
面　粉	Wheat flour			101.21	99.94	99.45
棉　花	Cotton (unginned cotton)	103.75	97.40	93.74	101.37	98.84
花生仁	Peanut kernel			104.95	102.36	100.71
油菜籽	Rapeseeds			101.43	106.84	98.51
花生油	Peanut oil	99.30	99.47	104.35	100.97	99.47
菜籽油	Rape oil	98.41	96.99	98.36	100.79	100.77
豆　油	Soybean oil	99.09	96.37	100.71	100.80	98.77
烤　烟	Flue-cured tobacco			98.22	103.86	102.64
活　猪	Hog	97.96	98.24	101.38	98.78	100.88
仔　猪	Piglet	100.57	96.94	97.61	97.24	100.66
猪　肉	Pork	99.78	98.71	100.97	99.50	101.50
牛　肉	Beef	99.92	100.55	102.78	99.14	100.20
羊　肉	Mutton	99.79	99.23	100.56	98.56	98.88
活　鸡	Live chicken			98.22	98.36	102.55
鸡　蛋	Eggs	99.59	101.55	103.32	98.55	99.80
草　鱼	Grass carp	102.92	99.36	100.28	100.36	104.66
鲤　鱼	Carp	105.93	98.37	101.97	101.07	109.03
鲢　鱼	Silver carp			101.22	101.13	105.25
带　鱼	Hairtail			100.23	99.67	104.11
大白菜	Chinese cabbage			106.79	70.58	91.80
黄　瓜	Cucumber			86.12	58.22	75.75
西红柿	Tomato			85.20	70.49	79.64
菜　椒	Green bell			89.17	62.78	81.56
四季豆	Kidney Beans			80.01	67.52	79.78
红富士苹果	Hongfushi Apple			100.85	107.23	106.80
香　蕉	Banana			93.84	97.77	103.65
橙　子	Orange			102.80	99.49	103.61

3－11 全国农产品集贸市场月度价格及走势
Monthly RMF Prices of the Agricultural Products

（6月份） （Jun.）

		2000	2001	2002	2003	2004
一、价 格	Price					
（元/公斤）	(yuan/ kg)					
籼 稻	Long-grained nonglutinous rice	1.00	1.07	1.07	1.04	1.59
优质籼稻	High quality long-grained nonglutinous rice	1.22	1.25	1.19	1.22	1.80
粳 稻	Round-grained rice	1.23	1.36	1.18	1.16	1.79
小 麦	Wheat	1.00	1.09	1.03	1.09	1.54
玉 米	Corn	0.87	1.10	1.06	1.14	1.45
大 豆	Soybeans	2.64	2.46	2.37	2.90	4.06
籼 米	Polished long-grained nonglutinous rice			1.63	1.74	2.59
优质籼米	High quality polished long-grained nonglutinous rice			1.91	2.05	2.97
粳 米	Polished round-grained rice			1.94	1.95	2.94
面 粉	Wheat flour			1.71	1.75	2.39
棉 花	Cotton (unginned cotton)	3.44	3.80	3.14	4.34	5.93
花生仁	Peanut kernel			4.40	5.60	6.86
油菜籽	Rapeseeds			1.86	2.28	2.82
花生油	Peanut oil	8.46	8.19	7.83	9.09	11.12
菜籽油	Rape oil	6.63	5.96	5.53	6.64	8.13
豆 油	Soybean oil	6.52	5.59	5.26	6.45	7.83
烤 烟	Flue-cured tobacco			8.20	8.83	9.76
活 猪	Hog	5.16	5.60	5.31	5.53	8.46
仔 猪	Piglet	7.20	7.77	7.22	7.34	11.87
猪 肉	Pork	9.25	9.81	9.60	9.83	14.02
牛 肉	Beef	12.39	12.66	13.52	14.72	15.95
羊 肉	Mutton	14.27	14.39	14.83	15.87	16.76
活 鸡	Live chicken			8.28	8.34	9.96
鸡 蛋	Eggs	4.74	5.08	5.34	4.96	6.41
草 鱼	Grass carp	7.47	7.34	7.09	7.24	9.94
鲤 鱼	Carp	8.20	7.72	6.95	6.96	10.25
鲢 鱼	Silver carp			5.93	5.73	7.63
带 鱼	Hairtail			8.80	9.19	10.53
大白菜	Chinese cabbage			0.87	0.83	0.98
黄 瓜	Cucumber			1.03	0.92	1.13
西红柿	Tomato			1.38	1.35	1.39
菜 椒	Green bell			1.46	1.64	1.80
四季豆	Kidney Beans			1.65	1.52	1.86
红富士苹果	Hongfushi Apple			3.38	3.65	3.89
香 蕉	Banana			2.81	2.98	3.77
橙 子	Orange			3.02	3.46	3.62

3—11 续表 continued

		2000	2001	2002	2003	2004
二、价格变动	Index					
（上月＝100）	(preceding month＝100)					
籼 稻	Long-grained nonglutinous rice	100.00	98.94	99.67	99.22	100.69
优质籼稻	High quality long-grained nonglutinous rice	102.52	97.32	99.01	101.19	100.59
粳 稻	Round-grained rice	100.00	104.99	100.60	101.08	99.80
小 麦	Wheat	100.00	95.84	96.43	99.07	99.13
玉 米	Corn	103.57	99.05	102.47	100.85	99.86
大 豆	Soybeans	100.38	98.56	100.19	99.52	101.00
籼 米	Polished long-grained nonglutinous rice			100.72	100.63	100.30
优质籼米	High quality polished long-grained nonglutinous rice			100.66	99.77	99.84
粳 米	Polished round-grained rice			100.25	98.85	99.53
面 粉	Wheat flour			99.27	99.71	99.64
棉 花	Cotton (unginned cotton)	101.24	101.42	103.35	97.62	97.94
花生仁	Peanut kernel			103.88	101.07	101.02
油菜籽	Rapeseeds			103.03	101.02	99.20
花生油	Peanut oil	99.18	100.91	100.66	99.34	98.95
菜籽油	Rape oil	97.07	99.27	100.39	100.95	99.47
豆 油	Soybean oil	99.69	101.07	100.61	98.03	98.66
烤 烟	Flue-cured tobacco			103.36	101.78	100.43
活 猪	Hog	97.91	99.61	98.61	99.47	103.75
仔 猪	Piglet	102.27	100.60	98.20	101.32	105.39
猪 肉	Pork	100.54	98.86	99.97	100.11	103.65
牛 肉	Beef	98.57	99.38	101.34	101.20	100.35
羊 肉	Mutton	98.28	99.79	98.26	100.83	99.81
活 鸡	Live chicken			100.25	100.45	101.55
鸡 蛋	Eggs	97.73	101.17	99.07	99.59	108.46
草 鱼	Grass carp	100.95	101.82	99.61	100.94	103.02
鲤 鱼	Carp	99.76	101.55	101.79	100.84	105.46
鲢 鱼	Silver carp			103.24	101.70	105.44
带 鱼	Hairtail			99.51	98.50	103.86
大白菜	Chinese cabbage			115.95	86.29	95.39
黄 瓜	Cucumber			66.42	66.33	70.77
西红柿	Tomato			76.49	67.58	70.46
菜 椒	Green bell			62.52	66.47	63.52
四季豆	Kidney Beans			70.06	62.72	67.03
红富士苹果	Hongfushi Apple			110.81	106.86	105.95
香 蕉	Banana			90.29	97.71	95.72
橙 子	Orange			104.33	107.93	99.31

3－12　全国农产品集贸市场月度价格及走势
Monthly RMF Prices of the Agricultural Products

（7月份）　　　　　　　　　　　　　　　　　　　　　　　　　　　　　　　　(Jul.)

		2000	2001	2002	2003	2004
一、价　格	Price					
（元/公斤）	(yuan/ kg)					
籼　稻	Long-grained nonglutinous rice	0.95	1.07	1.05	1.04	1.57
优质籼稻	High quality long-grained nonglutinous rice	1.11	1.26	1.17	1.21	1.80
粳　稻	Round-grained rice	1.27	1.32	1.16	1.16	1.78
小　麦	Wheat	0.94	1.09	1.04	1.08	1.53
玉　米	Corn	0.88	1.15	1.06	1.13	1.46
大　豆	Soybeans	2.65	2.42	2.37	2.91	4.09
籼　米	Polished long-grained nonglutinous rice			1.62	1.75	2.59
优质籼米	High quality polished long-grained nonglutinous rice			1.90	2.04	2.96
粳　米	Polished round-grained rice			1.92	1.96	2.95
面　粉	Wheat flour			1.71	1.75	2.39
棉　花	Cotton (unginned cotton)	3.45	3.89	3.16	4.42	5.75
花生仁	Peanut kernel			4.40	5.56	6.86
油菜籽	Rapeseeds			1.93	2.36	2.90
花生油	Peanut oil	8.51	8.09	7.80	9.12	11.27
菜籽油	Rape oil	6.60	5.91	5.56	6.68	8.03
豆　油	Soybean oil	6.21	5.42	5.36	6.49	7.70
烤　烟	Flue-cured tobacco			8.02	8.79	10.22
活　猪	Hog	5.38	5.62	5.35	5.78	8.63
仔　猪	Piglet	7.32	7.46	7.09	7.51	12.59
猪　肉	Pork	9.48	9.92	9.60	10.19	14.44
牛　肉	Beef	12.30	12.72	13.36	14.78	16.13
羊　肉	Mutton	14.45	14.22	14.72	15.89	16.72
活　鸡	Live chicken			8.40	8.52	10.20
鸡　蛋	Eggs	4.71	5.14	5.17	4.93	6.36
草　鱼	Grass carp	7.60	7.28	7.30	7.30	9.74
鲤　鱼	Carp	8.28	7.49	7.07	7.05	9.77
鲢　鱼	Silver carp			5.84	5.72	7.56
带　鱼	Hairtail			9.19	9.17	10.49
大白菜	Chinese cabbage			0.97	0.94	1.22
黄　瓜	Cucumber			0.90	0.89	1.21
西红柿	Tomato			1.17	1.08	1.34
菜　椒	Green bell			1.16	1.33	1.58
四季豆	Kidney Beans			1.45	1.37	1.83
红富士苹果	Hongfushi Apple			3.20	3.83	3.99
香　蕉	Banana			2.49	2.90	3.51
橙　子	Orange			2.91	3.37	3.75

3－12 续表 continued

		2000	2001	2002	2003	2004
二、价格变动	Index					
（上月＝100）	（preceding month＝100）					
籼　稻	Long-grained nonglutinous rice	95.00	100.58	98.84	100.00	99.04
优质籼稻	High quality long-grained nonglutinous rice	90.98	100.44	98.69	99.62	100.18
粳　稻	Round-grained rice	103.25	97.03	98.25	99.78	99.87
小　麦	Wheat	94.00	99.95	100.20	98.63	99.20
玉　米	Corn	101.15	104.26	99.82	99.21	100.61
大　豆	Soybeans	100.38	98.46	100.10	100.38	100.68
籼　米	Polished long-grained nonglutinous rice			99.70	100.31	99.73
优质籼米	High quality polished long-grained nonglutinous rice			99.20	99.64	99.56
粳　米	Polished round-grained rice			99.07	100.36	100.22
面　粉	Wheat flour			99.65	100.01	100.06
棉　花	Cotton (unginned cotton)	100.26	102.34	100.80	101.88	96.89
花生仁	Peanut kernel			100.10	99.19	100.11
油菜籽	Rapeseeds			103.90	103.23	103.06
花生油	Peanut oil	100.59	98.74	99.71	100.33	101.35
菜籽油	Rape oil	99.55	99.31	100.50	100.49	98.76
豆　油	Soybean oil	95.25	96.91	101.93	100.65	98.30
烤　烟	Flue-cured tobacco			97.75	99.52	104.69
活　猪	Hog	104.26	100.40	100.76	104.42	102.10
仔　猪	Piglet	101.67	96.04	98.32	102.26	106.03
猪　肉	Pork	102.49	101.18	100.06	103.61	102.98
牛　肉	Beef	99.27	100.47	98.78	100.39	101.10
羊　肉	Mutton	101.26	98.83	99.29	100.08	99.74
活　鸡	Live chicken			101.40	102.16	102.35
鸡　蛋	Eggs	99.37	101.25	96.87	99.21	99.12
草　鱼	Grass carp	101.74	99.19	102.93	100.82	97.96
鲤　鱼	Carp	100.98	96.98	101.77	101.19	95.34
鲢　鱼	Silver carp			98.57	99.83	99.01
带　鱼	Hairtail			104.47	99.86	99.56
大白菜	Chinese cabbage			111.16	113.41	123.93
黄　瓜	Cucumber			87.38	96.50	106.51
西红柿	Tomato			85.25	79.92	96.37
菜　椒	Green bell			79.32	80.85	87.73
四季豆	Kidney Beans			87.82	89.85	98.45
红富士苹果	Hongfushi Apple			94.78	104.83	102.55
香　蕉	Banana			88.55	97.04	92.90
橙　子	Orange			96.27	97.21	103.59

3－13 全国农产品集贸市场月度价格及走势
Monthly RMF Prices of the Agricultural Products

（8月份） (Aug.)

		2000	2001	2002	2003	2004
一、价 格	Price					
（元/公斤）	(yuan/ kg)					
籼 稻	Long-grained nonglutinous rice	0.97	1.06	1.04	1.05	1.55
优质籼稻	High quality long-grained nonglutinous rice	1.15	1.22	1.16	1.21	1.78
粳 稻	Round-grained rice	1.30	1.34	1.16	1.17	1.77
小 麦	Wheat	0.98	1.09	1.06	1.08	1.56
玉 米	Corn	0.89	1.13	1.06	1.15	1.45
大 豆	Soybeans	2.64	2.41	2.38	2.94	4.08
籼 米	Polished long-grained nonglutinous rice			1.63	1.75	2.57
优质籼米	High quality polished long-grained nonglutinous rice			1.92	2.04	2.97
粳 米	Polished round-grained rice			1.93	1.97	2.96
面 粉	Wheat flour			1.71	1.75	2.39
棉 花	Cotton (unginned cotton)	3.50	3.78	3.11	4.46	5.66
花生仁	Peanut kernel			4.43	5.65	6.90
油菜籽	Rapeseeds			1.88	2.38	2.89
花生油	Peanut oil	8.48	7.94	7.87	9.16	11.21
菜籽油	Rape oil	6.36	5.96	5.77	6.71	8.06
豆 油	Soybean oil	6.23	5.45	5.62	6.52	7.73
烤 烟	Flue-cured tobacco			7.96	8.57	10.36
活 猪	Hog	5.57	5.74	5.58	6.00	9.01
仔 猪	Piglet	7.43	7.59	7.33	7.81	13.69
猪 肉	Pork	9.82	10.13	9.93	10.56	15.01
牛 肉	Beef	12.66	12.60	13.65	14.90	16.32
羊 肉	Mutton	14.58	14.41	15.07	15.95	16.77
活 鸡	Live chicken			8.32	8.70	10.57
鸡 蛋	Eggs	5.17	5.44	5.59	5.23	6.84
草 鱼	Grass carp	7.34	7.28	7.08	7.30	9.65
鲤 鱼	Carp	7.89	7.53	7.03	7.15	9.29
鲢 鱼	Silver carp			5.98	5.75	7.48
带 鱼	Hairtail			8.97	9.28	10.45
大白菜	Chinese cabbage			0.99	1.15	1.34
黄 瓜	Cucumber			1.23	1.38	1.49
西红柿	Tomato			1.30	1.45	1.70
菜 椒	Green bell			1.45	1.59	1.73
四季豆	Kidney Beans			1.90	1.83	2.19
红富士苹果	Hongfushi Apple			3.02	3.86	3.92
香 蕉	Banana			2.61	2.95	3.47
橙 子	Orange			2.97	3.62	3.70

3—13 续表 continued

		2000	2001	2002	2003	2004
二、价格变动	Index					
(上月=100)	(preceding month=100)					
籼 稻	Long-grained nonglutinous rice	102.11	99.19	98.52	100.15	98.62
优质籼稻	High quality long-grained nonglutinous rice	103.60	97.25	98.62	99.95	98.81
粳 稻	Round-grained rice	102.36	101.29	100.01	100.55	99.43
小 麦	Wheat	104.26	100.12	101.84	100.55	102.30
玉 米	Corn	101.14	98.34	99.68	101.49	99.03
大 豆	Soybeans	99.62	99.82	100.27	100.88	99.90
籼 米	Polished long-grained nonglutinous rice			100.66	100.34	99.46
优质籼米	High quality polished long-grained nonglutinous rice			100.93	100.19	100.36
粳 米	Polished round-grained rice			100.39	100.79	100.24
面 粉	Wheat flour			100.04	99.79	99.95
棉 花	Cotton (unginned cotton)	101.39	97.17	98.29	100.89	98.39
花生仁	Peanut kernel			100.75	101.71	100.47
油菜籽	Rapeseeds			97.32	101.09	99.50
花生油	Peanut oil	99.65	98.22	100.90	100.40	99.47
菜籽油	Rape oil	96.36	100.70	103.82	100.45	100.41
豆 油	Soybean oil	100.32	100.57	104.76	100.45	100.45
烤 烟	Flue-cured tobacco			99.31	97.54	101.37
活 猪	Hog	103.53	102.06	104.22	103.90	104.41
仔 猪	Piglet	101.50	101.69	103.32	103.99	108.77
猪 肉	Pork	103.59	102.09	103.35	103.63	103.93
牛 肉	Beef	102.93	99.07	102.14	100.82	101.20
羊 肉	Mutton	100.90	101.33	102.35	100.42	100.30
活 鸡	Live chicken			99.10	102.14	103.65
鸡 蛋	Eggs	109.77	105.64	108.19	106.15	107.64
草 鱼	Grass carp	96.58	100.12	96.88	100.01	99.03
鲤 鱼	Carp	95.29	100.62	99.45	101.42	95.04
鲢 鱼	Silver carp			102.29	100.61	98.99
带 鱼	Hairtail			97.54	101.17	99.69
大白菜	Chinese cabbage			102.61	122.87	109.53
黄 瓜	Cucumber			137.54	156.06	123.43
西红柿	Tomato			111.20	134.77	127.26
菜 椒	Green bell			125.23	119.54	109.18
四季豆	Kidney Beans			130.85	133.98	119.81
红富士苹果	Hongfushi Apple			94.47	100.72	98.13
香 蕉	Banana			104.71	101.90	99.09
橙 子	Orange			102.13	107.59	98.79

3－14 全国农产品集贸市场月度价格及走势
Monthly RMF Prices of the Agricultural Products

（9月份） (Sep.)

		2000	2001	2002	2003	2004
一、价 格	Price					
（元/公斤）	(yuan/ kg)					
籼 稻	Long-grained nonglutinous rice	0.96	1.07	1.05	1.05	1.57
优质籼稻	High quality long-grained nonglutinous rice	1.13	1.24	1.16	1.23	1.78
粳 稻	Round-grained rice	1.26	1.39	1.16	1.18	1.80
小 麦	Wheat	0.97	1.12	1.05	1.10	1.57
玉 米	Corn	0.90	1.13	1.05	1.16	1.46
大 豆	Soybeans	2.51	2.45	2.42	2.94	4.04
籼 米	Polished long-grained nonglutinous rice			1.63	1.77	2.57
优质籼米	High quality polished long-grained nonglutinous rice			1.93	2.05	2.98
粳 米	Polished round-grained rice			1.96	1.98	2.99
面 粉	Wheat flour			1.72	1.76	2.41
棉 花	Cotton (unginned cotton)	3.34	3.40	3.48	4.85	5.32
花生仁	Peanut kernel			4.54	5.67	6.86
油菜籽	Rapeseeds			1.94	2.44	2.92
花生油	Peanut oil	8.40	7.93	8.25	9.24	11.28
菜籽油	Rape oil	6.34	5.85	6.10	6.76	8.02
豆 油	Soybean oil	6.09	5.42	5.88	6.56	7.68
烤 烟	Flue-cured tobacco			7.89	8.61	10.36
活 猪	Hog	5.58	5.87	5.60	6.25	9.32
仔 猪	Piglet	7.54	7.58	7.29	8.13	14.59
猪 肉	Pork	9.98	10.32	9.96	10.98	15.29
牛 肉	Beef	12.81	12.76	13.85	15.04	16.65
羊 肉	Mutton	14.54	14.24	15.19	16.02	16.95
活 鸡	Live chicken			8.42	8.88	10.85
鸡 蛋	Eggs	5.29	5.54	5.62	5.52	7.27
草 鱼	Grass carp	7.35	7.27	7.11	7.25	9.52
鲤 鱼	Carp	7.74	7.46	7.00	7.14	9.09
鲢 鱼	Silver carp			5.81	5.87	7.29
带 鱼	Hairtail			9.13	9.20	10.48
大白菜	Chinese cabbage			1.05	1.19	1.30
黄 瓜	Cucumber			1.36	1.53	1.63
西红柿	Tomato			1.52	1.72	1.94
菜 椒	Green bell			1.56	1.94	1.93
四季豆	Kidney Beans			1.98	2.12	2.30
红富士苹果	Hongfushi Apple			2.93	3.56	3.67
香 蕉	Banana			2.67	3.15	3.33
橙 子	Orange			2.98	3.98	3.70

3－14 续表 continued

		2000	2001	2002	2003	2004
二、价格变动	Index					
（上月＝100）	(preceding month＝100)					
籼稻	Long-grained nonglutinous rice	98.97	100.64	101.22	100.47	101.22
优质籼稻	High quality long-grained nonglutinous rice	98.26	101.39	100.28	100.97	100.19
粳稻	Round-grained rice	96.92	103.33	100.03	101.38	101.55
小麦	Wheat	98.98	103.29	99.11	101.55	100.31
玉米	Corn	101.12	100.28	99.59	100.44	100.80
大豆	Soybeans	95.08	101.42	101.91	100.29	98.82
籼米	Polished long-grained nonglutinous rice			99.54	100.93	99.96
优质籼米	High quality polished long-grained nonglutinous rice			100.92	100.37	100.33
粳米	Polished round-grained rice			101.49	100.46	100.98
面粉	Wheat flour			100.77	100.85	100.76
棉花	Cotton (unginned cotton)	95.45	89.96	111.78	108.80	94.05
花生仁	Peanut kernel			102.29	100.37	99.53
油菜籽	Rapeseeds			103.00	102.56	101.01
花生油	Peanut oil	99.06	99.82	104.79	100.88	100.66
菜籽油	Rape oil	99.69	98.16	105.70	100.86	99.57
豆油	Soybean oil	97.75	99.50	104.67	100.49	99.31
烤烟	Flue-cured tobacco			99.16	100.44	100.06
活猪	Hog	100.18	102.35	100.42	104.20	103.42
仔猪	Piglet	101.48	99.91	99.50	104.14	106.56
猪肉	Pork	101.63	101.88	100.38	104.00	101.89
牛肉	Beef	101.18	101.23	101.52	100.94	102.04
羊肉	Mutton	99.73	98.82	100.82	100.45	101.05
活鸡	Live chicken			101.24	102.06	102.69
鸡蛋	Eggs	102.32	101.97	100.55	105.66	106.21
草鱼	Grass carp	100.14	99.82	100.54	99.32	98.70
鲤鱼	Carp	98.10	98.98	99.59	99.92	97.81
鲢鱼	Silver carp			97.27	102.08	97.41
带鱼	Hairtail			101.81	99.14	100.23
大白菜	Chinese cabbage			106.42	102.87	97.45
黄瓜	Cucumber			110.20	110.32	109.54
西红柿	Tomato			116.82	118.84	113.73
菜椒	Green bell			107.43	121.98	111.82
四季豆	Kidney Beans			104.62	115.67	104.74
红富士苹果	Hongfushi Apple			97.04	92.19	93.60
香蕉	Banana			102.39	106.75	95.94
橙子	Orange			100.14	109.98	100.00

3－15 全国农产品集贸市场月度价格及走势
Monthly RMF Prices of the Agricultural Products

(10月份) (Oct.)

		2000	2001	2002	2003	2004
一、价格	Price					
(元/公斤)	(yuan/kg)					
籼稻	Long-grained nonglutinous rice	0.98	1.06	1.02	1.07	1.55
优质籼稻	High quality long-grained nonglutinous rice	1.16	1.24	1.14	1.25	1.76
粳稻	Round-grained rice	1.29	1.32	1.13	1.24	1.78
小麦	Wheat	1.00	1.12	1.02	1.14	1.58
玉米	Corn	0.90	1.10	0.97	1.16	1.43
大豆	Soybeans	2.47	2.40	2.42	3.06	3.93
籼米	Polished long-grained nonglutinous rice			1.62	1.80	2.56
优质籼米	High quality polished long-grained nonglutinous rice			1.91	2.09	2.95
粳米	Polished round-grained rice			1.93	2.03	2.96
面粉	Wheat flour			1.67	1.80	2.41
棉花	Cotton (unginned cotton)	3.50	3.20	3.93	5.90	4.93
花生仁	Peanut kernel			4.39	5.83	6.85
油菜籽	Rapeseeds			1.95	2.54	2.89
花生油	Peanut oil	8.32	7.85	7.86	9.92	11.24
菜籽油	Rape oil	6.63	5.85	6.10	7.25	7.88
豆油	Soybean oil	6.01	5.42	5.72	7.47	7.51
烤烟	Flue-cured tobacco			6.95	8.47	10.58
活猪	Hog	5.65	5.85	5.62	6.74	9.26
仔猪	Piglet	7.44	7.40	7.36	8.60	14.41
猪肉	Pork	10.16	10.30	9.91	11.79	15.07
牛肉	Beef	12.77	12.86	14.02	15.30	16.65
羊肉	Mutton	14.37	14.70	15.19	16.25	17.13
活鸡	Live chicken			8.27	9.08	10.82
鸡蛋	Eggs	5.09	5.45	5.44	5.66	6.90
草鱼	Grass carp	7.31	7.20	7.00	7.30	9.30
鲤鱼	Carp	7.65	7.32	6.87	7.14	8.76
鲢鱼	Silver carp			5.69	5.85	7.17
带鱼	Hairtail			8.86	9.44	10.37
大白菜	Chinese cabbage			0.75	1.02	0.90
黄瓜	Cucumber			1.52	1.94	1.80
西红柿	Tomato			1.63	2.14	2.05
菜椒	Green bell			1.84	2.24	2.23
四季豆	Kidney Beans			2.03	2.30	2.24
红富士苹果	Hongfushi Apple			2.73	3.16	3.29
香蕉	Banana			2.70	3.15	3.22
橙子	Orange			2.91	3.67	3.57

3—15 续表 continued

		2000	2001	2002	2003	2004
二、价格变动	Index					
（上月＝100）	(preceding month＝100)					
籼稻	Long-grained nonglutinous rice	102.33	99.03	97.39	101.72	98.94
优质籼稻	High quality long-grained nonglutinous rice	102.68	100.23	98.56	101.80	98.71
粳稻	Round-grained rice	102.59	94.94	97.39	105.02	98.84
小麦	Wheat	103.01	99.47	97.84	103.41	100.67
玉米	Corn	99.92	97.19	91.89	100.77	98.09
大豆	Soybeans	98.31	98.17	99.78	103.91	97.33
籼米	Polished long-grained nonglutinous rice			99.83	101.55	99.42
优质籼米	High quality polished long-grained nonglutinous rice			98.57	101.87	99.27
粳米	Polished round-grained rice			98.74	102.58	99.30
面粉	Wheat flour			97.03	101.95	100.21
棉花	Cotton (unginned cotton)	104.82	94.19	112.98	121.53	92.64
花生仁	Peanut kernel			96.76	102.82	99.78
油菜籽	Rapeseeds			100.41	104.09	99.21
花生油	Peanut oil	99.10	99.00	95.29	107.41	99.64
菜籽油	Rape oil	104.57	100.11	99.95	107.17	98.26
豆油	Soybean oil	98.73	99.97	97.27	113.88	97.82
烤烟	Flue-cured tobacco			88.05	98.34	102.11
活猪	Hog	101.21	99.59	100.39	107.84	99.34
仔猪	Piglet	98.65	97.60	100.85	105.81	98.78
猪肉	Pork	101.83	99.83	99.43	107.38	98.58
牛肉	Beef	99.66	100.83	101.21	101.69	100.02
羊肉	Mutton	98.86	103.22	99.98	101.42	101.09
活鸡	Live chicken			98.10	102.28	99.70
鸡蛋	Eggs	96.16	98.26	96.74	102.46	94.93
草鱼	Grass carp	99.52	98.96	98.34	100.63	97.74
鲤鱼	Carp	98.79	98.11	98.08	99.97	96.43
鲢鱼	Silver carp			97.83	99.62	98.34
带鱼	Hairtail			97.09	102.62	98.96
大白菜	Chinese cabbage			71.48	86.37	69.25
黄瓜	Cucumber			111.79	126.72	110.36
西红柿	Tomato			107.31	124.40	106.02
菜椒	Green bell			118.46	115.64	115.44
四季豆	Kidney Beans			102.21	108.65	97.42
红富士苹果	Hongfushi Apple			92.98	88.77	89.67
香蕉	Banana			101.20	100.00	96.56
橙子	Orange			97.79	92.08	96.40

3－16 全国农产品集贸市场月度价格及走势
Monthly RMF Prices of the Agricultural Products

(11月份) (Nov.)

		2000	2001	2002	2003	2004
一、价 格	Price					
(元/公斤)	(yuan/ kg)					
籼 稻	Long-grained nonglutinous rice	1.00	1.06	1.02	1.19	1.54
优质籼稻	High quality long-grained nonglutinous rice	1.19	1.25	1.14	1.41	1.75
粳 稻	Round-grained rice	1.26	1.28	1.10	1.36	1.74
小 麦	Wheat	1.02	1.11	1.05	1.26	1.56
玉 米	Corn	0.92	1.05	1.00	1.25	1.37
大 豆	Soybeans	2.46	2.36	2.46	3.40	3.78
籼 米	Polished long-grained nonglutinous rice			1.61	1.98	2.52
优质籼米	High quality polished long-grained nonglutinous rice			1.91	2.33	2.94
粳 米	Polished round-grained rice			1.90	2.25	2.90
面 粉	Wheat flour			1.70	2.01	2.41
棉 花	Cotton (unginned cotton)	3.57	2.90	4.11	6.28	4.72
花生仁	Peanut kernel			4.50	6.21	6.77
油菜籽	Rapeseeds			2.01	2.87	2.87
花生油	Peanut oil	8.16	7.88	8.13	10.78	11.04
菜籽油	Rape oil	6.24	5.88	6.15	7.93	7.80
豆 油	Soybean oil	5.94	5.36	5.82	7.67	7.31
烤 烟	Flue-cured tobacco			6.92	8.74	11.08
活 猪	Hog	5.79	5.92	5.70	7.23	8.88
仔 猪	Piglet	7.56	7.42	7.27	9.12	13.67
猪 肉	Pork	10.35	10.32	9.97	12.59	14.63
牛 肉	Beef	12.62	13.08	14.30	15.74	16.51
羊 肉	Mutton	14.63	14.62	15.37	16.60	17.15
活 鸡	Live chicken			8.34	9.52	10.52
鸡 蛋	Eggs	5.09	5.33	5.39	6.14	6.65
草 鱼	Grass carp	7.25	7.15	6.93	7.43	9.12
鲤 鱼	Carp	7.50	7.17	6.72	7.20	8.60
鲢 鱼	Silver carp			5.64	5.93	6.99
带 鱼	Hairtail			9.01	9.40	10.31
大白菜	Chinese cabbage			0.64	0.92	0.72
黄 瓜	Cucumber			2.12	2.33	1.96
西红柿	Tomato			1.98	2.49	2.06
菜 椒	Green bell			2.13	2.63	2.31
四季豆	Kidney Beans			2.50	2.65	2.52
红富士苹果	Hongfushi Apple			2.76	3.07	3.22
香 蕉	Banana			2.69	3.31	3.17
橙 子	Orange			2.60	3.44	3.40

3—16 续表 continued

		2000	2001	2002	2003	2004
二、价格变动	Index					
(上月=100)	(preceding month=100)					
籼稻	Long-grained nonglutinous rice	102.11	99.52	100.08	111.81	99.05
优质籼稻	High quality long-grained nonglutinous rice	102.74	100.25	99.55	113.03	99.53
粳稻	Round-grained rice	97.83	97.38	97.61	109.54	97.66
小麦	Wheat	101.82	98.83	102.47	110.76	99.15
玉米	Corn	102.64	95.04	103.69	107.16	95.65
大豆	Soybeans	99.60	98.00	101.64	111.10	96.15
籼米	Polished long-grained nonglutinous rice			99.29	110.03	98.52
优质籼米	High quality polished long-grained nonglutinous rice			100.03	111.72	99.42
粳米	Polished round-grained rice			98.08	110.70	97.85
面粉	Wheat flour			101.53	112.01	99.94
棉花	Cotton (unginned cotton)	102.14	90.43	104.66	106.49	95.75
花生仁	Peanut kernel			102.45	106.49	98.82
油菜籽	Rapeseeds			103.47	112.93	99.15
花生油	Peanut oil	97.99	100.39	103.40	108.63	98.21
菜籽油	Rape oil	94.17	100.50	100.93	109.33	98.91
豆油	Soybean oil	98.73	98.93	101.87	102.69	97.24
烤烟	Flue-cured tobacco			99.59	103.20	104.70
活猪	Hog	102.60	101.14	101.46	107.25	95.92
仔猪	Piglet	101.57	100.37	98.80	106.03	94.87
猪肉	Pork	101.86	100.18	100.60	106.77	97.04
牛肉	Beef	98.82	101.70	101.98	102.89	99.14
羊肉	Mutton	101.79	99.41	101.19	102.16	100.11
活鸡	Live chicken			100.86	104.87	97.25
鸡蛋	Eggs	100.04	97.86	99.00	108.51	96.40
草鱼	Grass carp	99.14	99.31	99.01	101.87	97.98
鲤鱼	Carp	98.11	97.97	97.88	100.85	98.12
鲢鱼	Silver carp			99.23	101.42	97.57
带鱼	Hairtail			101.64	99.50	99.45
大白菜	Chinese cabbage			84.55	89.76	79.28
黄瓜	Cucumber			139.74	120.47	108.84
西红柿	Tomato			121.17	116.33	100.13
菜椒	Green bell			115.22	117.34	103.77
四季豆	Kidney Beans			123.34	115.07	112.71
红富士苹果	Hongfushi Apple			101.19	97.15	97.95
香蕉	Banana			99.68	105.16	98.35
橙子	Orange			89.35	93.66	95.31

3－17 全国农产品集贸市场月度价格及走势
Monthly RMF Prices of the Agricultural Products

（12月份） (Dec.)

		2000	2001	2002	2003	2004
一、价 格	Price					
（元/公斤）	(yuan/ kg)					
籼 稻	Long-grained nonglutinous rice	1.01	1.08	1.03	1.21	1.54
优质籼稻	High quality long-grained nonglutinous rice	1.19	1.27	1.15	1.39	1.74
粳 稻	Round-grained rice	1.27	1.28	1.11	1.36	1.74
小 麦	Wheat	1.06	1.13	1.05	1.34	1.56
玉 米	Corn	0.97	1.03	1.02	1.28	1.33
大 豆	Soybeans	2.46	2.34	2.52	3.38	3.77
籼 米	Polished long-grained nonglutinous rice			1.63	2.00	2.51
优质籼米	High quality polished long-grained nonglutinous rice			1.93	2.37	2.93
粳 米	Polished round-grained rice			1.91	2.24	2.89
面 粉	Wheat flour			1.71	2.11	2.40
棉 花	Cotton (unginned cotton)	3.60	2.91	4.12	5.88	4.66
花生仁	Peanut kernel			4.64	6.33	6.72
油菜籽	Rapeseeds			2.06	2.84	2.87
花生油	Peanut oil	8.30	7.72	8.20	11.10	11.09
菜籽油	Rape oil	6.21	5.71	6.28	7.94	7.72
豆 油	Soybean oil	5.89	5.29	6.18	7.68	7.30
烤 烟	Flue-cured tobacco			7.65	8.87	11.49
活 猪	Hog	5.88	5.98	5.79	7.34	8.84
仔 猪	Piglet	7.56	7.44	7.35	9.02	13.48
猪 肉	Pork	10.21	10.34	10.12	12.55	14.40
牛 肉	Beef	12.74	13.17	14.60	15.77	16.54
羊 肉	Mutton	14.58	14.98	15.78	16.68	17.52
活 鸡	Live chicken			8.39	9.48	10.47
鸡 蛋	Eggs	5.10	5.38	5.43	6.09	6.74
草 鱼	Grass carp	7.28	7.22	6.87	7.34	9.07
鲤 鱼	Carp	7.56	7.17	6.62	7.16	8.64
鲢 鱼	Silver carp			5.64	5.85	6.96
带 鱼	Hairtail			8.94	9.22	10.20
大白菜	Chinese cabbage			0.71	0.89	0.65
黄 瓜	Cucumber			2.62	2.88	2.36
西红柿	Tomato			2.30	2.76	2.15
菜 椒	Green bell			2.49	2.87	2.67
四季豆	Kidney Beans			2.79	3.08	3.03
红富士苹果	Hongfushi Apple			2.90	3.03	3.17
香 蕉	Banana			2.77	3.35	3.20
橙 子	Orange			2.83	3.48	3.26

3－17 续表 continued

		2000	2001	2002	2003	2004
二、价格变动	Index					
(上月＝100)	(preceding month＝100)					
籼 稻	Long-grained nonglutinous rice	100.26	102.36	100.86	101.43	99.96
优质籼稻	High quality long-grained nonglutinous rice	99.68	101.65	100.86	98.83	99.57
粳 稻	Round-grained rice	100.58	99.65	101.34	99.97	100.04
小 麦	Wheat	104.23	101.86	100.51	106.15	99.68
玉 米	Corn	104.55	98.22	101.47	102.23	97.45
大 豆	Soybeans	99.95	99.27	102.59	99.52	99.70
籼 米	Polished long-grained nonglutinous rice			100.99	101.41	99.55
优质籼米	High quality polished long-grained nonglutinous rice			101.13	101.69	99.78
粳 米	Polished round-grained rice			101.02	99.69	99.52
面 粉	Wheat flour			100.75	104.96	99.83
棉 花	Cotton (unginned cotton)	100.79	100.30	100.22	93.73	98.83
花生仁	Peanut kernel			103.26	101.97	99.33
油菜籽	Rapeseeds			102.24	99.01	100.06
花生油	Peanut oil	101.78	97.98	100.86	102.98	100.50
菜籽油	Rape oil	99.52	97.02	102.15	100.11	98.94
豆 油	Soybean oil	99.15	98.71	106.18	100.16	99.93
烤 烟	Flue-cured tobacco			110.58	101.49	103.71
活 猪	Hog	101.43	101.13	101.44	101.44	99.45
仔 猪	Piglet	100.04	100.26	101.09	98.87	98.63
猪 肉	Pork	98.65	100.15	101.58	99.70	98.42
牛 肉	Beef	100.98	100.71	102.11	100.19	100.19
羊 肉	Mutton	99.68	102.46	102.64	100.46	102.18
活 鸡	Live chicken			100.65	99.52	99.51
鸡 蛋	Eggs	100.21	101.01	100.82	99.18	101.31
草 鱼	Grass carp	100.34	101.09	99.23	98.79	99.43
鲤 鱼	Carp	100.82	99.97	98.46	99.48	100.47
鲢 鱼	Silver carp			99.89	98.66	99.53
带 鱼	Hairtail			99.21	98.19	98.93
大白菜	Chinese cabbage			111.73	96.66	90.20
黄 瓜	Cucumber			123.59	123.53	120.72
西红柿	Tomato			116.15	110.91	104.67
菜 椒	Green bell			117.31	109.06	115.43
四季豆	Kidney Beans			111.47	116.54	120.18
红富士苹果	Hongfushi Apple			105.13	98.95	98.44
香 蕉	Banana			102.74	101.21	101.12
橙 子	Orange			108.70	101.40	95.95

3—18 全国农产品集贸市场月度价格走势(2004 年 1 月)
Monthly RMF Prices of the Agricultural Products(Jan. 2004)

		价 格 (元/公斤) Price (yuan/ kg)	价格走势 Increase rate		
			本月比上月上涨 Increase rate over the last month (%)	本月比上年同月上涨 Increase rate over the same month of the preceding year (%)	1—1 月比上年同期上涨 Jan. -Jan. increase rate over the same period of the preceding year (%)
籼 稻	Long-grained nonglutinous rice	1.23	1.25	16.22	16.22
优质籼稻	High quality long-grained nonglutinous rice	1.43	2.42	18.50	18.50
粳 稻	Round-grained rice	1.39	2.01	24.27	24.27
小 麦	Wheat	1.34	−0.09	18.09	18.09
玉 米	Corn	1.29	0.91	22.80	22.80
大 豆	Soybeans	3.52	3.98	29.45	29.45
籼 米	Polished long-grained nonglutinous rice	2.03	1.37	17.80	17.80
优质籼米	High quality polished long-grained nonglutinous rice	2.40	1.09	17.73	17.73
粳 米	Polished round-grained rice	2.29	2.20	16.60	16.60
面 粉	Wheat flour	2.15	1.91	21.24	21.24
棉花(籽棉)	Cotton (unginned cotton)	5.95	1.16	44.82	44.82
花生仁	Peanut kernel	6.55	3.44	30.45	30.45
油菜籽	Rapeseeds	2.81	−1.38	25.15	25.15
花生油	Peanut oil	10.99	−1.04	24.98	24.98
菜籽油	Rape oil	8.04	1.32	26.60	26.60
豆 油	Soybean oil	7.76	1.13	23.66	23.66
烤 烟	Flue-cured tobacco	9.33	5.20	18.74	18.74
活 猪	Hog	7.46	1.65	26.25	26.25
仔 猪	Piglet	9.22	2.16	22.47	22.47
猪 肉	Pork	12.73	1.43	24.82	24.82
牛 肉	Beef	16.10	2.12	7.84	7.84
羊 肉	Mutton	17.05	2.24	3.84	3.84
活 鸡	Live chicken	10.12	6.83	10.74	10.74
鸡 蛋	Eggs	6.18	1.37	12.10	12.10
草 鱼	Grass carp	7.70	4.80	6.01	6.01
鲤 鱼	Carp	7.60	6.08	8.38	8.38
鲢 鱼	Silver carp	6.26	6.98	10.10	10.10
带 鱼	Hairtail	9.64	4.51	−0.18	−0.18
大白菜	Chinese cabbage	0.88	−0.66	9.01	9.01
黄 瓜	Cucumber	3.53	22.41	5.25	5.25
西红柿	Tomato	3.23	16.80	16.66	16.66
菜 椒	Green bell	3.50	22.07	−2.15	−2.15
四季豆	Kidney Beans	3.66	18.69	1.58	1.58
红富士苹果	Hongfushi Apple	3.14	3.43	−1.08	−1.08
香 蕉	Banana	3.57	6.42	14.92	14.92
橙 子	Orange	3.53	1.37	7.70	7.70

3－19 全国农产品集贸市场月度价格走势(2004 年 2 月)
Monthly RMF Prices of the Agricultural Products(Feb. 2004)

		价 格(元/公斤) Price (yuan/ kg)	价格走势 Increase rate		
			本月比上月上涨 Increase rate over the last month (%)	本月比上年同月上涨 Increase rate over the same month of the preceding year (%)	1－2 月比上年同期上涨 Jan. -Feb. increase rate over the same period of the preceding year (%)
籼 稻	Long-grained nonglutinous rice	1.28	4.12	21.41	18.81
优质籼稻	High quality long-grained nonglutinous rice	1.47	3.14	19.86	19.19
粳 稻	Round-grained rice	1.44	3.86	27.62	25.95
小 麦	Wheat	1.35	0.67	19.90	18.99
玉 米	Corn	1.29	0.00	21.54	22.17
大 豆	Soybeans	3.56	1.30	31.41	30.43
籼 米	Polished long-grained nonglutinous rice	2.09	3.03	21.27	19.54
优质籼米	High quality polished long-grained nonglutinous rice	2.45	2.26	20.88	19.30
粳 米	Polished round-grained rice	2.36	2.77	19.02	17.81
面 粉	Wheat flour	2.17	0.58	20.51	20.87
棉花(籽棉)	Cotton (unginned cotton)	5.99	0.71	41.74	43.26
花生仁	Peanut kernel	6.49	－0.91	28.53	29.49
油菜籽	Rapeseeds	2.77	－1.33	20.85	22.98
花生油	Peanut oil	10.96	－0.22	23.52	24.25
菜籽油	Rape oil	7.95	－1.14	25.12	25.86
豆 油	Soybean oil	7.78	0.23	23.88	23.77
烤 烟	Flue-cured tobacco	9.25	－0.83	13.51	16.08
活 猪	Hog	7.42	－0.57	29.22	27.71
仔 猪	Piglet	9.37	1.68	24.57	23.52
猪 肉	Pork	12.49	－1.93	24.51	24.66
牛 肉	Beef	15.96	－0.91	7.39	7.61
羊 肉	Mutton	16.85	－1.19	3.13	3.49
活 鸡	Live chicken	9.00	－11.14	3.38	7.15
鸡 蛋	Eggs	5.82	－5.84	9.99	11.07
草 鱼	Grass carp	7.89	2.57	11.74	8.84
鲤 鱼	Carp	7.85	3.29	14.95	11.63
鲢 鱼	Silver carp	6.32	1.00	16.88	13.41
带 鱼	Hairtail	9.58	－0.63	1.30	0.55
大白菜	Chinese cabbage	0.87	－0.93	－0.97	3.80
黄 瓜	Cucumber	2.75	－21.92	－8.01	－1.00
西红柿	Tomato	3.08	－4.60	7.37	11.93
菜 椒	Green bell	3.36	－3.96	－1.91	－2.03
四季豆	Kidney Beans	3.62	－1.06	－4.81	－1.70
红富士苹果	Hongfushi Apple	3.11	－0.94	－0.61	－0.84
香 蕉	Banana	3.46	－3.12	9.87	12.38
橙 子	Orange	3.42	－3.08	8.79	8.23

3－20 全国农产品集贸市场月度价格走势(2004 年 3 月)
Monthly RMF Prices of the Agricultural Products(Mar. 2004)

		价 格(元/公斤) Price (yuan/ kg)	价格走势 Increase rate		
			本月比上月上涨 Increase rate over the last month (%)	本月比上年同月上涨 Increase rate over the same month of the preceding year (%)	1—3 月比上年同期上涨 Jan. -Mar. increase rate over the same period of the preceding year (%)
籼 稻	Long-grained nonglutinous rice	1.56	22.46	49.60	29.02
优质籼稻	High quality long-grained nonglutinous rice	1.78	21.27	45.31	27.95
粳 稻	Round-grained rice	1.78	23.49	51.46	34.72
小 麦	Wheat	1.50	11.50	36.87	24.84
玉 米	Corn	1.36	5.44	25.81	23.40
大 豆	Soybeans	3.74	4.96	33.72	31.55
籼 米	Polished long-grained nonglutinous rice	2.55	21.98	47.76	28.96
优质籼米	High quality polished long-grained nonglutinous rice	2.91	18.59	42.65	27.10
粳 米	Polished round-grained rice	2.84	20.44	46.00	27.12
面 粉	Wheat flour	2.34	7.87	32.37	24.67
棉花(籽棉)	Cotton (unginned cotton)	6.07	1.17	40.35	42.27
花生仁	Peanut kernel	6.63	2.14	26.22	28.37
油菜籽	Rapeseeds	2.79	0.64	30.09	25.26
花生油	Peanut oil	11.05	0.83	24.33	24.28
菜籽油	Rape oil	8.04	1.14	23.04	24.90
豆 油	Soybean oil	7.97	2.44	25.33	24.30
烤 烟	Flue-cured tobacco	9.31	0.57	8.65	13.49
活 猪	Hog	7.73	4.29	36.30	30.53
仔 猪	Piglet	10.38	10.75	36.83	27.98
猪 肉	Pork	12.69	1.64	28.07	25.79
牛 肉	Beef	15.93	−0.17	8.58	7.93
羊 肉	Mutton	17.04	1.11	5.20	4.05
活 鸡	Live chicken	9.21	2.38	8.14	7.47
鸡 蛋	Eggs	5.79	−0.45	14.55	12.18
草 鱼	Grass carp	8.43	6.76	18.97	12.19
鲤 鱼	Carp	8.31	5.93	23.42	15.49
鲢 鱼	Silver carp	6.55	3.59	20.80	15.83
带 鱼	Hairtail	9.59	0.10	3.04	1.37
大白菜	Chinese cabbage	0.94	7.39	−19.70	−5.80
黄 瓜	Cucumber	2.77	0.48	−2.48	−1.46
西红柿	Tomato	2.79	−9.32	−7.57	5.12
菜 椒	Green bell	3.78	12.31	−0.98	−1.66
四季豆	Kidney Beans	4.11	13.57	2.43	−0.25
红富士苹果	Hongfushi Apple	3.17	2.08	2.47	0.25
香 蕉	Banana	3.49	1.05	11.04	11.93
橙 子	Orange	3.52	2.76	13.62	9.99

3－21 全国农产品集贸市场月度价格走势(2004 年 4 月)
Monthly RMF Prices of the Agricultural Products(Apr. 2004)

		价 格 (元/公斤) Price (yuan/ kg)	价格走势 Increase rate		
			本月比上月上涨 Increase rate over the last month (%)	本月比上年同月上涨 Increase rate over the same month of the preceding year (%)	1－4 月比上年同期上涨 Jan. -Apr. increase rate over the same period of the preceding year (%)
籼 稻	Long-grained nonglutinous rice	1.58	0.92	51.76	34.66
优质籼稻	High quality long-grained nonglutinous rice	1.80	0.63	49.63	33.30
粳 稻	Round-grained rice	1.81	1.59	52.55	39.31
小 麦	Wheat	1.57	4.53	42.39	29.18
玉 米	Corn	1.44	6.22	31.00	25.35
大 豆	Soybeans	3.97	6.17	38.46	33.33
籼 米	Polished long-grained nonglutinous rice	2.60	1.97	50.27	34.30
优质籼米	High quality polished long-grained nonglutinous rice	3.01	3.39	46.85	32.06
粳 米	Polished round-grained rice	3.01	6.12	51.99	33.38
面 粉	Wheat flour	2.41	3.09	37.04	27.74
棉花(籽棉)	Cotton (unginned cotton)	6.13	1.06	39.82	41.64
花生仁	Peanut kernel	6.74	1.64	24.45	27.35
油菜籽	Rapeseeds	2.88	3.46	36.24	27.90
花生油	Peanut oil	11.30	2.17	24.62	24.36
菜籽油	Rape oil	8.11	0.85	24.16	24.71
豆 油	Soybean oil	8.04	0.84	23.12	24.00
烤 烟	Flue-cured tobacco	9.47	1.73	13.31	13.44
活 猪	Hog	8.08	4.48	43.52	33.71
仔 猪	Piglet	11.19	7.84	50.15	33.47
猪 肉	Pork	13.33	5.00	34.99	28.06
牛 肉	Beef	15.86	−0.41	8.10	7.97
羊 肉	Mutton	16.99	−0.29	6.35	4.62
活 鸡	Live chicken	9.57	3.88	13.40	8.90
鸡 蛋	Eggs	5.92	2.32	17.09	13.37
草 鱼	Grass carp	9.22	9.42	29.01	16.40
鲤 鱼	Carp	8.92	7.27	30.50	19.23
鲢 鱼	Silver carp	6.88	5.04	23.55	17.78
带 鱼	Hairtail	9.74	1.58	4.09	2.04
大白菜	Chinese cabbage	1.12	19.68	−17.24	−9.48
黄 瓜	Cucumber	2.11	−23.68	−11.32	−3.49
西红柿	Tomato	2.48	−11.36	−12.35	0.83
菜 椒	Green bell	3.48	−7.81	−11.63	−4.32
四季豆	Kidney Beans	3.48	−15.47	−3.15	−0.94
红富士苹果	Hongfushi Apple	3.44	8.41	7.92	2.19
香 蕉	Banana	3.80	8.91	21.77	14.38
橙 子	Orange	3.52	0.01	9.05	9.75

3—22 全国农产品集贸市场月度价格走势(2004年5月)
Monthly RMF Prices of the Agricultural Products (May. 2004)

		价 格(元/公斤) Price (yuan/ kg)	价格走势 Increase rate		
			本月比上月上涨 Increase rate over the last month (%)	本月比上年同月上涨 Increase rate over the same month of the preceding year (%)	1—5月比上年同期上涨 Jan. -May. increase rate over the same period of the preceding year (%)
籼 稻	Long-grained nonglutinous rice	1.58	−0.24	49.68	37.68
优质籼稻	High quality long-grained nonglutinous rice	1.79	−0.58	48.26	36.27
粳 稻	Round-grained rice	1.79	−0.94	55.67	42.58
小 麦	Wheat	1.55	−1.07	40.66	31.46
玉 米	Corn	1.45	0.90	28.36	25.98
大 豆	Soybeans	4.02	1.25	37.98	34.30
籼 米	Polished long-grained nonglutinous rice	2.59	−0.72	49.38	37.32
优质籼米	High quality polished long-grained nonglutinous rice	2.97	−1.13	44.99	34.66
粳 米	Polished round-grained rice	2.96	−1.80	49.88	36.69
面 粉	Wheat flour	2.40	−0.55	36.37	29.45
棉花(籽棉)	Cotton (unginned cotton)	6.06	−1.16	36.33	40.54
花生仁	Peanut kernel	6.79	0.71	22.45	26.31
油菜籽	Rapeseeds	2.84	−1.49	25.61	27.43
花生油	Peanut oil	11.24	−0.53	22.76	24.04
菜籽油	Rape oil	8.17	0.77	24.13	24.60
豆 油	Soybean oil	7.94	−1.23	20.63	23.30
烤 烟	Flue-cured tobacco	9.72	2.64	11.97	13.14
活 猪	Hog	8.15	0.88	46.57	36.22
仔 猪	Piglet	11.26	0.66	55.43	37.73
猪 肉	Pork	13.53	1.50	37.71	29.96
牛 肉	Beef	15.90	0.20	9.26	8.23
羊 肉	Mutton	16.80	−1.12	6.69	5.02
活 鸡	Live chicken	9.81	2.55	18.22	10.70
鸡 蛋	Eggs	5.91	−0.20	18.58	14.37
草 鱼	Grass carp	9.65	4.66	34.54	20.04
鲤 鱼	Carp	9.72	9.03	40.79	23.57
鲢 鱼	Silver carp	7.24	5.25	28.59	19.98
带 鱼	Hairtail	10.14	4.11	8.73	3.37
大白菜	Chinese cabbage	1.03	−8.20	7.63	−6.31
黄 瓜	Cucumber	1.60	−24.25	15.37	−1.47
西红柿	Tomato	1.97	−20.36	−0.98	0.56
菜 椒	Green bell	2.84	−18.44	14.81	−1.58
四季豆	Kidney Beans	2.77	−20.22	14.44	1.20
红富士苹果	Hongfushi Apple	3.67	6.80	7.48	3.32
香 蕉	Banana	3.94	3.65	29.09	17.27
橙 子	Orange	3.64	3.61	13.57	10.52

3－23　全国农产品集贸市场月度价格走势(2004年6月)
Monthly RMF Prices of the Agricultural Products(Jun. 2004)

		价　格 (元/公斤) Price (yuan/ kg)	价格走势 Increase rate		
			本月比上月上涨 Increase rate over the last month (%)	本月比上年同月上涨 Increase rate over the same month of the preceding year (%)	1－6月比上年同期上涨 Jan. -Jun. increase rate over the same period of the preceding year (%)
籼　稻	Long-grained nonglutinous rice	1.59	0.69	51.90	40.04
优质籼稻	High quality long-grained nonglutinous rice	1.80	0.59	47.38	38.13
粳　稻	Round-grained rice	1.79	－0.20	53.69	44.44
小　麦	Wheat	1.54	－0.87	40.76	32.99
玉　米	Corn	1.45	－0.14	27.10	26.17
大　豆	Soybeans	4.06	1.00	40.05	35.29
籼　米	Polished long-grained nonglutinous rice	2.59	0.30	48.89	39.26
优质籼米	High quality polished long-grained nonglutinous rice	2.97	－0.16	45.09	36.40
粳　米	Polished round-grained rice	2.94	－0.47	50.91	39.04
面　粉	Wheat flour	2.39	－0.36	36.28	30.58
棉花(籽棉)	Cotton (unginned cotton)	5.93	－2.06	36.78	39.91
花生仁	Peanut kernel	6.86	1.02	22.39	25.62
油菜籽	Rapeseeds	2.82	－0.80	23.35	26.73
花生油	Peanut oil	11.12	－1.05	22.27	23.74
菜籽油	Rape oil	8.13	－0.53	22.30	24.21
豆　油	Soybean oil	7.83	－1.34	21.41	22.99
烤　烟	Flue-cured tobacco	9.76	0.43	10.49	12.67
活　猪	Hog	8.46	3.75	52.87	38.93
仔　猪	Piglet	11.87	5.39	61.66	41.67
猪　肉	Pork	14.02	3.65	42.58	32.04
牛　肉	Beef	15.95	0.35	8.34	8.25
羊　肉	Mutton	16.76	－0.19	5.61	5.12
活　鸡	Live chicken	9.96	1.55	19.52	12.13
鸡　蛋	Eggs	6.41	8.46	29.15	16.75
草　鱼	Grass carp	9.94	3.02	37.31	22.95
鲤　鱼	Carp	10.25	5.46	47.24	27.56
鲢　鱼	Silver carp	7.63	5.44	33.31	22.26
带　鱼	Hairtail	10.53	3.86	14.64	5.21
大白菜	Chinese cabbage	0.98	－4.61	18.98	－2.83
黄　瓜	Cucumber	1.13	－29.23	23.10	0.16
西红柿	Tomato	1.39	－29.54	3.24	0.80
菜　椒	Green bell	1.80	－36.48	9.72	－0.59
四季豆	Kidney Beans	1.86	－32.97	22.31	2.89
红富士苹果	Hongfushi Apple	3.89	5.95	6.58	3.93
香　蕉	Banana	3.77	－4.28	26.46	18.75
橙　子	Orange	3.62	－0.69	4.50	9.44

3－24 全国农产品集贸市场月度价格走势(2004 年 7 月)
Monthly RMF Prices of the Agricultural Products (Jul. 2004)

		价 格 (元/公斤) Price (yuan/ kg)	价格走势 Increase rate		
			本月比上月上涨 Increase rate over the last month (%)	本月比上年同月上涨 Increase rate over the same month of the preceding year (%)	1－7 月比上年同期上涨 Jan. -Jul. increase rate over the same period of the preceding year (%)
籼 稻	Long-grained nonglutinous rice	1.57	－0.96	50.44	41.52
优质籼稻	High quality long-grained nonglutinous rice	1.80	0.18	48.20	39.57
粳 稻	Round-grained rice	1.78	－0.13	53.84	45.79
小 麦	Wheat	1.53	－0.80	41.57	34.19
玉 米	Corn	1.46	0.61	28.89	26.57
大 豆	Soybeans	4.09	0.68	40.47	36.05
籼 米	Polished long-grained nonglutinous rice	2.59	－0.27	48.02	40.52
优质籼米	High quality polished long-grained nonglutinous rice	2.96	－0.44	44.97	37.62
粳 米	Polished round-grained rice	2.95	0.22	50.70	40.70
面 粉	Wheat flour	2.39	0.06	36.34	31.40
棉花(籽棉)	Cotton (unginned cotton)	5.75	－3.11	30.08	38.47
花生仁	Peanut kernel	6.86	0.11	23.52	25.31
油菜籽	Rapeseeds	2.90	3.06	23.14	26.19
花生油	Peanut oil	11.27	1.35	23.50	23.70
菜籽油	Rape oil	8.03	－1.24	20.20	23.62
豆 油	Soybean oil	7.70	－1.70	18.58	22.35
烤 烟	Flue-cured tobacco	10.22	4.69	16.24	13.20
活 猪	Hog	8.63	2.10	49.48	40.46
仔 猪	Piglet	12.59	6.03	67.63	45.40
猪 肉	Pork	14.44	2.98	41.70	33.45
牛 肉	Beef	16.13	1.10	9.10	8.37
羊 肉	Mutton	16.72	－0.26	5.26	5.14
活 鸡	Live chicken	10.20	2.35	19.75	13.21
鸡 蛋	Eggs	6.36	－0.88	29.03	18.44
草 鱼	Grass carp	9.74	－2.04	33.42	24.47
鲤 鱼	Carp	9.77	－4.66	38.73	29.19
鲢 鱼	Silver carp	7.56	－0.99	32.22	23.71
带 鱼	Hairtail	10.49	－0.44	14.30	6.48
大白菜	Chinese cabbage	1.22	23.93	30.02	1.61
黄 瓜	Cucumber	1.21	6.51	35.87	2.31
西红柿	Tomato	1.34	－3.63	24.50	2.40
菜 椒	Green bell	1.58	－12.27	19.05	0.70
四季豆	Kidney Beans	1.83	－1.55	34.02	4.98
红富士苹果	Hongfushi Apple	3.99	2.55	4.25	3.98
香 蕉	Banana	3.51	－7.10	21.07	19.06
橙 子	Orange	3.75	3.59	11.36	9.73

3－25 全国农产品集贸市场月度价格走势(2004 年 8 月)
Monthly RMF Prices of the Agricultural Products(Aug. 2004)

		价 格 (元/公斤) Price (yuan/ kg)	价格走势 Increase rate		
			本月比上月上涨 Increase rate over the last month (%)	本月比上年同月上涨 Increase rate over the same month of the preceding year (%)	1－8 月比上年同期上涨 Jan. -Aug. increase rate over the same period of the preceding year (%)
籼 稻	Long-grained nonglutinous rice	1. 55	－1. 38	48. 13	42. 34
优质籼稻	High quality long-grained nonglutinous rice	1. 78	－1. 19	46. 51	40. 44
粳 稻	Round-grained rice	1. 77	－0. 57	52. 13	46. 59
小 麦	Wheat	1. 56	2. 30	44. 04	35. 40
玉 米	Corn	1. 45	－0. 97	25. 77	26. 47
大 豆	Soybeans	4. 08	－0. 10	39. 10	36. 44
籼 米	Polished long-grained nonglutinous rice	2. 57	－0. 54	46. 73	41. 30
优质籼米	High quality polished long-grained nonglutinous rice	2. 97	0. 36	45. 22	38. 57
粳 米	Polished round-grained rice	2. 96	0. 24	49. 88	41. 85
面 粉	Wheat flour	2. 39	－0. 05	36. 57	32. 04
棉花(籽棉)	Cotton (unginned cotton)	5. 66	－1. 61	26. 86	38. 23
花生仁	Peanut kernel	6. 90	0. 47	22. 01	24. 88
油菜籽	Rapeseeds	2. 89	－0. 50	21. 20	25. 53
花生油	Peanut oil	11. 21	－0. 53	22. 35	23. 53
菜籽油	Rape oil	8. 06	0. 41	20. 15	23. 18
豆 油	Soybean oil	7. 73	0. 45	18. 57	21. 87
烤 烟	Flue-cured tobacco	10. 36	1. 37	20. 80	14. 16
活 猪	Hog	9. 01	4. 41	50. 21	41. 73
仔 猪	Piglet	13. 69	8. 77	75. 33	49. 30
猪 肉	Pork	15. 01	3. 93	42. 10	34. 58
牛 肉	Beef	16. 32	1. 20	9. 51	8. 51
羊 肉	Mutton	16. 77	0. 30	5. 13	5. 14
活 鸡	Live chicken	10. 57	3. 65	21. 51	14. 26
鸡 蛋	Eggs	6. 84	7. 64	30. 83	20. 02
草 鱼	Grass carp	9. 65	－0. 97	32. 12	25. 44
鲤 鱼	Carp	9. 29	－4. 96	30. 01	29. 30
鲢 鱼	Silver carp	7. 48	－1. 01	30. 10	24. 53
带 鱼	Hairtail	10. 45	－0. 31	12. 63	7. 24
大白菜	Chinese cabbage	1. 34	9. 53	15. 91	3. 64
黄 瓜	Cucumber	1. 49	23. 43	7. 46	2. 75
西红柿	Tomato	1. 70	27. 26	17. 57	3. 67
菜 椒	Green bell	1. 73	9. 18	8. 73	1. 28
四季豆	Kidney Beans	2. 19	19. 81	19. 85	6. 21
红富士苹果	Hongfushi Apple	3. 92	－1. 87	1. 58	3. 64
香 蕉	Banana	3. 47	－0. 91	17. 74	18. 90
橙 子	Orange	3. 70	－1. 21	2. 25	8. 70

3－26 全国农产品集贸市场月度价格走势(2004 年 9 月)
Monthly RMF Prices of the Agricultural Products(Sep. 2004)

		价 格(元/公斤) Price (yuan/ kg)	价格走势 Increase rate		
			本月比上月上涨 Increase rate over the last month (%)	本月比上年同月上涨 Increase rate over the same month of the preceding year (%)	1－9 月比上年同期上涨 Jan. -Sep. increase rate over the same period of the preceding year (%)
籼 稻	Long-grained nonglutinous rice	1.57	1.22	49.25	43.11
优质籼稻	High quality long-grained nonglutinous rice	1.78	0.19	45.37	40.99
粳 稻	Round-grained rice	1.80	1.55	52.38	47.25
小 麦	Wheat	1.57	0.31	42.27	36.16
玉 米	Corn	1.46	0.80	26.23	26.44
大 豆	Soybeans	4.04	－1.18	37.06	36.51
籼 米	Polished long-grained nonglutinous rice	2.57	－0.04	45.32	41.76
优质籼米	High quality polished long-grained nonglutinous rice	2.98	0.33	45.16	39.31
粳 米	Polished round-grained rice	2.99	0.98	50.64	42.83
面 粉	Wheat flour	2.41	0.76	36.44	32.53
棉花(籽棉)	Cotton (unginned cotton)	5.32	－5.95	9.67	33.63
花生仁	Peanut kernel	6.86	－0.47	20.99	24.43
油菜籽	Rapeseeds	2.92	1.01	19.37	24.80
花生油	Peanut oil	11.28	0.66	22.08	23.37
菜籽油	Rape oil	8.02	－0.43	18.62	22.65
豆 油	Soybean oil	7.68	－0.69	17.18	21.34
烤 烟	Flue-cured tobacco	10.36	0.06	20.34	14.86
活 猪	Hog	9.32	3.42	49.10	42.62
仔 猪	Piglet	14.59	6.56	79.41	52.89
猪 肉	Pork	15.29	1.89	39.22	35.14
牛 肉	Beef	16.65	2.04	10.70	8.76
羊 肉	Mutton	16.95	1.05	5.76	5.21
活 鸡	Live chicken	10.85	2.69	22.26	15.18
鸡 蛋	Eggs	7.27	6.21	31.51	21.38
草 鱼	Grass carp	9.52	－1.30	31.30	26.10
鲤 鱼	Carp	9.09	－2.19	27.26	29.06
鲢 鱼	Silver carp	7.29	－2.59	24.15	24.49
带 鱼	Hairtail	10.48	0.23	13.87	7.97
大白菜	Chinese cabbage	1.30	－2.55	9.80	4.43
黄 瓜	Cucumber	1.63	9.54	6.71	3.09
西红柿	Tomato	1.94	13.73	12.51	4.47
菜 椒	Green bell	1.93	11.82	－0.33	1.15
四季豆	Kidney Beans	2.30	4.74	8.51	6.41
红富士苹果	Hongfushi Apple	3.67	－6.40	3.13	3.58
香 蕉	Banana	3.33	－4.06	5.81	17.40
橙 子	Orange	3.70	0.00	－7.03	6.64

3－27 全国农产品集贸市场月度价格走势(2004年10月)
Monthly RMF Prices of the Agricultural Products(Oct. 2004)

		价 格 (元/公斤) Price (yuan/ kg)	价格走势 Increase rate		
			本月比上月上涨 Increase rate over the last month (%)	本月比上年同月上涨 Increase rate over the same month of the preceding year (%)	1－10月比上年同期上涨 Jan. -Oct. increase rate over the same period of the preceding year (%)
籼 稻	Long-grained nonglutinous rice	1.55	－1.06	45.18	43.32
优质籼稻	High quality long-grained nonglutinous rice	1.76	－1.29	40.96	40.99
粳 稻	Round-grained rice	1.78	－1.16	43.41	46.84
小 麦	Wheat	1.58	0.67	38.50	36.40
玉 米	Corn	1.43	－1.91	22.88	26.07
大 豆	Soybeans	3.93	－2.67	28.38	35.65
籼 米	Polished long-grained nonglutinous rice	2.56	－0.58	42.27	41.81
优质籼米	High quality polished long-grained nonglutinous rice	2.95	－0.73	41.46	39.53
粳 米	Polished round-grained rice	2.96	－0.70	45.82	43.14
面 粉	Wheat flour	2.41	0.21	34.11	32.69
棉花(籽棉)	Cotton (unginned cotton)	4.93	－7.36	－16.40	27.14
花生仁	Peanut kernel	6.85	－0.22	17.42	23.68
油菜籽	Rapeseeds	2.89	－0.79	13.77	23.58
花生油	Peanut oil	11.24	－0.36	13.25	22.27
菜籽油	Rape oil	7.88	－1.74	8.76	21.14
豆 油	Soybean oil	7.51	－2.18	0.66	18.99
烤 烟	Flue-cured tobacco	10.58	2.11	24.94	15.86
活 猪	Hog	9.26	－0.66	37.34	42.01
仔 猪	Piglet	14.41	－1.22	67.49	54.53
猪 肉	Pork	15.07	－1.42	27.81	34.30
牛 肉	Beef	16.65	0.02	8.88	8.77
羊 肉	Mutton	17.13	1.09	5.42	5.23
活 鸡	Live chicken	10.82	－0.30	19.17	15.60
鸡 蛋	Eggs	6.90	－5.07	21.83	21.43
草 鱼	Grass carp	9.30	－2.26	27.52	26.24
鲤 鱼	Carp	8.76	－3.57	22.75	28.42
鲢 鱼	Silver carp	7.17	－1.66	22.56	24.29
带 鱼	Hairtail	10.37	－1.04	9.80	8.16
大白菜	Chinese cabbage	0.90	－30.75	－11.96	2.80
黄 瓜	Cucumber	1.80	10.36	－7.07	2.09
西红柿	Tomato	2.05	6.02	－4.12	3.60
菜 椒	Green bell	2.23	15.44	－0.49	1.01
四季豆	Kidney Beans	2.24	－2.58	－2.69	5.62
红富士苹果	Hongfushi Apple	3.29	－10.33	4.17	3.64
香 蕉	Banana	3.22	－3.44	2.17	15.84
橙 子	Orange	3.57	－3.60	－2.66	5.64

3—28 全国农产品集贸市场月度价格走势(2004 年 11 月)
Monthly RMF Prices of the Agricultural Products (Nov. 2004)

		价 格 (元/公斤) Price (yuan/ kg)	价格走势 Increase rate		
			本月比上月上涨 Increase rate over the last month (%)	本月比上年同月上涨 Increase rate over the same month of the preceding year (%)	1—11 月比上年同期上涨 Jan. -Nov. increase rate over the same period of the preceding year (%)
籼 稻	Long-grained nonglutinous rice	1.54	−0.95	28.62	41.82
优质籼稻	High quality long-grained nonglutinous rice	1.75	−0.47	24.13	39.24
粳 稻	Round-grained rice	1.74	−2.34	27.86	44.86
小 麦	Wheat	1.56	−0.85	23.98	35.13
玉 米	Corn	1.37	−4.35	9.68	24.42
大 豆	Soybeans	3.78	−3.85	11.11	33.05
籼 米	Polished long-grained nonglutinous rice	2.52	−1.48	27.39	40.34
优质籼米	High quality polished long-grained nonglutinous rice	2.94	−0.58	25.88	38.13
粳 米	Polished round-grained rice	2.90	−2.15	28.90	41.68
面 粉	Wheat flour	2.41	−0.06	19.65	31.35
棉花(籽棉)	Cotton (unginned cotton)	4.72	−4.25	−24.83	20.83
花生仁	Peanut kernel	6.77	−1.18	8.95	22.17
油菜籽	Rapeseeds	2.87	−0.85	−0.11	20.96
花生油	Peanut oil	11.04	−1.79	2.38	20.17
菜籽油	Rape oil	7.80	−1.09	−1.61	18.71
豆 油	Soybean oil	7.31	−2.76	−4.68	16.51
烤 烟	Flue-cured tobacco	11.08	4.70	26.76	16.88
活 猪	Hog	8.88	−4.08	22.84	39.91
仔 猪	Piglet	13.67	−5.13	49.86	54.03
猪 肉	Pork	14.63	−2.96	16.16	32.33
牛 肉	Beef	16.51	−0.86	4.91	8.40
羊 肉	Mutton	17.15	0.11	3.30	5.05
活 鸡	Live chicken	10.52	−2.75	10.52	15.09
鸡 蛋	Eggs	6.65	−3.60	8.24	20.04
草 鱼	Grass carp	9.12	−2.02	22.65	25.91
鲤 鱼	Carp	8.60	−1.88	19.43	27.58
鲢 鱼	Silver carp	6.99	−2.43	17.91	23.68
带 鱼	Hairtail	10.31	−0.55	9.75	8.30
大白菜	Chinese cabbage	0.72	−20.72	−22.24	0.75
黄 瓜	Cucumber	1.96	8.84	−16.04	0.16
西红柿	Tomato	2.06	0.13	−17.47	1.39
菜 椒	Green bell	2.31	3.77	−12.00	−0.19
四季豆	Kidney Beans	2.52	12.71	−4.69	4.69
红富士苹果	Hongfushi Apple	3.22	−2.05	5.03	3.75
香 蕉	Banana	3.17	−1.65	−4.45	13.87
橙 子	Orange	3.40	−4.69	−0.95	5.03

3—29 全国农产品集贸市场月度价格走势(2004 年 12 月)
Monthly RMF Prices of the Agricultural Products(Dec. 2004)

		价 格(元/公斤) Price (yuan/ kg)	价格走势 Increase rate		
			本月比上月上涨 Increase rate over the last month (%)	本月比上年同月上涨 Increase rate over the same month of the preceding year (%)	1—12 月比上年同期上涨 Jan. -Dec. increase rate over the same period of the preceding year (%)
籼 稻	Long-grained nonglutinous rice	1.54	−0.04	26.75	40.41
优质籼稻	High quality long-grained nonglutinous rice	1.74	−0.43	25.06	37.92
粳 稻	Round-grained rice	1.74	0.04	27.96	43.26
小 麦	Wheat	1.56	−0.32	16.42	33.30
玉 米	Corn	1.33	−2.55	4.56	22.57
大 豆	Soybeans	3.77	−0.30	11.31	30.98
籼 米	Polished long-grained nonglutinous rice	2.51	−0.45	25.05	38.91
优质籼米	High quality polished long-grained nonglutinous rice	2.93	−0.22	23.52	36.75
粳 米	Polished round-grained rice	2.89	−0.48	28.69	40.48
面 粉	Wheat flour	2.40	−0.17	13.80	29.65
棉花(籽棉)	Cotton (unginned cotton)	4.66	−1.17	−20.74	16.59
花生仁	Peanut kernel	6.72	−0.67	6.14	20.66
油菜籽	Rapeseeds	2.87	0.06	0.94	18.98
花生油	Peanut oil	11.09	0.50	−0.08	18.18
菜籽油	Rape oil	7.72	−1.06	−2.76	16.64
豆 油	Soybean oil	7.30	−0.07	−4.90	14.47
烤 烟	Flue-cured tobacco	11.49	3.71	29.54	17.98
活 猪	Hog	8.84	−0.55	20.43	37.97
仔 猪	Piglet	13.48	−1.37	49.49	53.60
猪 肉	Pork	14.40	−1.58	14.67	30.60
牛 肉	Beef	16.54	0.19	4.91	8.10
羊 肉	Mutton	17.52	2.18	5.07	5.05
活 鸡	Live chicken	10.47	−0.49	10.51	14.68
鸡 蛋	Eggs	6.74	1.31	10.56	19.14
草 鱼	Grass carp	9.07	−0.57	23.45	25.70
鲤 鱼	Carp	8.64	0.47	20.62	26.98
鲢 鱼	Silver carp	6.96	−0.47	18.95	23.28
带 鱼	Hairtail	10.20	−1.07	10.59	8.49
大白菜	Chinese cabbage	0.65	−9.80	−27.43	−1.32
黄 瓜	Cucumber	2.36	20.72	−17.95	−1.94
西红柿	Tomato	2.15	4.67	−22.11	−1.07
菜 椒	Green bell	2.67	15.43	−6.87	−0.79
四季豆	Kidney Beans	3.03	20.18	−1.72	4.08
红富士苹果	Hongfushi Apple	3.17	−1.56	4.50	3.81
香 蕉	Banana	3.20	1.12	−4.53	12.22
橙 子	Orange	3.26	−4.05	−6.27	4.07

3—30 2004年各地区农产品集贸市场价格
Annual RMF Prices of Agricultural Products by Region(2004)

单位:元/公斤 Unit:yuan/ kg

地区 Region	粮食 Grain					
	籼稻 long-grained nonglutinous rice	优质籼稻 High quality long-grained nonglutinous rice	粳稻 Round-grained rice	小麦 Wheat	玉米 Corn	大豆 Soybeans
北京 Beijing			1.93	1.42	1.36	3.68
天津 Tianjin	1.50	1.62	1.66	1.60	1.25	4.01
河北 Hebei			1.58	1.54	1.21	3.88
山西 Shanxi				1.53	1.16	3.98
内蒙古 Inner Mongolia				1.43	1.10	3.86
辽宁 Liaoning			1.71	1.80	1.12	3.53
吉林 Jilin			1.49		1.02	3.34
黑龙江 Heilongjiang			1.56		0.98	3.12
上海 Shanghai					2.00	4.60
江苏 Jiangsu	1.68	1.70	1.84	1.47	1.45	3.92
浙江 Zhejiang	1.59	2.04	1.87	1.74	2.84	4.59
安徽 Anhui	1.50	1.64	1.74	1.45	1.33	3.59
福建 Fujian	1.64	1.88	1.69	1.58	1.60	4.28
江西 Jiangxi	1.48	1.66	1.58	1.14		3.77
山东 Shandong			1.59	1.51	1.28	3.82
河南 Henan				1.45	1.26	3.83
湖北 Hubei	1.48	1.58	1.57	1.41	1.51	3.86
湖南 Hunan	1.42	1.62	1.60	2.03	1.57	4.71
广东 Guangdong	1.51	1.66	1.50	2.22		4.45
广西 Guangxi	1.57	1.94	1.90	2.12	1.57	4.33
海南 Hainan	1.53	2.03	1.50			3.84
重庆 Chongqing	1.36	1.61	1.94	1.35	1.47	3.74
四川 Sichuan	1.43	1.66	1.63	1.43	1.44	3.75
贵州 Guizhou	1.43	1.72	1.42	1.28	1.38	3.94
云南 Yunnan	1.57	2.10	1.75	1.47	1.47	3.50
陕西 Shaanxi				1.44	1.20	3.48
甘肃 Gansu				1.41	1.17	4.05
青海 Qinghai			1.70	1.66	1.15	2.80
宁夏 Ningxia			1.62	1.58	1.20	2.92
新疆 Xinjiang				1.41	1.12	3.07

3—30 续表 1 continued 1

地 区 Region	粮食 Grain				油料 Oil-bearing crops	
	籼 米 Polished long-grained nonglutinous rice	优质籼米 High quality polished long-grained nonglutinous rice	粳 米 Polished round-grained rice	面 粉 Wheat flour	花生仁 Peanut kernel	油菜籽 Rapeseeds
北 京 Beijing	2.70	2.91	2.61	2.04	6.36	
天 津 Tianjin	2.34	2.62	2.66	2.13	7.01	
河 北 Hebei	2.39	2.67	2.79	2.03	6.57	
山 西 Shanxi			2.88	2.10	6.67	
内蒙古 Inner Mongolia	2.90	3.28	2.59	2.22	6.50	2.83
辽 宁 Liaoning			2.63	2.40	6.95	
吉 林 Jilin			2.49	2.32	6.05	
黑龙江 Heilongjiang			2.48	2.23	7.06	
上 海 Shanghai	2.71	2.55	3.06	2.61	7.62	
江 苏 Jiangsu	2.57	2.63	2.83	2.23	6.88	2.75
浙 江 Zhejiang	2.50	2.85	3.01	2.67	7.08	3.13
安 徽 Anhui	2.38	2.64	2.84	2.22	6.06	2.65
福 建 Fujian	2.65	3.09	3.02	2.75	7.35	3.43
江 西 Jiangxi	2.46	2.70	2.61	2.62	7.01	2.70
山 东 Shandong			2.81	2.05	6.36	3.48
河 南 Henan	2.45	2.80	2.82	1.87	6.25	2.65
湖 北 Hubei	2.49	2.83	2.64	2.39	6.71	2.52
湖 南 Hunan	2.44	2.85	2.99	2.95	6.94	2.77
广 东 Guangdong	2.91	3.06	3.33	2.86	7.39	
广 西 Guangxi	2.54	3.13	2.97	2.92	6.67	3.11
海 南 Hainan	2.86	3.35	2.64	3.44	7.18	
重 庆 Chongqing	2.26	2.71	3.56	2.78	6.44	3.02
四 川 Sichuan	2.36	2.91	2.99	2.51	6.70	2.96
贵 州 Guizhou	2.28	2.70	2.18	2.32	6.72	2.55
云 南 Yunnan	2.39	3.31	2.85	2.64	7.27	2.78
陕 西 Shaanxi	2.22	2.40	2.98	2.16	6.36	
甘 肃 Gansu	2.84	3.22	3.35	2.08	7.56	3.22
青 海 Qinghai	2.65	3.13	3.35	2.23	7.49	
宁 夏 Ningxia			2.81	2.22	7.22	
新 疆 Xinjiang	2.40		2.85	2.02	7.61	2.24

3－30 续表 2 continued 2

地 区	Region	棉 花（籽棉）Cotton (unginned cotton)	食用油 Edible oil 花生油 Peanut oil	菜籽油 Rape oil	豆 油 Soybean oil	烤 烟 Flue-cured tobacco
北 京	Beijing	5.80	11.23	8.18	7.29	12.60
天 津	Tianjin		9.44	7.58	7.85	
河 北	Hebei	5.76	11.31	7.88	8.27	
山 西	Shanxi	5.63	6.89	7.88	7.28	
内蒙古	Inner Mongolia		11.92	8.63	8.32	
辽 宁	Liaoning	6.21	13.00		7.65	
吉 林	Jilin				7.84	6.62
黑龙江	Heilongjiang				7.59	
上 海	Shanghai			7.71	7.90	
江 苏	Jiangsu	5.36	9.11	7.71	7.73	8.07
浙 江	Zhejiang	4.48	10.99	7.84	8.32	
安 徽	Anhui	5.66	10.33	7.51	8.11	10.00
福 建	Fujian		9.70	8.53	8.16	10.69
江 西	Jiangxi	6.57	11.75	8.46	8.16	
山 东	Shandong	5.60	11.35	5.54	7.50	8.92
河 南	Henan	5.28	9.84	7.30	7.37	5.62
湖 北	Hubei	5.34	11.09	7.11	7.63	
湖 南	Hunan	5.47	11.78	8.97	8.80	7.20
广 东	Guangdong		13.26	8.77		
广 西	Guangxi		12.13	8.96	8.62	12.49
海 南	Hainan		15.32	7.64	9.23	12.00
重 庆	Chongqing	4.40	12.13	8.23	3.55	9.06
四 川	Sichuan	3.90	13.76	8.43	9.98	8.50
贵 州	Guizhou		11.37	7.86	7.15	
云 南	Yunnan		9.71	8.56		8.90
陕 西	Shaanxi	4.81	12.95	7.54	7.93	8.61
甘 肃	Gansu	5.20	13.05	8.47	8.98	5.98
青 海	Qinghai		7.50	7.82	7.90	
宁 夏	Ningxia		7.99	7.83	7.75	
新 疆	Xinjiang	4.89		7.74		7.53

3—30 续表 3 continued 3

地 区	Region	畜产品 Livestock products						
		活 猪 Hog	仔 猪 Piglet	猪 肉 Hog	牛 肉 Beef	羊 肉 Mutton	活 鸡 Live chicken	鸡 蛋 Eggs
北 京	Beijing	8.50	11.68	12.53	15.64	17.17	9.15	5.44
天 津	Tianjin	9.08	14.59	14.82	15.21	17.70	6.70	5.23
河 北	Hebei	8.47	11.76	14.15	14.39	15.68	7.26	5.39
山 西	Shanxi	8.26	15.89	13.54	14.20	14.73	8.60	5.28
内蒙古	Inner Mongolia	7.96	12.91	12.76	15.25	14.53	8.54	5.53
辽 宁	Liaoning	8.17	17.27	13.65	15.57	16.64	10.43	5.35
吉 林	Jilin	7.96	13.54	12.36	14.81	16.28	8.82	5.54
黑龙江	Heilongjiang	7.86	11.67	12.08	14.74	15.56	7.75	5.26
上 海	Shanghai			16.02	19.71	21.30	10.45	6.37
江 苏	Jiangsu	8.42	9.27	15.12	17.29	17.01	8.13	5.83
浙 江	Zhejiang	8.26	9.58	15.48	21.33	21.10	10.74	6.34
安 徽	Anhui	9.06	12.18	15.13	15.98	14.69	10.88	6.83
福 建	Fujian	9.78	12.33	14.28	19.89	22.53	14.80	7.92
江 西	Jiangxi	9.19	12.20	15.14	16.81	18.18	11.00	8.32
山 东	Shandong	8.55	10.09	14.38	15.11	16.48	7.88	5.42
河 南	Henan	8.74	13.27	13.94	14.26	15.52	7.66	5.40
湖 北	Hubei	8.65	15.05	15.13	14.70	13.41	10.74	6.86
湖 南	Hunan	8.70	13.17	14.66	17.38	17.76	11.36	7.39
广 东	Guangdong	11.13	9.77	14.01	18.67	19.06	11.94	7.14
广 西	Guangxi	8.37	9.93	14.26	18.73	24.06	14.58	7.10
海 南	Hainan	10.41	16.27	19.55	19.47	33.12	15.65	7.81
重 庆	Chongqing	7.46	8.28	13.07	14.43	12.72	12.80	7.26
四 川	Sichuan	7.24	8.69	11.88	14.67	14.35	11.68	7.97
贵 州	Guizhou	8.64	10.38	13.15	16.97	17.31	12.52	9.14
云 南	Yunnan	7.77	9.45	13.57	18.06	20.47	11.91	7.88
陕 西	Shaanxi	7.98	17.26	13.38	15.97	15.11	9.11	5.81
甘 肃	Gansu	8.38	16.76	13.41	15.70	15.28	11.14	5.55
青 海	Qinghai	8.72		12.63	15.57	14.47	11.54	6.12
宁 夏	Ningxia	8.20	13.94	12.14	15.88	15.25	8.17	5.94
新 疆	Xinjiang	8.37	10.96	13.12	17.69	21.00	9.67	6.20

3—30 续表 4 continued 4

地区	Region	水产品 Aquatic products 草鱼 Grass carp	鲤鱼 Carp	鲢鱼 Silver carp	带鱼 Hairtail	水果 Fruits 红富士苹果 Hongfushi apple	香蕉 Banana	橙子 Orange
北京	Beijing	11.42	9.24	7.60	9.62	2.42	3.48	4.18
天津	Tianjin	8.50	8.54	5.83	7.65	2.69	3.96	2.81
河北	Hebei	9.63	9.52	6.14	9.56	2.14	3.59	2.90
山西	Shanxi	12.59	9.77	6.65	10.00	2.33	4.08	
内蒙古	Inner Mongolia		10.44	6.72	7.69	3.25	4.38	3.88
辽宁	Liaoning	9.73	10.20	7.54	9.80	3.10	4.56	4.03
吉林	Jilin	9.71	10.07	7.48	8.85	3.80	4.67	4.51
黑龙江	Heilongjiang		10.45	6.95	8.94	4.09	4.99	4.27
上海	Shanghai	10.08	7.63	7.28	16.65	4.78	4.47	5.26
江苏	Jiangsu	8.26	7.70	6.14	10.11	3.16	3.45	4.08
浙江	Zhejiang	9.11	8.89	7.23		5.11	3.64	
安徽	Anhui	7.95	7.84	5.91	9.69	2.82	3.18	3.22
福建	Fujian	10.64	9.66	8.17	10.57	4.37	2.76	4.81
江西	Jiangxi	8.92	7.55	6.34	8.92	3.45	2.64	3.54
山东	Shandong	9.18	9.14	6.16	8.00	2.12	3.39	3.15
河南	Henan	9.01	8.82	6.01	8.61	2.21	2.91	2.11
湖北	Hubei	7.67	6.39	4.72	11.29	3.54	3.60	3.20
湖南	Hunan	8.75	7.51	5.41	14.00	4.42	3.17	4.05
广东	Guangdong	9.34	7.02	7.18	12.79	4.99	2.39	2.89
广西	Guangxi	9.39	8.80	5.97	10.42	5.56	2.11	2.61
海南	Hainan	6.76	6.89	7.27	11.78	5.46	1.34	3.79
重庆	Chongqing	9.10	9.85	8.01	11.13	4.13	3.41	2.66
四川	Sichuan	8.47	8.91		10.06	4.18	3.35	2.21
贵州	Guizhou	9.81	10.06		10.48	3.04	2.64	2.35
云南	Yunnan	8.58	9.55	7.54	10.38	3.77	2.02	3.09
陕西	Shaanxi	10.04	9.66	6.56	10.37	2.24	3.91	2.50
甘肃	Gansu	10.75	9.90	8.83	11.31	2.71	4.76	3.09
青海	Qinghai	13.56	11.35	6.81	10.44	4.00	4.93	3.69
宁夏	Ningxia	9.79	10.13	5.30	9.94	1.93	4.11	2.78
新疆	Xinjiang	12.14	9.26	5.54	9.56	3.08	4.73	3.39

3—30 续表 5 continued 5

地区 Region	蔬菜 Vegetable				
	大白菜 Chinese cabbage	黄瓜 Cucumber	西红柿 Tomato	菜椒 Green bell	四季豆 Kidney beans
北京 Beijing	0.74	1.92	1.98	2.56	3.17
天津 Tianjin	0.71	2.04	2.25	2.59	2.95
河北 Hebei	0.76	1.92	1.92	2.64	3.12
山西 Shanxi	0.82	2.21	2.20	3.24	3.38
内蒙古 Inner Mongolia	0.78	2.07	2.24	2.96	2.90
辽宁 Liaoning	0.86	2.14	2.18	3.06	3.50
吉林 Jilin	0.73	2.29	2.39	2.93	3.67
黑龙江 Heilongjiang	0.93	2.43	2.63	3.27	
上海 Shanghai	1.50	2.59	3.02	3.60	4.24
江苏 Jiangsu	0.92	2.19	2.35	2.43	2.70
浙江 Zhejiang	1.56	3.19	3.33	3.89	4.62
安徽 Anhui	0.80	1.87	2.22	2.05	2.58
福建 Fujian	1.34	2.00	2.38	2.90	2.20
江西 Jiangxi	0.89	1.87	2.32	2.29	2.00
山东 Shandong	0.76	1.82	1.81	2.54	3.20
河南 Henan	0.82	1.80	1.78	2.02	2.83
湖北 Hubei	1.16	2.13	2.36	2.45	3.04
湖南 Hunan	1.26	1.99	2.47	2.47	2.68
广东 Guangdong	1.77	2.21	2.31	2.79	2.68
广西 Guangxi	1.49	1.60	1.84	2.26	2.12
海南 Hainan	1.69	1.19	1.80	2.21	1.91
重庆 Chongqing	1.05	2.19	2.39	2.30	2.28
四川 Sichuan	0.98	1.73	2.05	2.13	1.85
贵州 Guizhou	0.91	1.59	1.84	1.78	1.53
云南 Yunnan	0.93	1.55	1.61	2.19	1.58
陕西 Shaanxi	0.75	1.97	1.99	2.53	2.74
甘肃 Gansu	0.81	2.14	2.12	3.02	3.37
青海 Qinghai	1.24	2.56	2.55	3.40	
宁夏 Ningxia	0.92	2.05	1.85	2.86	3.44
新疆 Xinjiang	1.03	2.38	2.53	3.42	3.98

4

国际市场农产品价格

Prices of the Agricultural Products at the International Market

4—1 2004年1月国际市场粮食期货价格
Grain Futures Prices at the International Market (Jan. 2004)

日期 date	小 麦 Wheat	稻 谷 Rough rice	大 豆 Soybean	玉 米 Corn
1—1				
1—2	394	874	801	252
1—3				
1—4				
1—5	401	887	798	254
1—6	399	912	800	253
1—7	393	900	791	250
1—8	394	907	793	251
1—9	391	911	796	251
1—10				
1—11				
1—12	395	891	823	265
1—13	398	846	836	267
1—14	393	852	838	268
1—15	391	851	836	269
1—16	393	844	832	270
1—17				
1—18				
1—19				
1—20	399	845	834	275
1—21	391	842	833	275
1—22	390	839	841	277
1—23	387	833	844	276
1—24				
1—25				
1—26	383	847	848	280
1—27	382	826	839	278
1—28	379	802	816	272
1—29	377	790	808	270
1—30	386	803	813	274
1—31				

注：期货价格为芝加哥期货交易所(CBOT)小麦成交价。

交割日期：2004年3月。单位：小麦、玉米、大豆为美分/蒲式耳；稻谷为美分/英担。

1蒲式耳小麦、大豆=0.027216吨小麦、大豆，1英担稻谷=0.045359吨稻谷，1蒲式耳玉米=0.025401吨玉米。

Notes: The prices of futures are taken as transacted prices of wheat at CBOT.

Contract month: March 2004. Price Quotes: wheat, corn, soybean: cents/bushel; rough rice: cents/cwt.

1 bushel wheat, soybean=0.027216 ton, 1 cwt rough rice=0.045359 ton, 1bushel corn=0.025401ton.

4—2 2004年2月国际市场粮食期货价格
Grain Futures Prices at the International Market (Fed. 2004)

日期 date	小 麦 Wheat	稻 谷 Rough rice	大 豆 Soybean	玉 米 Corn
2—1				
2—2	385	791	799	272
2—3	385	777	798	273
2—4	379	777	808	272
2—5	379	769	819	273
2—6	381	766	840	278
2—7				
2—8				
2—9	379	776	838	280
2—10	384	779	844	283
2—11	389	779	840	282
2—12	388	787	824	282
2—13	382	784	823	281
2—14				
2—15				
2—16				
2—17	377	798	847	285
2—18	370	817	853	282
2—19	369	826	867	282
2—20	371	825	890	285
2—21				
2—22				
2—23	385	833	912	287
2—24	391	858	917	288
2—25	388	879	930	290
2—26	386	881	925	293
2—27	382	884	932	296
2—28				
2—29				

注：交割日期：2004年3月。

Notes：Contract month：March 2004.

4—3 2004年3月国际市场粮食期货价格
Grain Futures Prices at the International Market (Mar. 2004)

日期 date	小麦 Wheat	稻谷 Rough rice	大豆 Soybean	玉米 Corn
3—1	389	934	948	302
3—2	383	939	951	301
3—3	379	953	935	297
3—4	376	982	936	297
3—5	375	977	933	297
3—6				
3—7				
3—8	368	1000	918	293
3—9	370	1016	936	298
3—10	367	1023	940	300
3—11	365	1005	941	300
3—12	364	1017	952	300
3—13				
3—14				
3—15	369	1019	974	306
3—16	374	1023	986	306
3—17	383	1025	991	306
3—18	396	1027	1011	312
3—19	396	1004	1024	312
3—20				
3—21				
3—22	410	999	1053	317
3—23	418	1001	1049	316
3—24	414	1015	1038	313
3—25	409	1009	1028	309
3—26	404	976	1024	306
3—27				
3—28				
3—29	403	965	1009	304
3—30	412	950	1018	309
3—31				

注:交割日期:2004年5月

Notes:Contract month:May 2004.

4—4 2004年4月国际市场粮食期货价格
Grain Futures Prices at the International Market (Apr. 2004)

日期 date	小 麦 Wheat	稻 谷 Rough rice	大 豆 Soybean	玉 米 Corn
4—1	413	970	1018	326
4—2	412	1003	1036	328
4—3				
4—4				
4—5	417	1013	1043	331
4—6	413	994	1012	327
4—7	416	1007	1021	330
4—8	413	991	1008	332
4—9				
4—10				
4—11				
4—12	412	979	977	324
4—13	398	991	970	315
4—14	397	986	990	314
4—15	390	987	990	308
4—16	387	992	965	312
4—17				
4—18				
4—19	394	1008	968	313
4—20	394	1011	962	309
4—21	387	1014	938	303
4—22	382	1046	945	305
4—23	373	1057	956	303
4—24				
4—25				
4—26	371	1063	963	300
4—27	379	1073	992	308
4—28	374	1065	996	307
4—29	378	1076	1012	311
4—30				

注：交割日期：2004年5月。

Notes：Contract month：May 2004.

4—5　2004年5月国际市场粮食期货价格
Grain Futures Prices at the International Market (May. 2004)

日期 date	小麦 Wheat	稻谷 Rough rice	大豆 Soybean	玉米 Corn
5—1				
5—2				
5—3	395	1118	1021	323
5—4	406	1099	1021	324
5—5	411	1093	1019	320
5—6	406	1109	1009	314
5—7	403	1134	1012	309
5—8				
5—9				
5—10	388	1129	1014	302
5—11	382	1134	1019	298
5—12	374	1108	1004	298
5—13	369	1068	974	296
5—14	364	1062	954	292
5—15				
5—16				
5—17	363	1072	896	292
5—18	370	1068	890	292
5—19	376	1063	896	296
5—20	371	1043	881	293
5—21	370	1047	866	291
5—22				
5—23				
5—24	375	1046	868	294
5—25	378	1060	885	303
5—26	380	1067	880	302
5—27	375	1046	843	301
5—28	366	1025	821	301
5—29				
5—30				
5—31				

注：交割日期：2004年7月。

Notes: Contract month: July 2004.

4－6 2004年6月国际市场粮食期货价格
Grain Futures Prices at the International Market (Jun. 2004)

日期 date	小 麦 Wheat	稻 谷 Rough rice	大 豆 Soybean	玉 米 Corn
6－1	384	1028	858	322
6－2	380	1022	856	324
6－3	371	1008	817	313
6－4	368	1000	828	310
6－5				
6－6				
6－7	364	1014	838	299
6－8	363	1013	855	298
6－9	361	1005	856	297
6－10	353	1010	848	289
6－11				
6－12				
6－13				
6－14	355	1032	880	288
6－15	352	1008	881	283
6－16	354	1004	868	282
6－17	353	1014	872	279
6－18	353	993	869	277
6－19				
6－20				
6－21	354	979	882	272
6－22	347	962	890	270
6－23	344	943	906	271
6－24	342	941	926	274
6－25	341	937	898	275
6－26				
6－27				
6－28	338	928	896	272
6－29	338	925	896	270
6－30				

注：交割日期：2004年7月。

Notes：Contract month：July 2004.

4—7 2004年7月国际市场粮食期货价格
Grain Futures Prices at the International Market (Jul. 2004)

日期 date	小 麦 Wheat	稻 谷 Rough rice	大 豆 Soybean	玉 米 Corn
7—1	343	821	694	261
7—2	340	807	697	260
7—3				
7—4				
7—5				
7—6	342	773	683	255
7—7	348	777	704	254
7—8	344	772	682	250
7—9	340	767	684	247
7—10				
7—11				
7—12	343	758	667	245
7—13	342	748	658	246
7—14	343	729	668	246
7—15	338	723	670	244
7—16	334	732	658	240
7—17				
7—18				
7—19	334	743	660	237
7—20	333	745	655	235
7—21	327	761	639	229
7—22	324	753	615	222
7—23	328	745	616	224
7—24				
7—25				
7—26	324	713	603	221
7—27	322	724	610	222
7—28	318	727	590	220
7—29	316	717	592	220
7—30	313	716	582	219
7—31				

注:交割日期:2004年9月。

Notes:Contract month:September 2004.

4—8 2004年8月国际市场粮食期货价格
Grain Futures Prices at the International Market (Aug. 2004)

日期 date	小 麦 Wheat	稻 谷 Rough rice	大 豆 Soybean	玉 米 Corn
8—1				
8—2	314	744	571	218
8—3	315	745	568	218
8—4	318	743	573	220
8—5	321	733	598	223
8—6	320	730	575	225
8—7				
8—8				
8—9	317	751	578	227
8—10	313	770	571	225
8—11	309	776	565	223
8—12	301	775	586	218
8—13	300	768	586	217
8—14				
8—15				
8—16	299	776	573	219
8—17	307	767	590	227
8—18	304	748	596	226
8—19	308	734	594	227
8—20	310	743	593	229
8—21				
8—22				
8—23	316	756	609	232
8—24	316	769	622	232
8—25	310	770	627	231
8—26	306	766	620	226
8—27	303	765	608	223
8—28				
8—29				
8—30	306	778	621	225
8—31				

注：交割日期：2004年9月。

Notes：Contract month：September 2004.

4—9 2004年9月国际市场粮食期货价格
Grain Futures Prices at the International Market (Sep. 2004)

日期 date	小麦 Wheat	稻谷 Rough rice	大豆 Soybean	玉米 Corn
9—1	327	789	638	241
9—2	324	781	628	237
9—3	319	763	616	232
9—4				
9—5				
9—6				
9—7	315	750	587	227
9—8	318	767	582	227
9—9	321	771	583	227
9—10	325	766	572	222
9—11				
9—12				
9—13	334	770	568	220
9—14	334	779	570	219
9—15	337	760	568	219
9—16	337	745	565	218
9—17	336	735	557	216
9—18				
9—19				
9—20	329	719	545	214
9—21	332	717	544	213
9—22	330	713	540	212
9—23	325	703	539	209
9—24	324	692	529	206
9—25				
9—26				
9—27	321	691	528	208
9—28	319	685	531	208
9—29	319	695	536	208
9—30				

注:小麦、玉米交割日期:2004年12月;稻谷、大豆交割日期:2004年11月。

Notes:Contract month of wheat and corn:December 2004;

Contract month of rough rice and soybean:November 2004.

4—10 2004年10月国际市场粮食期货价格
Grain Futures Prices at the International Market (Oct. 2004)

日期 date	小 麦 Wheat	稻 谷 Rough rice	大 豆 Soybean	玉 米 Corn
10—1	304	706	534	206
10—2				
10—3				
10—4	303	706	525	203
10—5	303	709	525	204
10—6	304	708	527	206
10—7	304	707	528	208
10—8	304	696	529	205
10—9				
10—10				
10—11	303	690	535	205
10—12	304	671	512	201
10—13	311	662	510	204
10—14	313	669	513	205
10—15	317	673	516	206
10—16				
10—17				
10—18	318	690	513	205
10—19	317	699	522	205
10—20	317	698	530	207
10—21	312	691	532	206
10—22	310	689	530	203
10—23				
10—24				
10—25	314	694	539	204
10—26	314	688	538	206
10—27	317	690	535	207
10—28	321	682	531	206
10—29	320	675	528	204
10—30				
10—31				

注：小麦、玉米交割日期：2004年12月；稻谷、大豆交割日期：2004年11月。

Notes: Contract month of wheat and corn: December 2004;

Contract month of rough rice and soybean: November 2004.

4－11　2004年11月国际市场粮食期货价格
Grain Futures Prices at the International Market (Nov. 2004)

日期 date	小　麦 Wheat	稻　谷 Rough rice	大　豆 Soybean	玉　米 Corn
11－1	309	688	524	201
11－2	306	677	524	200
11－3	301	681	524	200
11－4	301	681	512	198
11－5	305	681	507	199
11－6				
11－7				
11－8	306	695	507	198
11－9	307	711	508	198
11－10	307	718	529	201
11－11	303	725	523	198
11－12	300	717	521	198
11－13				
11－14				
11－15	305	718	537	204
11－16	308	709	537	203
11－17	317	709	550	207
11－18	318	698	553	204
11－19	312	699	551	201
11－20				
11－21				
11－22	307	704	552	199
11－23	302	713	558	198
11－24	300	713	557	198
11－25				
11－26	295	713	552	198
11－27				
11－28				
11－29	289	707	540	194
11－30				

注：小麦和玉米交割日期：2004年12月；稻谷和大豆交割日期：2005年1月。
Notes：Contract month of wheat and corn：December 2004；
Contract month of Rough rice and soybean：January 2005.

4—12 2004年12月国际市场粮食期货价格
Grain Futures Prices at the International Market (Dec. 2004)

日期 date	小 麦 Wheat	稻 谷 Rough rice	大 豆 Soybean	玉 米 Corn
12—1	300	742	533	204
12—2	297	750	524	203
12—3	301	758	524	206
12—4				
12—5				
12—6	306	760	530	209
12—7	301	744	526	205
12—8	298	740	525	203
12—9	302	744	527	203
12—10	299	743	533	203
12—11				
12—12				
12—13	300	729	546	204
12—14	299	723	547	205
12—15	302	735	549	206
12—16	301	727	548	204
12—17	301	738	544	203
12—18				
12—19				
12—20	307	758	557	207
12—21	305	758	550	206
12—22	307	757	547	205
12—23	308	759	550	206
12—24				
12—25				
12—26				
12—27	306	763	555	207
12—28	304	737	554	206
12—29	303	720	551	205
12—30		714	546	204
12—31				

注：小麦和玉米交割日期：2005年3月；稻谷和大豆交割日期：2005年1月。

Notes: Contract month of wheat and corn: March 2005;

Contract month of rough rice and soybean: January 2005.

4—13 2004年1月国际市场棉花期货价格
Cotton Future Prices at the International Market (Jan. 2004)

交割日期:2004年3月 单位:美分/磅 Contract month: Mar. 2004 Price quote: US cents/lb

日期 date	最高价 High	最低价 Low	收盘价 Close	平 均 Average	交易量 Volume
1—1					
1—2					
1—3					
1—4					
1—5	76.00	75.10	75.80	75.55	13,822
1—6	76.00	75.20	75.67	75.60	8,943
1—7	75.45	73.50	74.04	74.48	8,972
1—8	75.25	73.90	75.13	74.58	7,638
1—9	75.49	74.15	74.17	74.82	4,284
1—10					
1—11					
1—12	74.70	73.10	74.26	73.90	7,221
1—13	74.40	73.80	74.31	74.10	4,030
1—14	74.40	73.50	73.57	73.95	4,871
1—15	75.10	72.30	74.49	73.70	10,782
1—16	75.10	74.05	74.72	74.58	4,492
1—17					
1—18					
1—19					
1—20	75.30	73.35	75.27	74.33	8,415
1—21	75.80	75.10	75.66	75.45	7,502
1—22	75.90	75.20	75.82	75.55	4,698
1—23	76.00	75.55	75.94	75.78	7,113
1—24					
1—25					
1—26	76.18	75.00	75.64	75.59	6,559
1—27	75.25	73.41	73.76	74.33	13,629
1—28	73.30	70.76	70.76	72.03	17,625
1—29	70.60	67.76	68.66	69.18	28,471
1—30	71.60	69.80	70.73	70.70	15,191
1—31					

注:期货价格为纽约商品交易所(NYBOT)棉花成交价。1吨=2204.6磅。

Notes: The prices of futures are taken as transacted prices of cotton at NYBOT.

1 ton=2204.6 lb.

4—14 2004年2月国际市场棉花期货价格

Cotton Future Prices at the International Market (Fed. 2004)

交割日期:2004年3月 单位:美分/磅 Contract month: Mar. 2004 Price quote: US cents/lb

日期 date	最高价 High	最低价 Low	收盘价 Close	平 均 Average	交易量 Volume
2—1					
2—2	70.73	68.40	68.64	69.57	10,753
2—3	69.10	67.20	68.90	68.15	12,170
2—4	69.90	68.70	69.25	69.30	7,103
2—5	69.70	68.40	68.50	69.05	8,769
2—6	69.25	67.51	69.07	68.38	10,308
2—7					
2—8					
2—9	69.20	67.80	67.96	68.50	11,741
2—10	67.90	64.96	64.96	66.43	12,737
2—11	66.50	64.20	64.94	65.35	11,720
2—12	67.40	65.50	66.42	66.45	8,865
2—13	67.30	66.05	66.35	66.68	3,735
2—14					
2—15					
2—16					
2—17	67.25	66.40	67.20	66.83	6,163
2—18	67.35	66.30	66.40	66.83	4,492
2—19	68.00	66.62	67.89	67.31	5,734
2—20	68.80	67.25	67.69	68.03	7,146
2—21					
2—22					
2—23	68.85	67.80	68.70	68.33	531
2—24	70.00	68.50	69.00	69.25	502
2—25	69.40	68.80	69.10	69.10	47
2—26	71.60	68.35	71.50	69.98	55
2—27	73.05	71.90	72.10	72.48	40
2—28					
2—29					

4—15　2004年3月国际市场棉花期货价格
Cotton Future Prices at the International Market (Mar. 2004)

交割日期:2004年5月　单位:美分/磅　　Contract month:May. 2004　Price quote:US cents/lb

日期 date	最高价 High	最低价 Low	收盘价 Close	平　均 Average	交易量 Volume
3—1	73.91	73.05	73.53	73.48	5,887
3—2	72.90	70.53	70.73	71.72	8,654
3—3	71.40	68.70	70.02	70.05	12,726
3—4	70.50	68.40	68.97	69.45	8,547
3—5	70.95	68.20	69.48	69.58	9,627
3—6					
3—7					
3—8	68.70	66.60	67.01	67.65	11,082
3—9	65.90	64.01	64.01	64.96	12,682
3—10	65.70	63.75	64.63	64.73	14,955
3—11	66.45	64.75	65.93	65.60	8,377
3—12	65.75	64.58	64.62	65.17	5,357
3—13					
3—14					
3—15	65.50	62.97	65.43	64.24	11,276
3—16	66.30	65.15	65.79	65.73	5,173
3—17	66.40	65.00	66.10	65.70	5,477
3—18	67.79	66.90	67.75	67.35	5,889
3—19	68.35	67.20	67.92	67.78	3,911
3—20					
3—21					
3—22	68.85	66.80	67.00	67.83	5,348
3—23	67.00	64.60	64.86	65.80	10,536
3—24	65.95	64.00	65.26	64.98	5,763
3—25	65.80	63.76	64.20	64.78	8,186
3—26	65.05	64.01	64.90	64.53	5,901
3—27					
3—28					
3—29	65.70	64.30	65.55	65.00	5,740
3—30	65.65	64.85	65.10	65.25	4,874
3—31	64.45	62.10	62.10	63.28	12,235

4—16 2004年4月国际市场棉花期货价格
Cotton Future Prices at the International Market (Apr. 2004)

交割日期:2004年5月 单位:美分/磅 Contract month:May. 2004 Price quote:US cents/lb

日期 date	最高价 High	最低价 Low	收盘价 Close	平 均 Average	交易量 Volume
4—1	62.45	60.30	61.53	61.38	15,199
4—2	63.15	61.72	62.62	62.44	6,937
4—3					
4—4					
4—5	62.82	61.15	62.18	61.99	6,894
4—6	62.25	61.08	61.72	61.67	5,815
4—7	62.30	61.40	61.68	61.85	7,892
4—8	62.75	61.70	61.71	62.23	9,808
4—9					
4—10					
4—11					
4—12	61.70	58.71	58.76	60.21	11,300
4—13	59.00	56.76	57.37	57.88	13,450
4—14	60.37	57.90	60.37	59.14	13,576
4—15	62.30	60.90	61.40	61.60	11,619
4—16	62.90	61.60	61.99	62.25	11,626
4—17					
4—18					
4—19	62.50	61.40	62.21	61.95	5,976
4—20	61.85	61.10	61.50	61.48	3,695
4—21	63.97	61.05	63.45	62.51	7,142
4—22	64.55	62.40	64.48	63.48	3,431
4—23	65.00	63.50	63.95	64.25	2,294
4—24					
4—25					
4—26	65.90	64.10	64.18	65.00	932
4—27	64.90	63.20	64.85	64.05	332
4—28	65.50	57.00	60.00	61.25	134
4—29	61.00	58.50	60.32	59.75	50
4—30	61.25	61.25	59.50	61.25	6

4—17　2004年5月国际市场棉花期货价格

Cotton Future Prices at the International Market (May. 2004)

交割日期:2004年7月　单位:美分/磅　　Contract month:Jul. 2004　Price quote:US cents/lb

日期 date	最高价 High	最低价 Low	收盘价 Close	平　均 Average	交易量 Volume
5—1					
5—2					
5—3	60.75	59.05	60.24	59.90	5,575
5—4	60.70	59.35	59.68	60.03	3,661
5—5	60.60	59.35	60.54	59.98	3,338
5—6	61.80	60.55	61.75	61.18	5,291
5—7	64.75	62.60	64.75	63.68	14,573
5—8					
5—9					
5—10	65.75	64.30	64.54	65.03	10,614
5—11	64.70	62.40	64.15	63.55	6,849
5—12	64.25	62.10	63.15	63.18	5,371
5—13	65.60	63.20	65.34	64.40	8,530
5—14	66.19	63.65	64.97	64.92	9,601
5—15					
5—16					
5—17	64.50	63.50	64.21	64.00	5,232
5—18	64.70	62.65	62.94	63.68	6,808
5—19	64.00	62.07	63.97	63.04	6,330
5—20	64.50	63.20	63.54	63.85	2,625
5—21	63.90	62.50	63.00	63.20	3,259
5—22					
5—23					
5—24	63.75	62.50	63.54	63.13	2,348
5—25	64.00	62.90	63.68	63.45	2,844
5—26	64.20	61.95	62.35	63.08	7,821
5—27	61.85	59.35	61.15	60.60	13,331
5—28	62.60	60.85	61.19	61.73	7,259
5—29					
5—30					
5—31					

4—18 2004年6月国际市场棉花期货价格

Cotton Future Prices at the International Market (Jun. 2004)

交割日期:2004年7月 单位:美分/磅 Contract month:Jul. 2004 Price quote:US cents/lb

日期 date	最高价 High	最低价 Low	收盘价 Close	平 均 Average	交易量 Volume
6—1	61.50	58.19	58.23	59.85	41,600
6—2	59.15	55.50	57.38	57.33	41,740
6—3	57.85	56.20	57.04	57.03	41,779
6—4	58.70	57.30	57.80	58.00	41,317
6—5					
6—6					
6—7	58.20	56.25	56.53	57.23	39,596
6—8	56.96	55.05	55.69	56.01	36,648
6—9	56.90	55.45	56.59	56.18	36,510
6—10	58.75	56.90	58.17	57.83	34,378
6—11					
6—12					
6—13					
6—14	59.40	57.10	57.32	58.25	24,471
6—15	56.99	54.32	54.32	55.66	18,427
6—16	54.70	51.32	51.53	53.01	14,019
6—17	52.50	51.53	52.29	52.02	11,735
6—18	52.60	51.50	52.00	52.05	9,826
6—19					
6—20					
6—21	51.50	49.60	50.09	50.55	8,814
6—22	50.50	48.20	48.40	49.35	5,710
6—23	48.40	47.00	47.95	47.70	1,310
6—24	50.85	47.90	49.30	49.38	489
6—25	51.30	50.00	50.00	50.65	209
6—26					
6—27					
6—28	50.70	48.00	48.65	49.35	138
6—29	50.60	49.00	49.70	49.80	157
6—30	48.25	47.00	48.25	47.63	117

4－19 2004年7月国际市场棉花期货价格
Cotton Future Prices at the International Market (Jul. 2004)

交割日期:2004年10月 单位:美分/磅 Contract month:Oct. 2004 Price quote:US cents/lb

日期 date	最高价 High	最低价 Low	收盘价 Close	平均 Average	交易量 Volume
7—1	52.40	50.05	50.07	51.23	667
7—2	50.30	49.20	49.47	49.75	649
7—3					
7—4					
7—5					
7—6	49.50	48.60	49.49	49.05	271
7—7	50.00	48.80	48.85	49.40	552
7—8	48.65	47.75	48.00	48.20	499
7—9	48.25	47.75	47.85	48.00	283
7—10					
7—11					
7—12	47.20	45.50	46.60	46.35	485
7—13	47.20	46.10	46.60	46.65	226
7—14	47.95	46.60	46.80	47.28	303
7—15	47.35	46.40	47.28	46.88	203
7—16	47.90	47.30	47.30	47.60	137
7—17					
7—18					
7—19	47.60	46.90	47.50	47.25	194
7—20	48.75	47.70	48.68	48.23	393
7—21	49.10	47.90	48.00	48.50	385
7—22	47.35	46.20	46.85	46.78	508
7—23	47.14	45.90	46.45	46.52	368
7—24					
7—25					
7—26	45.75	43.80	44.31	44.78	587
7—27	44.50	43.50	43.94	44.00	496
7—28	44.80	43.60	44.45	44.20	409
7—29	45.40	43.50	43.73	44.45	288
7—30	44.20	43.50	43.83	43.85	265
7—31					

4—20 2004年8月国际市场棉花期货价格

Cotton Future Prices at the International Market (Aug. 2004)

交割日期：2004年10月 单位：美分/磅 Contract month：Oct. 2004 Price quote：US cents/lb

日期 date	最高价 High	最低价 Low	收盘价 Close	平 均 Average	交易量 Volume
8—1					
8—2	44.60	43.75	44.30	44.18	467
8—3	45.50	43.80	45.46	44.65	465
8—4	45.85	44.80	44.95	45.33	285
8—5	45.80	45.10	45.73	45.45	289
8—6	45.95	44.60	44.90	45.28	175
8—7					
8—8					
8—9	45.00	44.00	44.90	44.50	206
8—10	45.20	44.70	45.05	44.95	110
8—11	45.05	44.60	44.88	44.83	181
8—12	43.02	42.00	43.02	42.51	751
8—13	43.70	42.90	43.55	43.30	180
8—14					
8—15					
8—16	44.20	43.10	43.60	43.65	178
8—17	46.60	43.50	46.60	45.05	1,070
8—18	48.00	46.35	47.35	47.18	585
8—19	47.90	46.40	47.83	47.15	430
8—20	50.80	48.00	50.80	49.40	786
8—21					
8—22					
8—23	51.15	50.10	50.60	50.63	566
8—24	51.00	50.00	50.95	50.50	465
8—25	51.28	50.00	50.24	50.64	431
8—26	50.45	48.20	48.40	49.33	552
8—27	48.20	47.12	47.90	47.66	360
8—28					
8—29					
8—30	50.90	48.25	50.90	49.58	401
8—31	53.90	51.20	53.80	52.55	570

4—21 2004年9月国际市场棉花期货价格
Cotton Future Prices at the International Market (Sep. 2004)

交割日期:2004年10月 单位:美分/磅 Contract month:Oct. 2004 Price quote:US cents/lb

日期 date	最高价 High	最低价 Low	收盘价 Close	平 均 Average	交易量 Volume
9—1	55.20	53.05	53.40	54.13	588
9—2	55.00	53.50	54.00	54.25	810
9—3	53.00	51.00	51.00	52.00	492
9—4					
9—5					
9—6					
9—7	52.20	48.00	52.20	50.10	389
9—8	53.85	51.90	53.00	52.88	588
9—9	52.60	50.25	52.55	51.43	564
9—10	52.00	50.50	51.25	51.25	445
9—11					
9—12					
9—13	53.00	51.50	53.05	52.25	252
9—14	54.00	51.40	51.45	52.70	271
9—15	52.70	51.20	51.75	51.95	146
9—16	52.00	48.90	48.97	50.45	178
9—17	50.50	49.10	50.21	49.80	60
9—18					
9—19					
9—20	49.80	48.60	49.35	49.20	296
9—21	50.25	49.55	50.20	49.90	145
9—22	51.60	50.50	51.40	51.05	314
9—23	51.55	51.00	51.01	51.28	232
9—24	51.01	49.90	49.40	50.46	170
9—25					
9—26					
9—27	51.50	50.00	50.30	50.75	13
9—28	50.59	49.00	47.95	49.80	28
9—29	49.35	47.60	48.20	48.48	29
9—30	48.00	47.50	48.10	47.75	21

4—22 2004年10月国际市场棉花期货价格

Cotton Future Prices at the International Market (Oct. 2004)

交割日期:2004年12月 单位:美分/磅 Contract month:Dec. 2004 Price quote:US cents/lb

日期 date	最高价 High	最低价 Low	收盘价 Close	平 均 Average	交易量 Volume
10—1	47.03	46.10	46.98	46.57	5,620
10—2					
10—3					
10—4	47.55	46.60	47.33	47.08	2,968
10—5	48.64	47.15	47.23	47.90	8,489
10—6	48.50	47.10	48.47	47.80	4,669
10—7	48.70	47.30	47.37	48.00	3,999
10—8	47.95	46.81	47.35	47.38	2,806
10—9					
10—10					
10—11	47.40	46.40	46.52	46.90	4,026
10—12	45.50	43.75	44.79	44.63	12,406
10—13	46.25	44.50	45.95	45.38	10,417
10—14	48.50	46.45	46.52	47.48	12,018
10—15	47.13	45.65	45.82	46.39	6,229
10—16					
10—17					
10—18	46.50	45.50	46.42	46.00	5,094
10—19	47.75	46.00	47.54	46.88	10,116
10—20	48.90	47.10	47.99	48.00	10,444
10—21	47.40	45.80	45.81	46.60	6,881
10—22	46.25	45.11	45.67	45.68	5,080
10—23					
10—24					
10—25	47.15	45.90	46.54	46.53	7,136
10—26	47.00	46.40	46.62	46.70	2,624
10—27	47.20	46.50	46.83	46.85	3,961
10—28	46.40	45.00	45.31	45.70	9,073
10—29	45.80	44.65	44.98	45.23	8,679
10—30					
10—31					

4—23 2004年11月国际市场棉花期货价格
Cotton Future Prices at the International Market (Nov. 2004)

交割日期:2004年12月 单位:美分/磅 Contract month:Dec. 2004 Price quote:US cents/lb

日期 date	最高价 High	最低价 Low	收盘价 Close	平 均 Average	交易量 Volume
11—1	44.90	43.55	43.98	44.23	9,200
11—2	45.30	43.55	45.15	44.43	6,600
11—3	45.60	44.26	44.58	44.93	7,635
11—4	44.58	43.10	43.37	43.84	8,251
11—5	43.80	43.20	43.36	43.50	7,338
11—6					
11—7					
11—8	44.20	43.36	43.83	43.78	7,417
11—9	44.70	43.80	44.04	44.25	12,107
11—10	44.58	43.35	43.65	43.97	10,953
11—11	44.20	43.50	43.88	43.85	8,767
11—12	44.40	43.50	44.34	43.95	9,973
11—13					
11—14					
11—15	45.50	44.40	44.91	44.95	13,229
11—16	47.40	45.20	46.59	46.30	14,831
11—17	47.30	46.10	47.14	46.70	5,256
11—18	48.50	47.50	48.50	48.00	6,154
11—19	48.85	45.50	47.83	47.18	5,591
11—20					
11—21					
11—22	48.80	47.70	48.78	48.25	609
11—23	49.10	48.50	49.00	48.80	1,275
11—24	49.15	48.50	48.40	48.83	777
11—25					
11—26					
11—27					
11—28					
11—29	48.50	47.95	48.50	48.23	282
11—30	48.65	48.10	48.65	48.38	257

4—24 2004年12月国际市场棉花期货价格
Cotton Future Prices at the International Market (Dec. 2004)

交割日期:2005年3月 单位:美分/磅 Contract month: Mar. 2005 Price quote: US cents/lb

日期 date	最高价 High	最低价 Low	收盘价 Close	平 均 Average	交易量 Volume
12—1	44.78	43.25	43.89	44.02	8,117
12—2	43.90	43.30	43.62	43.60	2,828
12—3	43.70	42.00	42.42	42.85	12,099
12—4					
12—5					
12—6	42.65	41.72	42.53	42.19	8,320
12—7	43.20	42.45	43.19	42.83	5,740
12—8	42.95	42.50	42.60	42.73	3,817
12—9	43.05	42.60	42.86	42.83	3,371
12—10	43.75	42.10	42.31	42.93	7,989
12—11					
12—12					
12—13	43.25	42.60	43.22	42.93	5,623
12—14	43.55	42.60	42.63	43.08	5,809
12—15	43.50	42.65	42.76	43.08	4,772
12—16	43.48	42.76	43.46	43.12	3,623
12—17	44.15	43.30	44.13	43.73	8,880
12—18					
12—19					
12—20	44.50	43.90	43.99	44.20	6,853
12—21	44.25	43.60	43.62	43.93	4,388
12—22	43.70	42.21	42.72	42.96	10,954
12—23	43.00	42.51	42.90	42.76	2,801
12—24					
12—25					
12—26					
12—27	42.95	42.17	42.92	42.56	5,218
12—28	44.24	43.00	44.20	43.62	12,513
12—29	44.58	43.65	44.01	44.12	9,573
12—30	44.95	43.00	44.77	43.98	13,604
12—31					

5

全国农产品价格调查方案

Programmes for the Survey of the Prices of Agricultural Products in China

5—1　农产品生产价格调查与指数编报方案

一、调查目的

农产品生产价格是指农产品生产者第一手(直接)出售其产品时实际获得的单位产品价格。开展农产品生产价格调查是为了全面收集农产品生产价格资料,客观反映全国农产品生产价格水平和结构变动情况,满足农业与国民经济核算需要,为各级政府制定农业保护与农产品流通政策提供决策依据,向社会各界提供优质的农产品价格信息服务。

二、调查对象

抽选的农业生产经营单位。

三、调查方式

农产品生产价格调查采取抽样调查和重点调查相结合的调查方法。抽样调查将有农产品出售的农业生产经营单位列为调查对象,采取随机抽样的调查方法;对一些区域性比较强的农产品则采取在主产区主观选样的方法选择农业生产经营单位作为调查对象

四、调查内容

农产品生产价格调查的内容为被调查单位生产并出售的主要农产品,被调查单位在辅助调查员的指导下将在报告期出售的农产品的名称、出售数量、价格、金额即时记入农产品生产价格调查台帐(台帐表式附后)。

在充分征求部门、地方意见的基础上,根据新的行业分类标准,国家统计局农村司制定了《农产品参考目录》,各地必须执行全国统一的分类标准和代码。

五、调查周期和数据上报

农产品生产价格调查周期为季度,执行日历年度。

《农产品生产价格基层表》数据由县农调队(统计局)根据住户台帐或住户日记帐数据整理、录入、计算、审核并于季度最后月的 25 日前从网上上报所在省(区、市)农调队。季报表数据应包括农业生产经营单位在报告期出售的农产品的名称、产品代码、计量单位、出售数量、金额、价格以及相应的基期价格。基期价格由县队直接从相应的基期报表中过录。

《农产品生产价格指数表》综合定期报表由各省(区、市)农调队上报国家统计局农村司,时间为季(年)度最后月的 25 日前。

六、农产品生产价格的汇总方法

(一)调查单位每种农产品的平均价格(加权算术平均法):

某调查单位在报告期某产品出售金额之和除以报告期该产品出售数量之和。公式为:

$$p_i=\frac{\sum_{j=1}^{n}p_{ij}q_{ij}}{\sum_{j=1}^{n}q_{ij}}$$

式中,p_i 为第 i 个代表品的平均价格,p_{ij} 为第 i 个代表品第 j 次的出售价格,q_{ij} 为第 i 个代表品第 j 次的出售数量。

(二)全国及省(区、市)产品平均价格(加权算术平均法):

全部被调查单位报告期某产品出售金额之和除以报告期该产品出售数量之和。公式为:

$$P_i=\frac{\sum_{j=1}^{n}p_{ij}q_{ij}}{\sum_{j=1}^{n}q_{ij}}$$

式中,P_i 为第 i 个代表品的平均价格,p_{ij} 为第 i 个代表品第 j 个调查单位的出售价格,q_{ij} 为第 i 个代表品第 j 调查单位的出售数量。

七、农产品代表产品的确定

(一)代表产品选择的原则和要求:

1. 农、林、牧、渔四大类、各中类以及 90%以上的小类均选有代表品,以使价格指数能较好地反映各类别价格变动情况。

2. 选择对国计民生影响大的产品,一般生产量和销售量大的产品对国计民生影响较大。

3. 选择稳定性强的产品,因为代表品一经确定,就要连续观察几年。

4. 选择具有发展前景的新产品作为代表品。

5. 具有地方特色的产品,虽然在全国比重不大,但具有地方特色,也应选为代表品。一些季节性强的产品从全年看比重不大,但在某些季节是当

地的主要产品，也要考虑进来，以确保全年和各季度平均价格及指数的代表性。

代表品一般稳定五年。在五年期间，若产品结构调整较快，以致影响代表性时，可提前进行修订。

（二）国家代表产品的选择：

编制农产品生产价格指数是以代表产品（类别）的价格变动来反映全部农产品的价格变化趋势和变动幅度。确定科学、合理的代表品对于编制农产品生产价格指数具有重要意义。如果代表产品过少，会造成代表品不足、价格指数不准确；代表品过多，工作量过大，造成不必要的浪费。根据上述原则，在充分征求部门和地方意见的基础上，国家统计局农村司制订了全国农产品生产价格调查的代表类别和代表产品。即《农产品参考目录》中用"*"所列示的农、林、牧、渔 4 个大类、14 个中类、30 个小类、180 种代表品。上述代表产品代表的各类别销售额占当年全国农产品销售额的 70%以上，具有足够的代表性。

（三）地方代表产品的选择：

各省、自治区、直辖市执行全国统一的分类标准和代码，并根据国家下发的《农产品参考目录》，结合本地实际确定代表产品，包括目录中没有但在当地比较重要的产品。对于各地自行增加的代表品要报国家统计局农村司审定，取得统一编码。

八、农产品代表品权数的计算

权数是衡量每种产品重要性的指标。由于每种产品在农业经济中的地位和作用不同，其价格变动对全部农产品价格变动的影响也有所不同。所以在计算价格指数时，要科学、合理地确定权数。

（一）权数确定的原则和要求：

1. 只计算代表类别和代表产品的权数（如国家只给农产品参考目录中带※号的类别和产品分配权数），其他产品不分配权数。

2. 采用 2000～2002 年三年的资料平均计算权数，权数一般五年更换一次。在五年期间，若出现产品更新换代快，以致影响权数代表性的情况时，应及时进行合理修正。

3. 重点做好大类、中类权数和重要品种权数的审核。对生产量和销售量不大、资料又难以收集的商品，在计算其权数时，可先确定该商品所在类的类值，并确定该类别主要商品的权数，用分摊法将剩余的权数按其比例（重要程度的次序）分配给余下的商品。

4. 由于农产品生产与出售季节性比较强，为客观、准确地反映农业生产价格变动趋势和变动幅度，要对季度、季度累计和全年分别计算权数。

（二）权数的种类与资料来源：

1. 商品（销售）权数：用于计算农产品生产价格指数。农产品商品（销售）权数主要利用农产品销售额进行计算，各种代表产品的商品（销售）权数合计为 1000。权数资料来源于农村住户和农场的农产品出售金额资料，也可根据农村住户调查季报和帐页资料进行加工整理，或利用农产品产量与商品率资料推算。

2. 产值权数：用于缩减农业发展速度。

各种代表产品的产值权数合计为 1000。产值权数资料取自农林牧渔业产值统计，或通过重点调查、部门资料进行推算。

九、农产品生产价格指数的计算方法与步骤

农业生产价格指数是反映一定时期内，农产品生产者出售的农产品价格水平变动趋势及幅度的相对数。生产资料购买价格指数是反映农业生产者购买生产资料价格水平变动趋势及幅度的相对数。

（一）计算每个调查单位每个代表品的价格指数：

$$k_{ij}=\frac{P_{ij1}}{P_{ij0}}$$

式中，k_{ij} 为第 j 个调查单位第 i 个代表产品的个体指数，P_{ij1} 为第 j 个调查单位第 i 个代表产品的报告期平均价格，P_{ij0} 为第 j 个调查单位第 i 个代表产品的基期平均价格。

（二）计算代表品的价格指数 K_i：

$$K_i=\sqrt[n]{k_1\times k_2\times\cdots\cdots\times k_n}$$

式中，$k_1,k_2,\cdots k_n$ 分别为第 i 个代表产品在第 1 到第 n 个调查单位中的个体指数。

（三）计算小类价格指数：

$$K=\frac{\sum K_iW_i}{\sum W_i}$$

其中，K 为该小类指数，K_i 为该小类下第 i 个代表品价格指数，W_i 为第 i 个代表品的产值权数或销售额权数。

（四）计算中类价格指数：

$$K=\frac{\sum K_iW_i}{\sum W_i}$$

其中，K 为中类价格指数，K_i 为该中类下第 i 个小类价格指数，W_i 为第 i 个小类的产值权数或销售额权数。

大类及总指数的计算，同中类价格指数计算方法。

（五）季度累计价格指数的计算方法，与分季指数计算方法相同。

（六）国家和省级价格指数的计算方法一致。

十、有关问题说明

（一）农产品生产价格是农业生产经营单位第一次出售其产品时所获得的价格，因此，所调查的代表品是由被调查单位生产且出售的农产品，外购再出售的农产品不作为调查内容。

（二）如果抽中的调查单位在调查时没有任何销售活动，该记录的各项观测值均为零，在季报时仍应保留该样本，同时上报空记录的个数，并说明情况。如确定该调查户或单位在半年内都不可能有销售活动，则应以样本附近或相似特征的调查对象替换。

（三）县队在数据录入、审核时，如果发现某调查单位某些代表产品报告期与基期价格变动幅度较大，应查询该调查单位出售的该代表品在品种、品质、销售条件等方面是否发生了改变，如果是由于上述非价格变动因素引起的，则应该剔除非价格变动因素，使报告期与基期代表品同质可比；如果新的产品已成为市场主流，则一般应调整基期价格。调整的方法可以相邻农户或地域的同质产品价格代替，如果缺乏相邻农户或地域的同质产品价格，也可以为空。

Programme for the Survey of the Producer Prices of Agricultural Products and for the Calculation of the Price Indices

I. The Purpose of the Survey

The producer prices of agricultural products refer to the actual prices per unit of agricultural products at which the producers of the agricultural products directly sell them. The purpose of conducting the survey of producer prices of agricultural products is to comprehensively collect the data on the producer prices of agricultural products, objectively reflect the situations of the level and structural changes of the producer prices of agricultural products, meet the needs of conducting the agricultural accounts and national accounts, provide the government at different levels with the base data for making the policies of protecting agriculture and circulation of agricultural products and provide the various social circles with the high quality informationon the prices of agricultural products.

II. The Respondents of the Survey

The respondents of the survey are the units engaged in the agricultural production and management.

III. The Procedures of the Survey

The method of sample survey combined with the method of key-unit survey is used in the survey of producer prices of agricultural products. In the sample survey, the units engaged in the agricultural production and management are listed as the respondents of the survey and the method of random sample survey is used. For the agricultural products, which grow mainly in certain areas, the respondents of the survey are selected in the major producing areas with the subjective sampling method.

IV. The Contents of the Survey

The contents of the survey of producer prices of agricultural products include the data on the main agricultural products produced and sold by the respondents of the survey. Under the guidance of the auxiliary enumerators, the respondents of the survey should timely keep records on the names, quantities, prices and amount of the agricultural products sold in the reporting period in the accounts of the survey of producer prices of agricultural products or the household journals.

After soliciting the opinions of various departments and regions, the Department of Rural Survey (DRS), National Bureau of Statistics (NBS) has worked out the Reference Catalogue of Agricultural Products in accordance with the new Standard Classification of Economic Sectors. The national unified standard classification and their codes should be implemented in different regions.

V. The Cycle of the Survey and the Data Reporting to the Higher Authorities

The cycle of the survey of producer prices of agricultural products is a quarter. The calendar year is implemented.

The data in the Questionnaires of the Grass-roots Units on the Producer Prices of Agricultural Products are processed, made entries, calculated and checked by the rural survey organizations of the county bureaus of statistics in accordance with the household accounts or journals. They are finally reported to the rural survey organizations of the concerned bureaus of statistics at the provincial level by means of internets. The quarterly data should include the names, codes, calculation units, quantity sold, amount and prices of the agricultural products sold by the units engaged in the agricultural production and management in the reporting period as well as the concerned prices in the base period. The prices in the base period are directly copied by the county survey organizations from the corresponding questionnaires of the grassroots units.

The periodic tabulated tables on the producer prices of agricultural products and their indices are reported by the rural survey organizations of provinces, autonomous regions and municipalities directly under the central government to the Department of Rural Survey (DRS), National Bureau of Statistics (NBS) before 25th in the last month of the quarter.

VI. The method of tabulating the data on the producer prices of agricultural products

(1) The average price of a certain agricultural product in a unit surveyed equals to the sum of money obtained by the unit in selling the agricultural product in the reporting period divided by the total quantity of the agricultural product sold in the same period. (This is the method of weighted arithmetic average). The formula for the calculation is given below:

$$p_i = \frac{\sum_{j=1}^{n} p_{ij} q_{ij}}{\sum_{j=1}^{n} q_{ij}}$$

Where p_i stands for the average price of the ith representative product; p_{ij} stands for the selling price of the ith representative product at the jth time and q_{ij} stands for the quantity of the ith representative product sold at the jth time.

(2) The average price of a certain agricultural product in a certain province (autonomous region or municipality) and in the whole country equals to the sum of money obtained in selling the agricultural product in the reporting period in all the units surveyed divided by the total quantity of the agricultural product sold in the same period. (This is the method of weighted arithmetic average). The formula for the calculation is given below:

$$P_i = \frac{\sum_{j=1}^{n} p_{ij} q_{ij}}{\sum_{j=1}^{n} q_{ij}}$$

Where p_i stands for the average price of the ith representative product; p_{ij} stands for the selling price of the ith representative product of the jth unit and q_{ij} stands for the quantity of the ith representative product sold by the jth unit.

VII. The Determination of the Representative Agricultural Products

(1) The principles and requirements for the selection of representative products:

(i) The representative products should be selected from the four major divisions, namely farming, forestry, animal husbandry and fishery, and from the various divisions and more than 90% of the groups, so that the price indices can better reflect the changes of the prices in different categories.

(ii) The products which have great importance to the national economy and people's livelihood should be selected. The products, which have large yields and sales, are generally the products important to the national economy and people's livelihood.

(iii) We should select the products steadily produced, because they should be surveyed continuously for several years after they are selected.

(iv) The new products, which have good prospect for the future development, should be selected.

(v) The products, which have local characteristics, should be selected though their proportion to the total output in the whole country is not large. The products only produced in certain seasons should be selected too, because though not large in the proportion to the annual output, they are main products in certain seasons in the localities. The annual and quarterly average prices and their indices can be representative only when they are included.

The representative products should not changed generally in the period of five years after they are selected. However, if the structure of the products is readjusted quite quickly in the period of five years so that the products formerly selected are no longer representative, the list of representative products can be revised ahead of time.

(2) The selection of the representative products of the whole country:

The purpose of the calculation of the indices of the producer prices of agricultural products is to reflect the change trend and change extent of the prices of all agricultural products with the data on the changes of the prices of representative products in different categories. The determination of representative products in a scientific and reasonable way is of great significance to the calculation of the indices of producer prices of agricultural products. If the representative products are too few in number, it will result in the insufficiency of the representative products and the inaccuracy of the price indices. But if the representative products are too many in number, it will result in the too heavy workload and unnecessary waste. In accordance with the above-mentioned principles, after fully soliciting the opinions of the concerned departments and regions, the Department of Rural Survey of National Bureau of Statistics (DRS/NBS) has worked out the representative categories and the representative products in the national survey of the producer prices of agricultural products. They include the four major divisions, namely farming, forestry, animal husbandry and fishery, 14 divisions, 30 groups and 180 representative products, indicated with the symbol * in the Reference Catalogue of Agricultural Products. The sales of the various categories of the representative products account for more than 70% of the total sales of agricultural products in the whole country in the year. Therefore the categories and agricultural products selected are sufficiently representative.

(3) The selection of the representative products in different regions:

The rural survey organizations of provinces, autonomous regions and municipalities determine the representative products in the regions in accordance with the Reference Catalogue of Agricultural Products, in the light of the local actual conditions while implementing the national unified classifications and codes, including those relatively important products in the regions, though they are not included in the national Catalogue. The representative products supplemented by the regions should be reported to the national survey organization for examination, so as to have the unified codes.

VIII. The calculation of the weights of the representative agricultural products

Weights are the indicators measuring the importance of different products. Because each product is different in its position and role in the agricultural economy, the influence of its price change over the price change of all agricultural products is different too. Therefore we should determine the weights in a scientific and reasonable way in the calculation of price indices.

(1) The principles and requirements in determining the weights:

(i) Only the weights of the representative categories and the representative products are calculated. The Department of Rural Survey of National Bureau of Statistics (DRS/NBS) only distributes the weights of the categories and products indicated with the symbol * in the Reference Catalogue of Agricultural Products. As for the other products, no weights are distributed.

(ii) The weights are calculated as averages of the data of the three years 2000 — 2002. The weights are generally changed once in every five years. If the old products are quickly renewed or up grated by the new ones in the five years so that the formerly determined weights are no longer representative, the weights should be timely revised in a reasonable way.

(iii) Attention should be mainly paid to the examination of the weights of the major divisions and divisions as well as the weights of important products. As for the commodity, which is not large in its yield and sales and is difficult to collect the data, we can firstly determine the weight of the category, to which the commodity belongs, secondly determine the weights of the main commodities in that category and finally distribute the remainder of the weight of the category to the other commodities in that category in a proportional way, namely in the order of their importance.

(iv) Because the agricultural products are generally produced and sold in different seasons, we should calculate the weights for the quarter, for the accumulative data from the beginning of the year to the quarter and for the whole year respectively, so as to objectively and accurately reflect the change trend and change extent of the producer prices of agricultural products.

(2) Kinds of weights and data sources:

(i) Weights of sales of the commodities: They are used to calculate the indices of the producer prices of agricultural products.

The weights of sales of the commodities are calculated mainly on the basis of the data on the sales of agricultural products. The sum of the weights of sales of the various representative agricultural products equals to 100. The data sources for the calculation are the data on the sales of agricultural products of the rural households and farms. We can also process the data on the basis of the quarterly report of the survey of rural households and the concerned accounts or estimate on the basis of the data on the yields of agricultural products and their commodity rate.

(ii) Weights of output value. They are used to deflate the agricultural growth rate.

The sum of the output values of various representative products equals to 100. The data sources for the calculation of weights of output value are the statistical data on the output value of farming, forestry, animal husbandry and fishery. We can also estimate on the basis of the data of key-unit survey or the data from the concerned departments.

IX. The Methods and Steps for the Calculation of the Indices of the Producer Prices of Agricultural Products

The indices of the producer prices of agricultural products are relative numbers, which reflect the trends and extents of the changes of the producer prices of agricultural products sold by the producers in a certain period.

(1) The calculation of the price index of each product in each unit surveyed:

$$k_{ij}=\frac{P_{ij1}}{P_{ij0}}$$

Where K_y stands for the individual price index of the ith representative product in the jth unit surveyed; P_{y1} stands for the average price of the ith representative product in the jth unit surveyed in the reporting period and P_{y0} stands for the average price of the ith representative product in the jth unit surveyed in the base period.

(2) The calculation of the price index of the representative product K_i:

$$K_i=\sqrt[n]{k_1\times k_2\cdots\cdots\times k_n}$$

Where K_1, K_2, ······ K_n stands respectively for the individual price index of the ith representative product in the first, the second, ······ the nth unit surveyed.

(3) The calculation of the price index of the group:

$$K=\frac{\sum K_iW_i}{\sum W_i}$$

Where K stands for the price index of the group, K_i stands for the priceindex of the ith representative product in the group and W_i stands for the weight of output value or the weight of sales of the ith representative product.

(4) The calculation of the price index of the division:

$$K=\frac{\sum K_iW_i}{\sum W_i}$$

Where K stands for the price index of the division, K_i stands for the priceindex of the ith group in the division and W_i stands for the weight ofoutput value or the weight of sales of the ith group.

The calculation of the price index of the division and the calculation of the general price index are similar as that of the division.

(5) The method for the calculation of the price index in the period from the beginning of the year to the end of the quarter is similar to the calculation of the quarterly price index.

(6) The method for the calculation of the national price index is similar to the calculation of the provincial price index.

X. The Treatment of Some Problems

(1) The producer prices of agricultural products are the prices at which the units engaged in the agricultural production and management sell the products for the first time. Therefore the representative product surveyed refers to the agricultural product produced and sold by the unit surveyed. The agricultural product purchased from other units and resold should not be included in the survey.

(2) If the selected unit in the sample survey has no activities of sales, the observed value on sales is zero, the data of the sample unit should be still included in the quarterly report and the situations should be reported to the higher authorities. If the selected household or unit in the sample survey will definitely have no activities of sales in the future half year, the household or unit should be replaced by the household or unit in the nearby areas or other respondent, which has the similar characteristics.

(3) In the course of making data-entries and examination and verifying data, if the statisticians in the county survey organization find that the change extents of the prices of certain representative products in a certain unit surveyed between the reporting period and the base period are relatively large, they should inquire if there is any change in the variety, quality or selling condition of the representative product. If the change is caused by non-price factors, the non-price factors should be removed, so as to make the representative product in the reporting period comparable with that in the base period. If the new product represents the main trend in the market, its price in the base period should be readjusted. In the readjustment, the price of the product of the same quality in the neighbouring agricultural household or the neighbouring area can take its place. If no price of the product of the same quality in the neighbouring agricultural household or the neighbouring area can be found, the data in the base period can be blank.

5—2　农产品集贸市场价格调查方案

一、调查目的

农产品集贸市场价格是指全国农产品主产区集贸市场主要农产品的成交价格。开展农产品集贸市场价格调查旨在收集农产品集贸市场价格资料，准确把握全国大宗农产品在主产区的价格走势，为提高我国农产品主产区的区域优势和市场竞争力服务。

二、调查内容

农产品集贸市场价格调查内容包括农牧渔业36种主要产品的集贸市场价格（调查品种见《农产品集贸价格调查表》）。

三、调查对象

农产品集贸市场价格调查的统计范围为全国选中的农产品主产县。

四、调查周期与数据上报

（一）农产品集贸市场价格调查周期为月报。

（二）采价时间为每月20日左右，即每月19～21日内任一工作日。

（三）数据上报时间：价格资料由各省（区、市）农调队每月25日前上报国家统计局农村司。

五、采价办法

（一）各省（区、市）对调查品种要统一口径，不得随意变换。所有调查品种的采价范围都是指一般普通商品、中等规格。经过加工，带有品牌包装的商品不在调查之列；经过分拣后加入精美包装作为礼品出售的农产品也不在调查之内。

（二）对于固定采价集市上没有的品种（如稻谷、活猪和籽棉等），为了保证调查数据的完整性，可采取以下几种办法：①可到其他有出售的市场取得价格；②仅在调查日当天无出售的产品，可根据上一日的情况采价；③原粮和籽棉可用市场上的大米和皮棉按当地的折算比率取得或到大米和籽棉加工点取得；④活猪价格可到农户或屠宰场取得；⑤当地不生产、也不从外地调入的产品价格就空缺。

（三）对同一品种不同等级价格的采价不好把握时，可用交易量较大的三个以上摊位价格的简单平均价作为该产品的价格。对同一品种、同一摊位、同一等级成交价格不一致时，用交易量较大的成交价作为该摊位、该产品的价格。

（四）食用油：采普通散装油价格。

（五）猪、牛、羊肉如市场上出售的是带骨肉，采价时需按当地比率折成去骨价。

（六）水产品：淡水鱼要求是采活鱼价格；带鱼可采死鱼价（包括每条规格在0.5～1公斤重的冷冻带鱼段）。

（七）蔬菜：采新鲜蔬菜价格。

（八）水果：采新鲜水果价格。

六、填报说明

（一）农产品集贸市场价格调查表由省、自治区、直辖市农调队报送。

（二）产品代码与计量单位：产品代码按M405表规定填报；单价单位为元/公斤（如采价时为“元/斤”应换算为元/公斤）。

（三）价格数据保留两位小数。

（四）如部分产品缺项，单价项应空缺（不要补“0”）。

（五）各省（区、市）农调队对农产品集贸市场价格调查数据不作汇总处理，通过农调内网直接上报以调查县为单位的集贸市场价格原始数据。

（六）严格数据审核。当月单价与上月或上年同月相比增减幅度较大时应进行认真核实、确认，并随《农产品集贸市场价格调查上报表》报送文字说明。

（七）开展农产品市场价格专题分析，有关农副产品价格的重大信息与研究报告，及时报送文字材料。

（八）年度价格走势分析与调查数据质量评估报告随12月价格报表一同报送。

七、指标解释

（一）籼稻：水稻的一种，茎秆较高较软，叶子黄绿色，稻穗上的籽粒较稀，稻粒长而细。

（二）优质籼稻：经过杂交育种改良后的籼稻。

（三）粳稻：水稻的一种，茎秆较矮，叶子较窄，深绿色，稻粒短而粗。

（四）玉米：一年生草本植物，茎高二、三米，叶子长而大，子实比黄豆稍大。

（五）籼米：籼稻碾出的米，黏性小。

（六）优质籼米：优质籼稻碾出的米。

（七）粳米：粳稻碾出的米，黏性较大。

（八）面粉：小麦磨成的粉，调查规格品是普通标准粉。

（九）籽棉：是指棉农从棉枝上摘下的、未经轧花加工除籽的棉花。籽棉经过加工后去掉棉籽的棉花叫皮棉。籽棉加工成皮棉的比例一般是 10∶3，即 10 公斤籽棉可加工成 3 公斤皮棉。

（十）花生仁：去壳的生花生。

（十一）活猪：待宰的肥猪（也称毛猪，一般在 65 公斤以上）。

（十二）仔猪：待育肥的普通小猪（一般指 10 公斤以下刚断奶的猪）。

（十三）草鱼：身体圆筒形，微绿色，生活在淡水中，吃水草。

（十四）鲤鱼：身体侧扁，背部苍黑色，腹部黄白色，嘴边有须一对，淡水鱼。

（十五）鲢鱼：身体侧扁，鳞细，背部青黑色，腹部白色，淡水鱼。

（十六）菜椒：也称柿子椒。

（十七）四季豆：部分地区也称扁豆。

（十八）中等：产品规格栏的“中等”有两种含义。原粮的“中等”是指国家规定的中准级，其他品种的“中等”是指市场实际交易数量较多的质量等级。

Programme for the Survey of the Prices of Agricultural Products at the Rural Market Fairs

I. The Purpose of the Survey

The prices of agricultural products at the rural market fairs refer to the unit prices of main agricultural products, which have been stricken bargains at the rural market fairs in major producing areas in China. The purpose of conducting the survey of the prices of agricultural products at the rural market fairs is to collect the data on the prices of agricultural products at the rural market fairs, accurately keep abreast of the change trend of the prices of the staple agricultural products in the major producing areas in the whole country and serve for the purpose of improving the regional superiority and competitive power at the market of the major producing areas of agricultural products in China and their competitive power at the market.

II. The contents of the survey

The contents of the survey of the prices of agricultural products at the rural market fairs include prices of 36 main agricultural products of farming, forestry, animal husbandry and the fishery at the rural market fairs (As for the variety surveyed, see the questionnaires used in the survey of the prices of agricultural products at the rural market fairs).

III. Respondents of the survey

The statistical coverage of the survey of the prices of agricultural products at the rural market fairs includes the major producing counties of agricultural products selected in the sample survey in the whole country.

IV. Cycle of the Survey and Data Reporting

(1) The cycle of the survey of the prices of agricultural products at the rural market fairs is a month.

(2) The date for collecting the price data is about the 20th of every month, namely any working day in the period 19th—21th.

(3) The date for reporting data: The price data are reported by the rural socio-economic survey organizations of provinces, autonomous regions and municipalities under the central government to the Department of Rural Survey (DRS) before the 25th of every month.

V. Methods for Collecting the Data on Prices

(1) The rural survey organizations at the provincial level should pay attention that the specifications of the varieties surveyed should be unified in different time and should not be changed at will. All the varieties listed for collecting their prices refer to the ordinary commodities with medium standard. Those commodities, which have been processed and packaged with brands, are not to be surveyed. The agricultural products, which have been picked out, beautifully packaged and sold as gifts, are also not to be surveyed.

(2) For the varieties (such as paddy, live pig and unginned cotton, etc.) not sold at the specified rural market fairs for collecting price data, the following methods can be adopted so as to ensure the complete data coverage: (i) The price data can be collected from the other market fairs, at which these varieties are sold; (ii) For the varieties, which are not sold only on the day for the survey, the data on their prices on the preceding day can be collected; (iii) The data on the prices of the unhusked rice and unginned cotton can be converted on the basis of the data on the prices of husked rice and ginned cotton at the market with the local conversion rate or can be collected from the spots where the unhusked rice or unginned cotton are processed into husked rice or ginned

cotton; (iv) The data on the price of live pig can be collected from the rural households or slaughterhouse; (v) For the products neither produced in the locality nor transported from other places, their price data can be blank.

(3) When it is not easy to make decision for collecting the price data of the same variety with different grades, the simple average of the prices of more than three vendor's stands which have relatively bigger sales volumes can be taken as the price of that variety. When the prices at which the bargains are stricken are not the same for the same grade, same variety at the same vendor's stand, the price at which the bargain is stricken with the biggest sales volume can be taken as the price of that variety at that vendor's stand.

(4) For edible vegetable oil, the price in bulk and in ordinary grade can be collected.

(5) For pork, beef and mutton, if they are sold with bones, their prices without bones can be estimated with the local conversion rate.

(6) For aquatic products, the prices of live fish should be taken for the freshwater fish while the price of dead fish can be taken for the hairtail, including the frozen hairtail segments with the weight of 0.5—1 kg for each hairtail.

(7) For vegetable, the prices of fresh vegetable should be collected.

(8) For fruits, the prices of fresh fruits should be collected.

VI. Instructions

(1) The questionnaires for the survey of the prices of agricultural products at the rural market fairs should be reported by the rural survey organizations of provinces, autonomous regions and municipalities under the central government.

(2) Codes of products and units of calculation: The codes of products should be filled out in accordance with the stipulations for Table M405. The unit for calculation of the unit price is yuan / kg.

(3) Two decimals are required to be kept in price data.

(4) If the data of parts of products are unavailable, the item on unit price should be blank.

(5) The rural survey organizations of provinces, autonomous regions and municipalities should not tabulate the survey data on the prices of agricultural products at the rural market fairs, but should directly report the original data on the prices of agricultural products at the rural market fairs in every county by the means of the internet.

(6) The data should be strictly examined and verified. When the unit price of the month increases or decreases by a quite big margin as compared with the previous month or the same month in the previous year, it should be seriously checked and confirmed.

(7) The annual analysis report on the change trend of prices and appraisal report on the quality of survey data should be reported along with the price questionnaires of December.

VII. Explanatory Notes on the Indicators

(1) long-grained nonglutinous rice: a kind of paddy rice with quite tall and soft stem and its leaves are yellowish-green. The grains are sparsely grown in the ears of rice. The grains of rice are long and thin.

(2) High quality long-grained nonglutinous rice: The improved nonglutinous rice after cross-breeding.

(3) Round-grained rice: a kind of paddy rice. Its stalk is comparatively low. Its leaves are comparatively narrow and deep green. The grains of rice are short and wide.

(4) Corn: an annual herb. Its stalk is 2—3 meter tall. Its leaves are long and large. Its grains are a little larger than soybeans.

(5) Polished long-grained nonglutinous rice: rice husked from the long-grained nonglutinous rice. It has little stickiness.

(6) High quality polished long-grained nonglutinous rice: rice husked from the high quality long-grained nonglutinous rice.

(7) Polished round-grained rice: rice husked from the round-grained rice. It has comparatively high stickiness.

(8) Wheat flour: powder husked from wheat.

The specification for the survey is the ordinary standard flour.

(9) Unginned cotton: refers to the cotton picked down by the cotton farmers from the cotton branches and unginned. When the unginned cotton is ginned and the seeds are removed, it is called ginned cotton. 10 kg of unginned cotton can be generally processed into 3 kg of ginned cotton.

(10) Peanut kernel: refers to the shelled peanut.

(11) Hog: refers to the grown pig to be slaughtered. Its weight is generally greater than 65 kg.

(12) Piglet: refers to the ordinary young pig to be fattened up. It generally refers to the newly weanned pig. Its weight is generally less than 10 kg.

(13) Grass carp: Its body is shaped like a cylinder and is greenish. It live in freshwater and takes waterweeds as its food.

(14) Carp: Its body is squad shaped. Its back is black and its belly is yellowish white. It has a pair of beard near its mouth. It is a kind of freshwater fish.

(15) Silver carp: Its body is squad shaped. It has thin scales. Its back is greenish black and its belly is white. It is a kind of freshwater fish.

(16) Sweetbell: It is called shizijiao or caijiao in China.

(17) Kidney bean: It is called sijidou or biandou in different regions in China.

(18) Medium grade: There are two meanings. The medium grade of raw grain refers to the middle grade stipulated by the government. The medium grade of other products refers to the quality grade at which the bargain of a large quantity of products are stricken.

5—3 农产品批发价格调查方案

一、调查目的

农产品批发价格是指全国大中型农产品批发市场或从事农产品批发交易的经营单位进行农产品批发交易的成交价格。开展农产品批发价格调查旨在收集农产品批发价格资料,准确把握全国主要农产品价格走势与供求状况,满足各级政府和宏观决策部门研究制定农村经济政策的需要,为提高我国农产品市场竞争力服务。

二、调查内容

农产品批发价格调查内容为农林牧渔业主要农产品的批发交易价格,调查品种分为粮油、棉花、蔬菜、果品、花卉、肉禽蛋、水产品和木材共八个类别。

三、调查对象

农产品批发价格调查的对象为农产品批发市场或从事农产品批发交易的经营单位。调查网点根据交易品种和成交量综合确定,全国共调查 100 家农产品批发市场和经营单位。

四、调查周期与上报日期

农产品批发价格调查周期为月报,批发价格上报日期为每月 25 日。

粮油、蔬菜、果品、花卉、肉禽蛋和水产品价格的采价日期为上报日的前一个工作日。棉花和木材价格的报告期为上月 25 日至当月 24 日。遇法定节假日,采价和上报日期顺延,按实际采价日期填报。

五、调查方式

(一)粮油、蔬菜、果品、花卉、肉禽蛋和水产品的批发价格以市场内该种农产品最大批发商(摊位、商家或商号)单笔最大交易为准。最大交易量前三家为批发商调查样本,一般优先选择交易量最大的批发商作为采价对象,并在一年内保持相对稳定。

批发价格为采价日单笔最大交易量的成交价格。价格资料由调查员在采价日对批发商进行现场访问取得。

(二)棉花和木材批发价格按被抽中市场或经营单位在报告期内批发交易的全部成交情况填报。

批发价格为批发交易的加权平均价格。价格资料由被调查单位对报告期内相关产品的全部销售情况逐一分类登记,并定期整理、报送价格数据。

(三)实行全国统一的统计分类标准和编码。各地可根据需要适当增加调查指标,但不得改变指标排列顺序和编码。

六、数据报送与汇总

(一)各省(区、市)农调队通过国家统计系统内部信息传输系统(Openmail)直接报送批发市场和经营单位的价格资料。

(二)数据上报采用规定的 EXCEL 模板格式,价格保留两位小数。缺省指标可不予填报,但不得改变指标顺序和数据格式。

(三)批发价格数据汇总工作由国家统计局农村司负责。

Programme for the Survey of the Wholesale Prices of Agricultural Products

I. The Purpose of the Survey

The wholesale prices of agricultural products refer to the prices at which the bargain of the wholesale trade of agricultural products are stricken at the large and medium-sized wholesale market of agricultural products or at the units engaged in the wholesale trade of agricultural products. The purpose of conducting the survey of wholesale prices of agricultural products is to collect the data on the wholesale prices of agricultural products, accurately keep abreast of the change trend of prices of main agricultural products and the situation of their supply and demand in the whole country, so as to meet the needs of the government at different levels and the departments of macro-economic decision-making for formulating the rural economic policies.

II. The Contentsof the Survey

The contentsof the survey of wholesale prices of agricultural products include the prices of the main agricultural products in farming, forestry, animal husbandry and fishery in the wholesale trade. The varieties surveyed are classified into the following eight categories: (1) grain and edible oil, (2) cotton, (3) vegetable, (4) fruits, (5) flowers, (6) meat, poultry and eggs, (7) aquatic products and (8) wood.

III. Respondents

The respondents of the survey of wholesale prices of agricultural products are the wholesale marketsof agricultural products or the units engaged in the wholesale trade of agricultural products. The units to be surveyed are determined on the basis of the trade varieties and sales volume. A total of 100 wholesale markets of agricultural products and the units engaged in the wholesale trade of agricultural products are surveyed in the whole country.

IV. Survey Cycle and Reporting Date

The cycle of the survey of wholesale prices of agricultural products is a month. The date for reporting the wholesale prices is the 25th of every month.

The date for collecting the data on grain, edible oil, cotton, vegetable, fruits, flowers, meat, poultry, eggs and aquatic products is that working day preceding the reporting date. The period for reporting the data on the prices of cotton and wood is the period from the 25th of the previous month to the 24th of this month. When it happens to be a national festival or holiday, the date for collecting or reporting the price data is postponed correspondingly. The actual date for collecting the price data is to be reported.

V. Proceduresof the Survey

(1) For the wholesale prices of grain, edible oil, cotton, vegetable, fruits, flowers, meat, poultry, eggs and aquatic products, the data on the price of the product of the largest individual trade at the largest vendor's stand, store or shopin the market are to be collected. The first three largest vendor's stands, stores and (or) shops are the sample units. The largest vendor's stand, store or shopin the market is generally to be selected to be the respondents. The respondents should be stable in a year.

The wholesale price refers to the price of the product of the largest individual trade on the day for collecting price data. The price data are collected by the enumerator from the wholesale vendor's stand, store or shopin the interview on the day for collecting price data.

(2) For the wholesale prices of cotton and wood, the price data should be filled out in the

light of the actual conditions of the wholesale trade of the selected market or the unit engaged in the trade in the reporting period.

The wholesale prices are the weighted average prices in the wholesale trade. The price data on the wholesale of the concerned products should be recorded one by one by the respondents in a classified wayand should be periodically processed and reported.

(3) The national unified standard statistical classification and codes are implemented. The survey indicators can be implemented by the different regions in the light of their needs, but no changes should be made in the order and codes of the indicators.

VI. Data Reporting and Tabulation

(1) The rural survey organizations in different regions should directly report the price data of the wholesale markets and the units engaged in the wholesale trade by means of the Openmail, an internal system of information transmission in the national statistical system.

(2) The stipulated format Exell should be used in reporting data. Two decimals should be kept in the price data. The unavailable data can be left out but no changes should be made in the order of indicators and data format.

(3) The Department of Rural Survey of the National Bureau of Statistics (DRS/NBS) is responsible for the work of tabulation of the data on the wholesale prices.